Basic Buddhism

Exploring
Buddhism
and
Zen

Nan Huai-Chin

SAMUEL WEISER, INC.

York Beach, Maine

First published in 1997 by
Samuel Weiser, Inc.
P.O. Box 612
York Beach, ME 03910-0612

Library of Congress Cataloging-in-Publication Data
  Nan, Huai-chin.
    Basic Buddhism : exploring Buddhism and Zen / Nan, Huai-chin.
      p. cm.
    Based on "Chung-kuo fo chiao fa chan shih," by Huai-chin Nan.
    Includes index.
    ISBN 1-57863-020-7 (paper : alk. paper)
      1. Buddhism—History. 2. Buddhism—China—History. 3. Zen
  Buddhism—China—History. I. Nan, Huai-chin. Chung-kuo fo chiao
  fa chan shih. II. Title.
  BQ266.N36   1997
  294.3'0951—dc21   97-25613
                                                        CIP
BP

Translated by J. C. Cleary

Typeset in Galliard in 10 point

Printed in the United States of America

05 04 03 02 01 00 99 98 97
9 8 7 6 5 4 3 2 1

The paper used in this publication meets the minimum requirements of
the American National Standard for Permanence of Paper for Printed
Library Materials Z39.48-1984.

Contents

THE DEVELOPMENT OF INDIAN CULTURE

The formation and growth of any religion is sure to have a cultural background. As is common knowledge, in the present-day world, if we speak of civilizations with a long history and cultural tradition, there are only China and India in the East, and Egypt and Greece in the West. These are called the world's four great ancient civilizations.

The glorious history of Greece is already a thing of the past, but its cultural legacy has mixed with other elements and spread, contributing to the formation of the modern civilization of Europe and America. Egyptian civilization is already remote and hidden in the mists, and only some fragments of its grandeur remain. Indian civilization, especially the Buddhist civilization which has made such an impact on the world and has shone brightly from ancient to modern times, has already been completely assimilated in the territory of Chinese civilization, through a process that lasted from the end of the Han dynasty through the Song dynasty.

Greek civilization represents the West. It developed first from a religion to a philosophy; from a philosophy it evolved into science, bringing about the modern Western culture. Thus one can say that it has many flourishing offshoots.

If people in today's world want to inquire into the source of the various great religious civilizations, they soon find that, ultimately, all these civilizations had their origins in the East. This is particularly true of Buddhist civilization, which long ago became interconnected with Chinese civilization to form a single whole. Its widespread influence thus goes without saying. But when we trace the source and seek the background of the sudden rise of Buddhism in India, and examine its development into a great stream radiating in all directions after its transmission to China, we are sure to uncover a definite sequence of cause and effect. Therefore, to understand the birth of Buddhist civilization and its gestation in the civilization of the preceding period, we must first have some elementary knowledge of traditional Indian civilization.

The Background of Indian Culture

Humans are born between heaven and earth, and it is unavoidable that both climate and geographical circumstances are important factors in shaping a people's civilization. India is a peninsula in southern Asia, and its geography and climate have obvious differences from lands in other regions. Southern India extends into the tropics, while northern India is next to the Himalaya Mountains and central India has a temperate climate. For the people of ancient India, the yearly cycle, in accord with the climate, was divided into three seasons of four months each. Because of India's location between the temperate and the tropical zones, the physical and mental activity of its people, and, generally speaking, their way of thinking, was very lively. This is particularly true of the southern regions, which were even richer in mystical imagination.

From ancient times until today, the cultures and languages of India have never been unified. In ancient India, there were more than fifty or sixty writing systems. These are generally lumped together under the single term Sanskrit for all forms of Indian written language, but in reality, Sanskrit is just one of the many written languages of India. There are still several dozen languages current in India today. China was able to unify its weights and measures and its written language because of the great unification it underwent in the Qin and Han dynasties (c. 220 B.C.–A.D. 200). But such was not the case for India. Though from ancient times until now it has always been called one country, in reality, India is still divided into various ethnic groups, each occupying its own area. Hence Indian culture has never really been unified.

During the period from the Zhou dynasty to the Qin dynasty in Chinese history (c. eleventh to third centuries B.C.), India was divided into various small states, just as China was. There were two or three hundred small principalities, each occupying its own territory and each having its own ruler. During this period, many schools of learning were established. The various schools of thought all claimed to teach the truth, although in just a single region there were more than a hundred different schools. In the cultural life of the people, there was one special characteristic: class di-

visions were very strict, and so noble and humble were sharply separated into castes and received very different treatment. This out-
look remains deep-rooted and strong, despite all the attacks of
20th-century ideas of freedom and equality. Concerning this, we
can only quote the proverbial observation: Something that has
been so since ancient times will not change now.

The Indian system of four castes creates four traditional classes
of people. First, the *brahmans* were hereditary specialists in rituals
and sacrifices. They were the heart of instruction in religion and
culture and ranked the highest of the castes. Hence of all the
castes, they merited the highest respect. They were the upper stratum, functioning as spiritual and intellectual leaders. All military
and political affairs were influenced by them. Second were the
kshatriyas, the royal officers and warriors. They gathered together
military and political power in a single lineage and became hereditary rulers. Third, came the *vaisyas*, the class of merchants, who
possessed wealth and controlled trade, while the fourth class, the
sudras, were a class of peasants who worked tilling and planting the
land.

Besides these four, there was also a class of hereditary slaves
and debased people who performed lowly occupations like
butchering animals and so on. Their position was the lowest of all
and their lives were very difficult and full of suffering. This ancient
Indian system of four castes has remained solid and unbreakable
for over three thousand years. The remnants of this way of thinking have still not been totally obliterated.

The brahman class controlled cultural education and, relying
on the four *Vedas*, upheld the concepts of *Brahman* (the absolute)
and *Atman* (the true self). This formed the Brahmanical religion
that was the center of historical Indian civilization. This gradually
spread out and influenced the thinking and consciousness of the
three upper castes, the brahmans, kshatriyas, and vaisyas, toward
the way of life of the *shramana* who leaves home to cultivate the
path to self-realization.

For them, the ideal course of a person's life was divided into
four periods. The first was a period of pure conduct, a period of
life devoted to a young person's education. When they reached a
certain age, young people would leave home to study the *Vedas*
and other branches of learning. (For the disciples of brahmans, this
was from age 8 to 16; for the disciples of kshatriyas, from 11–20;

for the disciples of vaisyas, from age 12–24.) These disciples would spend a set period of time studying, for example, a term of twelve years, or twenty-four years, or thirty-six years, or forty-eight years. Only when the term was completed and their studies accomplished, could they return home to ordinary life.

The second period, the period of living as a householder, was one of maturity, when a person would marry and have children, undertaking the responsibilities of family life and fulfilling the duties of heading a household.

The third was a period of living in the forests. This was the period of middle age, when a person would live in seclusion in the forest, a period of life when the person concentrated on cultivating the path. Having already completed their obligations as householders during their mature years, from this point on people would live in seclusion to devote themselves to higher pursuits, diligently cultivate ascetic practices, and learn various methods of meditative concentration and contemplation, in order to seek the sublimation of the Atman to reach union with Brahman.

Fourth, came a period of withdrawal from the world. By means of cultivating practice in their middle years, when people entered their years of old age and decline, their life of cultivating practice would have reached a conclusion. Their bodies and minds would be absolutely purified, and they would have already perfected the fruits of the path. From this point on, they would seclude themselves in the forests, free from sensory entanglements and no longer participating in the affairs of the world.

This ideal human life was advocated and experienced not only by the brahmans themselves; the kshatriyas and vaisyas could also emulate it. But the sudras, the menial class, never had any way to share in it. This kind of religious life was thus fundamentally restricted. For this reason, there was a reaction among the kshatriyas, who gradually became dissatisfied with the old norms of thinking that placed the brahmans in the lead. The kshatriyas began to assert themselves and provided the impetus for new trends of thought in such fields as religion, philosophy, culture, and education. Thenceforth, they began to investigate the real truth about the world, to seek the ultimate of the Atman spirit, and to delve into the basic source of the myriad forms in the universe. Thus, as soon as the books of profound meaning called the *Upanishads* began to appear within Indian culture, they were pitted against the traditional spirit of the brahmans. But the position of the brahmans remained as preeminent as ever. Brahmanical thought had deeply penetrated Indian culture and was hard to change.

From the foregoing introduction, we can understand the source of the thought of the people of ancient India and their cultural background. Due to the specifics of their geographical circumstances and the natural climate, the ancient Indians liked contemplative pursuits and enjoyed setting their wills on lofty, far-reaching goals. Moreover, they already had the deeply rooted religion of Brahmanism and a pervasive system of religious thought. From the beginning of their history, the Indians tended toward the idea of leaving the world in order to seek to purify body and mind, and they considered living in retreat in the forest as the greatest enjoyment in human life. Thus their thought system was preoccupied with lofty concerns and tended toward empty imaginings. But most of all, returning from the lofty concept of Atman to ordinary human life, the intermediate level, a humanistic system of thought, was lacking. This contributed to the extremely rigid caste divisions and the extreme inequality of status between high and low. Even religious beliefs in ancient India could not arrive at concepts of equality and liberty.

Shakyamuni Buddha arose in response to these conditions. With his great vow of compassion, he founded the Buddhist religion, balancing out inequalities, keeping the good points from the preexisting culture and doing away with its shortcomings. He taught in response to what was good and beautiful in the human spirit, summing up a hundred generations of cultural tradition. He refuted the concept that humankind was divided into classes by nature, and pointed out how to elevate, refine, and perfect human nature.

The Religion and Philosophy of Ancient Indian Civilization

With the particular form and the rich contents of its thought systems, Indian civilization truly occupied an extremely important and preeminent position in world cultural history for about three thousand years, from roughly 2000 B.C. to A.D. 1000.

The following were major components of the thought of the ancient civilization of India:

The _Vedas:_ Ancient Indian civilization is commonly called Vedic civilization. This was the period when the brahmanical religion was the center of culture. The education propagated by the brahmans determined the people's cultural consciousness. They relied totally on the _Vedas_ for their central ideas. Veda means "treatise on wisdom" or "treatise of explanation." In other words, treatises which seek knowledge of the universe and of human life. They include three main sections: verses of praise and collections of mantras; books on pure conduct called _Brahmanas,_ books of the brahmans, and books of spiritual learning; and books of abstruse meaning, called _Upanishads,_ which are books of esoteric philosophy. There are four collections of verses of praise, called the four _Vedas:_ the _Rig-Veda,_ containing elegies and chants; the _Yajur-Veda,_ describing sacrifices; the _Sama-Veda,_ containing songs; and the _Atharva-Veda,_ containing prayers.

The Vedic elegies and explanations are the fount of Indian religion and philosophy. They pay homage to a multitude of gods and spirits. They offer worship and make songs of praise to Heaven and Earth, the Sun and Moon, the wind and clouds, the thunder and rain, and myriad natural phenomena, such as mountains and rivers and animals. Hence, the early Vedic religion can be called a primitive culture's pantheism. In their religious and philosophical message, the _Vedas_ do not talk of hell and do not talk of the past. They do not contain the concept of cause and effect, nor of karmic rewards and punishments. However, they do hold that the human soul does not perish. Their idea is that, after the body dies, the soul returns to Yama's heaven. The _Vedas_ teach that, in all matters relating to sacrificing to the gods and spirits, and all prayers to avoid calamities and attract blessings, the people can get a response by chanting the verses of the _Vedas._ This is quite similar to the prayers and incantations of the religious specialists in ancient Chinese culture. It is also like the primitive religious consciousness found among all the world's ethnic groups at a certain point in their history.

Gradually, in order to satisfy metaphysical needs, from this primitive religious belief there eventually arose accounts of the origin of humanity. The origin of humanity was due to a chief god who created everything. He was the supreme deity, the origin of the universe and of the human race. All the shapes and forms of myriad phenomena in the universe were also his creations along with humanity.

The books of pure conduct, called the *Brahmanas*, form the second section of the *Vedas*. As time moved forward, the philosophy of the *Vedas* could no longer fully meet people's needs. At this point, the books of pure conduct came into existence to spur on the brahman class and form a solidly constructed brahmanical religion. Most of the books of pure conduct still had as their essential message an affirmation of the sacrifices and songs that the *Vedas* used to offer praises to the gods and provide explanations of man and the world and formulas for praying to avert disasters and attract blessings.

As for their religious philosophy, the *Brahmanas* transformed the Vedic philosophy of a chief god who was the creator of all things and the origin of man. They revered a god who was the lord of creation, but held that this god was not apart from our true selves. This chief god was Brahman. The name "Brahman" means absolutely pure and perfectly real. The *Brahmanas* asserted that there is no duality between Atman, the true self of human beings, and the true self of Brahman. This is similar to the later Confucian idea of the unity of Heaven and mankind, and is similar to the message of other religions that God and mankind share the same essence.

Subsequently, this religious consciousness of Brahman, and the philosophy that there is no duality between Brahman and Atman, the true self of humans, became deeply implanted in Indian philosophical thought. This has endured all the way to the present day. The highest goal of modern Indian religion and its yogic techniques is still to reach the realm where Brahman and Atman are united as one.

Still, the brahmanical religion, based on revering and following the *Brahmanas,* the books of pure conduct, adhered at the same time to the Vedic traditions and paid homage to the grandeur of nature. It adopted the pervasive supernatural beings worshipped by the lower orders of society, namely the asuras, the rakshas, the evil spirits, and other spirits, and honored them all.

The only special point of the *Brahmanas,* compared to the brahmanical religion, is that they incorporated a religious philosophy of cause and effect and karmic reward and punishment. This is the theory that sentient beings revolve in the cycle of birth and death due to the force of karma. It explains that, because they planted different good and evil causal bases in their past lives, people receive different rewards of pleasure and suffering in their present lives. Based on this, there were also teachings concerning what they called "ascending to heaven" and "descending to hell." This is the original source of the teaching of karmic reward and punishment.

The third section of the *Vedas*, the books of abstruse meaning or the *Upanishads*, were what came into prominence after the *Brahmanas*, the books of pure conduct. The *Vedas* were the source of the traditional religion and philosophy of ancient India. After a transformation, the *Brahmanas* came into existence, vast all-inclusive collections, the holy scriptures of the primitive Indian religion, Brahmanism. After another transformation, the *Upanishads* came into existence, and brought together the Indian religious philosophy and the widespread philosophy of the intellectuals and the common people. At the end of the period of the *Brahmanas*, the religious and philosophical researches of people in India had already reached the stage of an enthusiastic outflow in all directions, reaching everywhere high and low. No matter whether male or female, young or old, everyone was studying issues like the liberation of the mind's spiritual awareness, the destination of the soul, and the formation of the world with all their mental strength. The Chinese transliteration of the word *Upanishad* has the connotation of a teacher and disciple sitting face to face communicating secrets.

The contents of the *Upanishads* are very rich, their thinking is profound and abstruse: the whole collection includes more than two hundred works. The German philosopher Schopenhauer was infatuated with the *Upanishads*, and his own philosophical thinking was very much influenced by them. He praised the *Upanishads* again and again. He said that they were filled with holiness and ardor, that every chapter could induce lofty and pure thinking, and that, of all the books in the world, it was hard to find any that could match them in excellence and profundity. He thought that these books could console him in life and give him repose in death.

The *Upanishads* have several special characteristics. They affirm the nonduality of Brahman and Atman. They assert that both the essence of the lord of creation, who is beyond form, and the essence of humans, who are at the level of form, are fundamentally a single whole. The myriad phenomena in the world are fundamentally born of the same root as we ourselves. The philosophy of the *Brahmanas* starts from the life of the physical body and goes on to talk of the life of the soul. But it stops there and does not explain why things are so. The *Upanishads*, on the other hand, take the self that is hidden within our bodies and minds, and analyze it into five treasuries and four states. The four states are wakefulness, dreaming, sound sleep, and death. The five treasuries are the self produced by tasting flavors, the self produced by the breath of life, the self produced by consciousness, the self produced by knowledge, and the self produced by joy. This self produced by joy is the realm where the soul by itself reaches its supreme point and is absolutely happy.

In sum, the ultimate aim of the *Upanishads'* philosophy of Brahman and Atman is to take the small self of the individual person, liberate it, elevate it, refine it, and return it to the great self of Brahman, like the hundred rivers returning to the sea, or a drop of water going back to its source. The whole universe and all the sentient beings in it, along with the dense array of myriad forms, are all no more than the transformations of the one great self, Brahman.

According to the *Upanishads*, the myriad apparent phenomena of this world, including devas, humans, animals, plants, and all living things, are all born from the transformations of Brahman. By means of the five great elements, earth, water, fire, wind, and space, Brahman gives birth by transformation to things born from eggs, things born from wombs, things born from heat, things born from moisture, horses, humans, elephants, plants and animals, and all kinds of things. Like the ocean rising up in waves, Brahman, through illusory transformations, produces the multitude of apparent phenomena. In doing this, Brahman has no particular aim, but is just playfully performing magical transformations. Therefore, all apparent phenomena are empty illusions. Only the one Atman/Brahman really exists.

The process by which Brahman gives rise to the world's myriad phenomena can be summed up into four phases. First, from the self of name and form (which can be said to be an abstract concept of subjective functioning), Brahman develops this world. Second,

Brahman also has an initial self, which gives rise to desires. From the imagination of desire flows forth water, fire, and earth, the three great original elements which form the personal self. Third, by transforming and combining with the personal self, Brahman enters into the other multitude of phenomena. Fourth, in making the world by means of selves, the sea and the wind come into existence, along with life and death. Brahman enters through the gate which living species have on the top of their heads, and makes their personal selves.

The personal self is the center of sentient beings. The term "sentient beings" is broadly inclusive. It includes the many kinds of devas and humans, as well as all the kinds of living things in the world. Brahman's own nature has two aspects. One aspect is the ability to maintain always the fundamental state of basic essence. Another aspect is the ability to develop into a living personal self. In other words, one aspect is the power to organize itself into the body belonging to a personal self (like a physical body), while the other aspect is the ability to transform into the life force and enter into the lives of all sentient beings (like a soul).

The physical-body part is analyzed into five kinds of winds and three qualities. The five kinds of winds are similar to what the Taoists call the energy system: exhalation, inhalation, the intermediate wind, the death wind, and the dissolving wind. The three qualities are joy, sorrow, and confusion. Atman is enclosed by the physical body and the mental consciousness and cannot go free. It is as if it is locked up in a prison. It is always within the small space at the base of the heart.

The Atman is always shut up within our relevant functions, that is, such functions as breathing, sensing, and intending. The eyes, ears, nose, tongue, and skin are called the organs of knowing: they are the source of knowledge. The hands, feet, tongue, excretory organs, reproductive organs, and others are called the organs, and they are the source of will. The controlling factor which links them together is intent.

When we are awake, because of the five winds and the various organs, we are entirely active and in motion. When we are dreaming, only the five winds and the intent are active. When we are sleeping without dreams, the intent stops and only the five winds are active. The state of awakening is the realm of liberation. This is exactly Atman's state of joy where there is no joy, no sorrow, no confusion, no pain, and no happiness.

There are only two roads the fate of sentient beings with personal selves can follow: cyclical existence and liberation. One is to follow apparent phenomena in their continuing transformations: this is cyclical existence. The other is to return to the fundamental state of Brahman: this is liberation. If sentient beings do not attain liberation, then they all go around and around within the three realms of heaven, earth, and space, in the three planes of existence and the four kinds of birth. The three planes of existence are: the plane of the devas; the plane of the ancestors or the plane of human beings; and the plane of animal existence and hell. The four forms of birth are birth from wombs, birth from eggs, birth from moisture, and birth from transformation.

The ultimate goal of the *Upanishads* is to find liberation, to get free of wrongdoings and afflictions. It is to awaken to the nondualistic purity of Brahman with human nature. The reason that people cannot return to the purity of Brahman is the barrier of ignorance and the absence of illumination. Conversely, with illumination, we can awaken to the purity of Brahman. How can humans return to the purity of Brahman? They must cultivate meditative concentration and yoga, control the movement of feelings and superficial phenomena, and chant the mantra OM, the symbol of Brahman. If they can chant it continuously, they can gradually get control of their bodies and minds and enter the nonduality where the real Atman and Brahman join.

THE RISE OF VARIOUS PHILOSOPHICAL TRENDS

In the process of change from the *Vedas* to the *Brahmanas*, and then to the *Upanishads*, the manner and the method of Indian religious philosophical investigations of the universe and human life became more and more rigorous. The content was also gradually enriched and became more all-inclusive. A welter of contradictions emerged in the thought of the *Upanishads*, however, and they still could not free themselves from the limited scope of the brahmanical religion. The spirit of seeking reality is the hidden basic nature of humanity, and at this point in Indian history this spirit asserted itself through religious philosophy.

The Six Schools of Philosophy

Around the period that Shakyamuni Buddha founded Buddhism, a profusion of various schools of philosophy, all seeking the truth for themselves, established their independence. Each had its own philosophical system and its own organized system of thought. It is customary in the study of Indian philosophy to speak of the six orthodox schools and the three heterodox schools. The six so-called orthodox schools were Samkhya, Yoga, Vaisheshika, Nyaya or Naiyayaka, Mimamsa, and Vedanta. These six schools accepted the authority of the philosophy that had come down from the *Vedas,* and they can be called the orthodox schools of the brahmanical religion. The three so-called heterodox schools were Buddhism, Jainism, and Worldly Secularism. These three schools were anti-orthodox: they did not accept the authority of Vedic thought.

The worldview of the Samkhya school was dualistic. It maintained that at the basic source of the world there were two original principles: a material inherent identity and a spiritual self. By the development of these two original principles, there came to be egotism, the five organs of knowledge, the five organs of action, the organ of mind, the five sense objects, and the five great elements. By means of these twenty-five truths, the Samkhya School accounted for the myriad forms of the world.

The Yoga school established its own philosophy based on the thought of the Samkya school. The Vaisheshika school, based on a pluralistic theory, put forward a materialistic view of the apparent world, and explained everything in terms of six fundamental categories: substances, qualities, actions, sameness, difference, and merging. The Nyaya school, with the thought of the Vaisheshika school as its background, developed a logic of causation and explanation in order to verify the validity of knowledge. The Mimamsa school continued the ritual forms of the *Brahmanas,* the books on pure conduct. The Vedanta school handed down and further expounded the philosophy of the *Upanishads.* In reality, all six orthodox schools were passing down the *Vedas,* with some small emendations, and putting a new face on them.

The Samkhya School: A characteristic of all the religions of India had been that, in their investigations of philosophical wisdom, they always went beyond the subjectivity of absolute faith. The philosophy of the Samkhya school affirmed from the first that the real world is characterized by suffering and the absence of bliss, and that people must seek liberation. It taught that people must first comprehend the causes of this suffering. It recognized that such methods as being born as a deva and offering sacrifices and prayers were surely not the means to ultimate liberation. It taught that this world is hard pressed by three kinds of suffering: internal suffering, the suffering associated with sickness (paralysis, fever, congestion), and psychological suffering (being parted from loved ones, being put together with hated enemies, not getting what you seek, the suffering that comes with birth); external suffering, not being able to get free of the pressures and harm done by the material world; and natural suffering, not being able to get free of the bondage imposed by the natural world.

The Samkhya philosophers propounded the theory that the result is there in the cause. They established the doctrine of two primal factors, material inherent nature and spiritual self, as their basic principle. At the same time, they established the twenty-five essences as the real truth of the universe and human life. They put forward a theory of three kinds of awareness: experiential awareness (also called immediate awareness, resembling direct awareness and experience); comparative awareness (the usual form of knowledge, the comparative judgment where things are known by inference); and awareness of the words of the sages. To these three kinds, the Nyaya school added awareness by metaphoric comparison. On the basis of these categories of awareness, the Nyaya philosophers thought that the existence of the gods could not be proven and thus could not be known with certainty, and so they approached a kind of atheism.

The so-called twenty-five essences are shown in the following chart:

Neither subject nor object of creation: the spiritual self
The creative subject: inherent nature
Both subjects and objects of creation:
    Egotism
    The five sense objects:
        form, sound, scent, taste, touch.
The objects of creation:
    The five great elements:

space, wind, fire, water, earth
The five organs of knowledge:
    ears, skin, eyes, tongue, nose
The five organs of action:
        tongue, hands, feet, sexual organs, excretory
        organs
The organ of mind

It is obvious that the philosophical thought of the Samkhya school
had emerged from the brahmanical religious consciousness, which
tended toward rational investigation and research on life. It was
seeking liberation from cyclical existence and realization of the
fruit of the path. In the Chinese Buddhist canon among the scriptures of the Samkhya school there is the *Golden Seventy Treatise,*
translated by Paramartha, which can provide research material. But
there are still many deficiencies in the Samkhya philosophical system as a whole and its theoretical structure, and it cannot make its
case convincingly.

The Yoga school: Basically, the philosophical thought of the Yoga
school came out of the same trend as that of the Samkhya school.
The difference is that, in the basic principles of the Samkhya
school, there was a great tendency toward atheism whereas the
Yoga school posited a transcendent god, Maheshvara Deva. "Yoga"
means contemplative practice and accord between god and man.
Thus some translate it as "accord" and some as "meditation" or
"meditative contemplation."

    There are four types of yoga scriptures. The first type are
those on *samadhi,* called *Samadhi Pada,* which explain the basic
nature of *samadhi.* The second type are those on method, called
Sadhana Pada, which explain methods to cultivate in order to
enter *samadhi.* The third type are those on spiritual powers, called
Vibhuti Pada, which explain the basic principles of spiritual powers
and classify them into types. The fourth type are those on existing
independently, called *Kaivalya Pada,* which explain the highest
goal, which is to reach the realm of the spiritual self which is absolutely free and without bonds.

    In the main, the philosophy of the Yoga school is similar to
the Samkhya school. The only difference is that it changes inherent
nature to the twenty-fourth truth, the spiritual self into the

twenty-fifth truth, and posits Maheshvara as the twenty-sixth essence. Maheshvara (the name means "Great Lord") has no sentiments, no thoughts, no karma. He is not subject to karmic reward and punishment: he is transcendent, beyond the pain and pleasure of karmic reward. He developed into a great spiritual self beyond time and space. He is the teacher of all devas and humans. His sign, his mantra, is the Sanskrit OM. By chanting that mantra, people can reach accord with Maheshvara. But the god posited by the Yoga school cannot be separated from the body and mind of the personal self. Therefore, the Yoga school's methods and principles of cultivation all proceed from the mental and the physical, and aim to cut off desires, purify the mind, and seek liberation.

The cultivation methods of the Yoga school proceed from eight methods of practice to reach the realm of spiritual powers and liberation. The so-called eight branches of practice are prohibitions against evil conduct, encouragements to good conduct, methods of sitting, tempering the breath, curbing confusion, holding steady, quieting thoughts, and equipoise. The first two branches of practice must be observed in common by everyone, whether they are cultivating the path or they are in conventional life. The remaining six branches are the special practices that must be cultivated by those who are cultivating Yoga practice.

1. **The prohibitions** are disciplinary precepts for conduct. One must observe the five precepts against killing, robbery, sexual excess, lying, and covetousness.

2. **The encouragements** urging pure conduct. One must do five things: be satisfied, practice austerities, learn how to chant mantras by reading and from memory, and piously serve the major gods.

3. **Methods of sitting**: altogether there are from eighty-four to over ninety-six methods. There is lotus sitting, lion sitting, rooster sitting, bowing and sitting, and so on. There are also many different mudras formed with the hands and fingers. These are all secret signs for attaining spiritual powers.

4. **Tempering the breath**: various methods for refining the breath, patterns of breathing, and methods of breath-work.

5. **Curbing confusion**: to control the confused feelings of the body, there are such methods as contracting like a turtle to rein in the six sense organs, which can be used to reach a state similar to that of animals when they hibernate.

6. **Holding steady**: to enable the mind to be unmoved, cut off all false thoughts, and fix the mind in one place.

7. **Quieting thoughts**: by holding the mind motionless, one can merge mind and objects, and attain meditative concentration where everything is unified.

8. **Equipoise** (which is *samadhi*): in the end, one causes the mind to be like empty space, like a mirror reflecting the myriad forms.

The three branches from holding steady to quieting thoughts and equipoise are the central cultivation methods of the Yoga school. By means of these, one attains inconceivable spiritual powers and wisdom. To put it another way, at last one attains the level where one's own inconceivable latent powers are unfurled. Through one's own inherent nature, one attains liberation and enters the realm of wisdom. But there are differences in the depth of *samadhi*. Generally, *samadhi* is divided into two types: with thought (with mind) and without thought (without mind). *Samadhi* without thought is the highest realm of concentration free from thought. If one can proceed from *samadhi* with thought and reach the wondrous realm without mind, then one can enable the spiritual self to shine alone, transcendent. By cultivating yoga, one can achieve spiritual powers.

According to what is recorded in the Buddhist *Treatise on the Mind of Skill in Means*, the Yoga school has eight subtle methods of explanation. They are the four great elements (earth, water, fire, and wind) along with space, intent, illumination, and lack of illumination. The Yoga school speaks of eight forms of sovereign mastery: the ability to become small, the ability to become large, the ability to lift things easily, the ability to go far, the ability to follow what the heart desires, the ability to divide the body and appear at many places at once, the ability to be honorable and excellent, and the ability to conceal the body.

We should rather say of the Yoga school's philosophy that it is a doctrine of realization rather than a learned system of thought. Its theories are a gradual transformation of the Upanishadic teachings that have come down from antiquity, but the Yoga school puts particular emphasis on meditation and contemplative practice, on using one's body and mind to seek realization of the truths of its religious philosophy. The methods it employs are almost scientific. In terms of their methods for seeking realization, none of the Indian religions and schools of learning can be separated from the Yoga school's meditation and contemplation, and Buddhism is no exception. It is just a matter of the degree of depth of what is realized, and differences in the accuracy of the perception of truth.

The Vaisheshika School: The name of this school is rendered into Chinese in various ways. The standard term means "school of victorious argument." The Sanskrit word means something like "differentiating special characteristics." At first, the school was founded on the theory of six categories for analyzing all phenomena and later this was developed into ten categories. In the Chinese Buddhist canon, there is included a translation by Dharma master Fazang of a treatise on the Vaisheshika school's ten categories by the shastra master Jnanacandra. His account of the ten analytic categories is approximately as follows:

1. **Substance:** This is a translation of the Sanskrit word *dravya.* This means that the intrinsic qualities of the real essence of the myriad forms of being in the universe include time and space. (In terms of Chinese philosophy, this is *ti,* substance.)

2. **Qualities:** This is a translation of the Sanskrit word *guna.* It means the phenomenal appearances of the myriad forms of being in the universe. (In terms of Chinese philosophy, this is *xiang,* form.)

3. **Actions:** This is a translation of the Sanskrit word *karma.* It means the functions and activities of the myriad forms of being. (In terms of Chinese philosophy, this is *yung,* function.)

4. **Sameness:** This means that, amid the difference in the multitude of apparent forms of being, there are basic principles which they have in common.

5. **Difference:** This means that, within the sameness of the myriad forms of being, there are all kinds of different specific qualities.

6. **Merging:** This means that substance and qualities, subject and object, are totally connected within the parts of things.

7. **Capability:** This means the inherent capacities of the substance, qualities, and actions of the myriad forms of beings.

8. **Without capability:** This refers to one's own results being born spontaneously, without involvement in the results of others.

9. **Categorical consistency:** This means that those with the same essence are similar to each other, like humans and other humans, and that those with a different essence are dissimilar to each other, like humans and animals.

10. **Nothingness:** This means that, ultimately, the myriad forms of being and the multitude of apparent phenomena do not exist.

The guiding principle of the Vaisheshika school was to use its ten categories to make deductions and analyses. These included theoretical discussions of psychology, physiology, material things, spiritual things, time, and space. The philosophers of the Vaisheshika school thought that the material world existed objectively. At the same time, they established a very subtle doctrine analyzing matter into major types, resembling the theories of molecular and atomic physics that are current today. They thought that atoms existed eternally in infinite numbers and, due to invisible forces, assembled together and scattered apart. They pushed their analysis to the point where things could not be further divided—the atomic level—and declared that there was no other master of creation. They said that atoms were invisible and could not be further divided, and that they endured forever without changing and without being destroyed, without beginning and without end.

The Vaisheshika philosophers said that atoms were spherical in shape and that they were one-sixth the size of the particles of floating dust visible in sunlight. They said that the atoms of the four great elements, earth, water, fire, and wind, were all different from each other, and that they had a color, a scent, and a feel, as liquids do. The atoms congealed together and formed double atoms, called child-atoms. When three double atoms joined together, they formed triple atoms, called grandchild-atoms, which were the same size as particles of floating dust visible in sunlight. When four triple atoms joined together, they formed a quadruple atom. The process of aggregation continued like this, through many stages, eventually forming the universe and all its worlds.

The Vaisheshika atomic theory is similar to the atomic theory and materialism of early Greek philosophy, and to the *yin-yang* theory of the Chinese *Book of Changes*. The people of several regions reached the same conclusions by different routes, and approached the atomic theories of modern science.

But traditionally, the ultimate spiritual aim of Indian civilization was always to seek liberation from the human world. Since this Vaisheshika theory was developed in India, its ultimate aim was still to seek spiritual liberation, not to investigate and develop knowledge of the material aspects of the world. A characteristic of the Vaisheshika school was its theory that results are not present in causes, and that moving along the path of liberation meant seeking true knowledge and clear perception. This was equivalent to a theory of pure knowledge. Vaisheshika theories were very numerous, and this account will stop here after this brief provisional introduction. In our Chinese Buddhist canons, there are works, such as the *Commentaries on the Hundred Treatises* and *Accounts of Consciousness Only,* that you can consult as sources on the Vaisheshika school.

The Nyaya School: The Sanskrit word *nyaya* has the meaning of logical inference and logical criteria. The common practice in Chinese is to translate it as "the school of correct logic." This is the ancestral school of Indian logic. The aim with which the Nyaya school was founded was still to seek true knowledge and reach the stage of the liberation of wisdom. Later, it developed into a system of formal logic with five branches: propositions, causation, metaphor, concatenation, and conclusions. The later Indian systems of strict logical inference were all successors to one of the Nyaya school's methods of seeking knowledge, namely, logic, but they did not have the great purpose of the Nyaya school. Some people think that the connection between the development of logic in the West and in India gives much food for thought, but this is beside the point for our present subject, and for now we will not discuss it.

The Mimamsa School: The Sanskrit word *mimamsa* has the meaning of pondering, investigating, or doing research. The Mimamsa school's philosophy can be described as a religious philosophy that researched the doctrines of the brahmanical religion and propagated the thought of the *Vedas*. The Mimamsa philosophers undertook to spread orthodox interpretations of the sacrifices and religious methods of the *Vedas*, and ponder and investigate the inner meaning of the *Upanishads*.

In the course of this, the Mimamsa philosophers propounded the doctrine of the eternal existence of the actual sounds of the Vedic teachings. They thought that the words of the Vedic scriptures had an intrinsic reality in addition to their meaning that endured forever, along with them, without changing. They thought that the texts of the *Vedas* were divinely created scriptures, that they were undeniably true, and moreover, that the sounds of their words had an esoteric spiritual power. They worshipped them as the supreme principle, so the sounds of the Sanskrit words were imbued with supreme authority.

This philosophical foundation provided the basis for the later Esoteric Buddhist theory of *mantrayoga*. It was extraordinarily powerful. As for the method by which this theory was established by the Mimamsa philosophers, it was by no means blind, dogmatic superstition. They used logical methods as their basis and established a theory of awareness. They distinguished immediate awareness through experience and realization, comparative awareness involving knowing by inference, awareness on the basis of metaphoric comparisons, and awareness by criteria of meaning. In order to uphold the brahmanical thought of the ancient scriptures, they completely opposed Buddhist anti-ritualism. But they were still not able to establish a theory that only god exists, and so Vedanta arose to repair this deficiency.

The Vedanta School: The Vedanta school arose as a continuation of the Mimamsa school. It too was a philosophy that opposed Buddhism and did its utmost to maintain the truth of the *Vedas* and *Upanishads*. It established a monistic concept of Brahman as the ultimate. As the name implies, Vedanta was a development of the *Vedas*.

Though Mimamsa and Vedanta developed comparatively late, and because they were in the main line of Indian religious philosophy, their theories had a great influence on people's minds. Thus they are generally mentioned along with the four great schools discussed previously.

The Buddhism of Shakyamuni versus non-Buddhist Paths

From the foregoing introduction, we have already become acquainted to some small degree with the civilization and religious thought of ancient India, and the profusion of different philosophies and various schools of learning. From our historical and cultural viewpoint as Chinese, the situation in ancient India was exactly like the period at the end of the Eastern Zhou dynasty, when a multitude of philosophies contended with each other and diverse schools of thought flourished. There was ideological confusion, and the ideas in which people believed began to waver under the impact. Added to this were political factors, the economic poverty of society, and warfare between ethnic groups and rival aristocrats. As the saying goes: "Armies bring famine."

In response to the needs of the time, there arose extraordinary personalities aiming to purify the world and bring relief to the people. There are only two roads which such extraordinary people can follow. One is to seek military power to resolve the situation, carrying out a unification of the country and bringing peace and security to the people. This is the road of the hero. The other is to spread a higher culture and a new way of thought, teaching by word and by example and, as a sage, causing civilizing doctrines to spread throughout the country and to be transmitted for generations to come. A hero conquers everyone and makes all the people in the country submit to him. But he cannot conquer his own afflictions and suffering, or the sorrows of life and death. A sage conquers himself and, on behalf of all people, takes on the burden of long-term affliction, with the bravery it takes to eliminate the sufferings of others.

Given contemporary circumstances in India, Shakyamuni's Buddhism arose in response to a need. Naturally, it had its background in the times and its historical causes. What were the results of Buddhist philosophy and its methods of practice? We will discuss that later. Here we will only deal with the period surrounding Shakyamuni Buddha's appearance, and with the other people who lived at the same time and carried on religious teachings opposed to his. There certainly were such people. We will cite them as illustrative examples, so we can recognize just where the true meaning and spirit of Shakyamuni's Buddhism lay.

The Worldly School

The theory of this school was similar to modern materialism and close to modern-day existentialism. Its followers proposed the theory of depending on the world of apparent reality in all things and holding onto sentiments and thoughts, so it is called the school of following along with the world.

The Worldly school denied the authority of all religions. They thought that, apart from direct sensation, there is nothing that can be believed. Hence, they thought that the conclusions reached by logical inference were also unreliable. They thought that nothing really exists in this world except the four great material elements of earth, water, fire, and wind, which can be seen and touched. The four great elements join together to form all living things, including the bodies and lives of humans; they produce feeling and knowing just as molds form by spontaneous transformation. In turn, spiritual states are but the functioning of matter. In sum, according to the worldly school, apart from matter, no such thing as the spirit exists. Thus, people need only rely on their own sensations and desires, and hunt for happiness. While this body is in existence, people should satisfy their own desires: this is the ultimate human goal. Beyond enjoying this world, there cannot be any other ideal world.

The adherents of this Worldly school were full of romantic sentiments, and were very similar in their way of thinking to such modern day philosophies as materialism, hedonism, and passivity. They advocated the theory that everything happens spontaneously, without a cause; thus there are no causes and no effects. Their refrain was: heaven does not exist; liberation does not exist; there is no spiritual existence; there are no other worlds; thus there is no such thing as karmic reward and punishment.

In fact, this kind of thinking has existed always and everywhere in the contradictory psychology of the human race. Sentient beings are always in an eternal night of dreams, and the morning bell and the evening drum can do nothing about it! But at the time when Shakyamuni Buddha was spreading his teaching, this way of thinking was very powerful. From this, we can imagine the state of unrest in Indian society at that time, and the trend toward decline.

Any society in a state of unrest, in a period of sadness and disillusionment, or when the history of its civilization is going down hill—any society like this, if it does not take vigorous determined action, will move into a state of passivity and intoxication with the enjoyment of immediate reality. When that happens, even if these kinds of ideas and these kinds of proposals do not become a school of thought, they will spontaneously exist in the widespread consciousness of the people. And if people advocate them, they will be enunciated as truths and demonstrated in people's conduct. In this way, they will come to have the power of a school of thought.

Jainism

The founding teacher of Jainism was Vardhamana Mahavira, a contemporary of Shakyamuni Buddha. He was born in a Kshatriya lineage in the region near the city of Vaishali. At the age of twenty-eight, he left home to seek the path. After cultivating practice for twelve years, he thought he had attained great penetrating enlightenment. He was called Jaina, which means "victorious." In the twenty or thirty years of the latter part of his lifetime, he organized a congregation of *shramanas* and wandered around teaching throughout the countries of Magadha and Vaishali. At last, he died in the village of Prava in Magadha.

Not long after Mahavira's death, his disciples divided into two great sects, the white-robed sect and the naked sect (also called the natural-body sect and the empty-robe sect). In the Buddhist scriptures, the Jainas are called Nirgranthas which means "free from all ties." When there was a great famine in Magadha, one group of Jaina monks moved to southern India under the leadership of the head of the group, Bhadrabahu. The group that remained in Magadha assembled a collection of holy scriptures. Later on, when the group that had gone to the south returned to Magadha, they refused to accept this collection of scriptures. In their opinion, only the southern group that advocated going naked was correct. Because of this, a movement gradually arose that split the Jainas in Magadha into a sect that wore white robes and a sect that went naked. By the first century A.D., this split was an accomplished fact. Subsequently, there were even more divisions into branch sects. Even at the present day, there are many men cultivating the path in southern India who still go naked like this.

The philosophical thought of the Jainas was similar in the main to the Samkhya doctrine that opposed mind and matter. They thought that spiritual life had a living soul and that material life did not. They were pure dualists, but they thought that spiritual life was not outside of matter. They also established a theory of seven truths: life, the nonliving, leakage, bonds, control, peaceful stillness, and liberation. When the two truths of good and evil were added to these, there were nine truths in all. From their fundamental philosophical standpoint, the Jainas were dualistic or else pluralistic, and this was always self-contradictory.

The Jainas used the two truths of life and the nonliving as the essential elements in their theory of the karmic rewards of birth and death, and liberation. The other truths were derived from these two. They thought that life is a real essence, basically inherently pure by nature. Because it is covered over by the nonliving (by material things), it loses its fundamental light. All the activities of living are karma. Karma percolates into life, and so it is called leakage. In the Jaina theory, what is called karma is a rarefied form of matter: when the body is in motion, it excretes a rarefied form of matter. Thus, this body is the karmic body. The karmic body ties down life with bonds and joins together with the nonliving to make us revolve in the planes of existence and receive pain and pleasure. To be liberated from cyclical existence, we must cultivate austerities and control the flow of karma into life: this is control.

Through control, we reach the level where old karma is obliterated and new karma is not born: this is peaceful stillness. When we progress further and annihilate all karma, life separates from matter and transcends the world: this at last is liberation.

There was another aspect of Jaina theory which showed similarities to the theory of magnetic fields in modern physics. This is very interesting. Now the Jainas divided their category of life into four components: space, dharmas, nondharmas, and matter. When these four components of life were united, they called it a real entity. These four components are what constructs the whole universe. Space is the field in which myriad beings and a multitude of apparent phenomena are formed and move. This field gives all things their basic principles: space itself is a single whole, infinite, eternal, and inactive. But the Jaina theory also said that space is space at the conceptual level. Dharmas are the conditions for movement, the space in which movement is possible. Nondharmas are the conditions for stillness, the space in which stillness is possible. Both dharmas and nondharmas are eternal, single, inactive, independent entities. Matter is comprised of the gross or fine forms made up by the joining together or dissolution of color, scent, taste, touch, sound, etc. It includes the material entities of darkness, shadows, light, and heat. The fine forms of matter are atoms; the coarse forms are compounded things. Atoms are not necessarily indivisible, but they are so rarefied that they occupy a point in space, and their movements are extremely swift. They join together like dryness and moisture, and so they form compound things, and from this they construct objects.

Life, dharmas, nondharmas, and matter coexist in space; they make up the apparent forms of the world. In Jaina theory, transcending this space (this material space) is what is meant by transcending the world. The Jainas thought that *nirvana* was liberation from the revolving flow. As Buddhism has the three jewels of the Buddha, the Dharma, and the Sangha, the Jainas also spoke of three jewels: correct faith, correct knowledge, and correct conduct. They advocated the cultivation of austerities. They accepted the caste system and some of their teachings are the same as those of the brahmanical religion. But they rejected the *Vedas,* forbade sacrifices, and prohibited the killing of living beings. In these ways, their spirit was similar to that of Buddhism.

The Outside Paths of the Six Teachers and Others

Next we will discuss the outside paths of the six teachers who were contemporaries of Shakyamuni Buddha. Although these teachers all propounded different theories and disputed among themselves, they were influential at the time and later, and each possessed his own faithful followers. At various points in the Buddhist scriptures, they are mentioned and criticized. But, apart from the Jainas, whose own scriptures are still extant as testimony, the other schools of thought have left only a few fragments from which we may catch glimpses of the contents of their theories. Even though not much remains of them and the ideas they propounded tend toward the preposterous, nevertheless, if they were able to become schools of thought, they certainly must have had some reasoning that could justify their absurd claims. What follows is an approximate account of them.

Purana taught that there is no good or evil in anything, that there is no karmic reward or punishment for merits or wrongdoings, and that there are no gradations of karmic power. This line of thought seems to be based on the concepts of the Worldly school of thought.

Maskarin taught that there are seven components to the bodies of all sentient beings: earth, water, fire, wind, suffering, pleasure, and life. These seven components are indestructible and remain forever without moving. Thus, they can be flung on a sharp blade and still not be injured, because there is nothing that is susceptible of injury and nothing that can die. This line of thought is close to materialism, but it seems to be a development based on the atomistic concepts of the Vaisheshika school.

Sanjayin taught that there are two essential points. The first is to respect the power of the apparent reality of the world. The second is the concept of the survival from previous lives. His followers thought the sovereignty exercised by a monarch could be reborn after his material death and that humans could be reborn after death, just like the plants that die in Fall, remain dormant in Winter, and then return to live again in the Spring. Thus, after dying, people return to be born again in this world. Levels of suffering and pleasure do not depend on the karma people create in their present lives; they are all due to past connections. The present has no causes and the future has no results.

But Sanjayin taught his followers that, if in their present conduct people uphold discipline, practice diligently, and work hard to progress and cover over the evil results in the present life, then they can attain a level where there are no leaks and thereby exhaust the karmic power of the past. Thus they can make all suffering end. When the multitude of sufferings has ended, this is liberation. This kind of thinking seems to be based on the Samkhya theory that results are present in causes.

Ajita-kesakambala's teaching also took the position that there is no good or evil, no disasters or blessings, and denied the theory of cause and effect, or karmic reward and punishment. It seems to be derived from a concept of inert emptiness.

Kakuda-katyayana's teaching took the position that if people kill living beings and feel no remorse in their minds, then in the end they cannot fall into the evil planes of existence, since their minds would be like empty space without a speck of dust or water. If they feel regret, then they enter hell. It is like water soaking in and wetting the earth. The lives of all sentient beings were created by Ishvara. Thus there is no question of human merit or wrongdoing; human behavior is all mechanical. The master craftsman who constructed this mechanism is Ishvara. This line of thought seems to be based on the theories of the Yoga school, progressively deteriorating and becoming more and more aberrant.

Nirgrantha's teaching took the position that there is no such thing as giving charity, no such thing as good, no such thing as father and mother, no present and no future, no arhats, no such thing as cultivation, and no such thing as the path. All sentient beings undergo the cycle of birth and death for eighty thousand eons and then spontaneously attain liberation, no matter whether or not they have faults. It is like the four great rivers of India all entering the ocean, with no distinctions among them. Sentient beings are also like this; when they attain liberation, there are no distinctions among them.

This kind of thought was a totally nihilistic theory of one-sided emptiness. Buddhism is good at speaking of emptiness, but emptiness in the Buddhist sense is not the materialistic concept of nothingness. If you study Buddhism without understanding this clearly, you will always take the emptiness of which the Buddha speaks as close to the outside paths' view of emptiness. But this is something that is not new. Go wrong by the slightest bit at the beginning, and you're off by a thousand miles at the end. In your study of cultivation, you must be alerted to this.

There is another account of the six teachers of the outside paths related in the notes to the *Vimalakirti Sutra*:

> Purana taught that nothing exists, that all phenomena are like empty space, and are neither born nor destroyed. Maskarin taught that the sins and defilements of sentient beings have no causal conditions.
>
> Sanjayin taught that it is not necessary to seek the path. He taught that after a certain number of eons going through birth and death, the end of suffering is attained spontaneously. It's like winding a thread around a mountain: when the thread is used up, it stops. Ajita-kesakambala taught that if you experience suffering in this life, in future incarnations you will experience eternal happiness.
>
> Kakuda-katyayana taught in terms of both existence and nonexistence, giving answers according to the questions he was asked, adopting views in response to people. If someone asked if phenomena exist, he would answer that they do exist. If someone asked if phenomena are nonexistent, he would answer that they are nonexistent.
>
> Nirgrantha taught that wrongdoing and merit, suffering and happiness, are all due to past lives, that you must pay back what you owe. Even if you practice the path in this life, you cannot cut off the results of past karma.

The notes to the *Vimalakirti Nirdesha Sutra* conclude that these six teachers all created misguided views. They claimed that going naked and practicing austerities constituted omniscience.

The common practice in discussing the sectarian divisions in classical Indian philosophical thought is to focus on the six major schools and the six heterodox teachers discussed above. But, according to what is recorded in the translations of the various Buddhist scriptures, there was a great profusion of separate sects which was not limited to these alone. The Buddhist sources commonly speak of more than ninety-six non-Buddhist views. The *Yoga Shastra* mentions sixteen opinions (sixteen theories based on subjective views), sixty-two views (sixty-two differing ideas), and so on.

Other examples are the *Treatise on the Nirvana of the Outside Paths and the Lesser Vehicle*, which lists twenty non-Buddhist sects, and the *Vairocana Sutra*, which, in its chapter, "The Mind Abiding in the Path," lists thirty non-Buddhist sects. Some taught that time is the basis for the formation of the universe and the myriad beings. Some proposed space as the principle formative factor, or the western direction, or the natural world. In voluminous writings, each school propounded its own theory.

If we want to study the world's philosophical thought and religious philosophy, Indian civilization alone already contains all the types of thinking found from ancient to modern times all over the world. We can acclaim Indian philosophy as an unsurpassed marvel.

But over the generations, those who have studied Indian philosophy have only paid attention to the different doctrines and theories of the various schools of thought. In general, they have overlooked the fact that all schools of thought in India adopted the method of seeking realization through experience. In regard to Indian philosophy, it is without doubt a great shortcoming to speak only of theories and not of practical methods. Thus, most students of the classical Indian philosophies have not viewed them in their entirety.

In sum, except for the Worldly philosophy which emphasized a doctrine of enjoying apparent reality, the main teaching of the other schools of Indian philosophy tended toward doctrines of transcending the world. All of them used yogic concentration and contemplation as the guiding principle for cultivating realization. In terms of differences in their methods of yogic concentration and contemplation, each of the various schools had its own theories and attainments. On this basis, there formed the overall Indian philosophical view of methods of cultivating realization, but this is beyond the scope of this book and, for now, we will not deal with it. Nevertheless, the Buddhist teachings and methods of seeking realization are inseparably linked to meditative contemplation and yoga, so we need to give an explanation of these things before proceeding to the main topic.

CHAPTER SUMMARY

The foregoing discussion of Indian religion and philosophy leads us to two conclusions. First, ancient India's learned thought had developed in many different directions and showed many marvels. This is understandable since, for any people with a long history, the legacy of culture and thought that they have accumulated over time will not be simple. Unfortunately, in the case of India, the country never passed through a long period of complete unification, and so the many branches of ancient Indian culture and philosophy appear jumbled and it is hard to distinguish clearly among them.

Developing from the *Vedas,* the *Brahmanas,* and the *Upanishads,* Indian religious philosophy evolved into various schools of thought and also brought forth the theories of the six major non-Buddhist teachers contemporary with Shakyamuni Buddha. But this was the situation in the culture and thought not only of ancient India, for it has turned out that, up to the present day in Indian religion, or in the various religious sects that are freely accepted in various parts of the country, they still preserve the ideas and forms of the traditions of the past. These traditions, with their history of several thousand years, have already fused into a single whole with everyday life. In other words, these things have already become part of the popular consciousness.

Therefore, if we do not arrive at a deep understanding of Indian culture, but instead just get a superficial impression and look at things on the surface, or we only study matters from a single point of view, then we may think that we have already understood the source of Buddhism. But in truth, we will have only a partial, misleading understanding. We will be like a crowd of blind men running their hands over an elephant, each of whom seizes upon one part of its body and thinks that that part typifies the whole elephant.

Moreover, if we do not proceed from the preexisting culture and philosophy of India in our attempt to understand and investigate Buddhism, even if we interpret the Buddhist scriptures as Buddhists, sometimes it is still very easy to mistakenly enter into the religion of the brahmans, or the thought of the other schools of philosophy. This is even more true of the explanations given by non-Buddhists who are estranged from Buddhism. Therefore, before giving an account of Buddhism, we must first deeply plumb the sources of the religious philosophies of Indian culture. At the same time, this will make those who study Buddhism more alert, so they can avoid getting tangled up in the intricacies of Buddhist philosophy.

The second conclusion concerns the rise of Buddhism. From the viewpoint of human life, there is sure to be a sequence of cause and effect that can be traced in the development of human civilization and the evolution of thought, as well as in the appearance of great personalities whose significant achievements in world-transcendence and worldly involvement have led them to found areas of learning and schools of thought. The founders of religions and the great philosophers cannot be exceptions to this rule. First of all, we must understand the religion and philosophy of the preexisting Indian culture, and from this we can discover the motive and goal of Shakyamuni Buddha's compassion and actions on behalf of the world. We can discover where the spirit of the Buddhism he founded lay and how it inherited its legacy from the past and opened the way for the future.

If we can temporarily put aside religious allegiances and let go of our tendencies to reject those who differ from ourselves, from the scholarly viewpoint we can see that there was not such a big difference between Shakyamuni Buddha's role in the ancient history of India and the role of Confucius in China. Confucius was afraid that the Tao of True Kingship was not being manifested, that human minds were getting bogged down, and that misguided doctrines were spreading everywhere. Therefore, he edited the *Classic of Poetry* and the *Classic of History*, defined the proper rituals and music, and wrote the *Spring and Autumn Annals* in order to clarify the principles of managing the world and preserve the tradition of the Tao, thereby perpetuating the spirit of civilization. In rejecting wrong paths, in expounding correct teachings, in concern for equity, in propagating civilizing teachings, in correcting thought and extending wisdom, the concern and spirit for saving the world and its people displayed by Confucius and Shakyamuni Buddha were not very far apart, though there are some slight differences between them. As for the differences in the relative profundity of the doctrines of the philosophies of Shakyamuni Buddha and Confucius, in all fairness, each has its strong points, but we should not force the comparison.

Shakyamuni Buddha was concerned to displace misguided doctrines and keep the true ones, and to cut away excessive complications and adhere to simplicity. But Buddhism itself, in the long run, could not take root and grow in India. As things turned out, the full glory of Buddhism had to wait until China accepted the entire legacy of its teachings and theories as a whole, and synthesized them together to establish a Chinese Buddhism whose glories have shone through ancient and modern times. This is really something inconceivable. But the same is true in the history of many of the world's great religions: in the region that produces the founder of a religion, the people are unwilling to value his contribution. They have to wait until people in other lands start to revere him, and only then can they see how precious he is. Gradually, it all flows back upstream to the source.

People all over the world, ancient and modern, have a common psychological pattern. Generally, they value what is far away and devalue what is close at hand; they revere the ancient and despise the modern; they like what is secret and hate what is manifest; they reject what is familiar and fall in love with what is strange. The common saying has it that: "A monk from far away chants the sutras better." Perhaps this is the same principle. In the future, will Chinese Buddhism have to wait for some monk from even farther away to come to chant the scriptures? This is enough to make people reflect deeply.

CHAPTER 2

Shakyamuni Buddha, the Founder of Buddhism

As previously stated, the formation and growth of a religion is sure to have its cultural background. There will be an even closer connection between the personal history of the founder of a religion and the religion which he founds. So before studying a religion, we must understand the life of its founder. This is something that cannot be overlooked.

In any religion, when it comes to speaking of the founder's life, believers are all sure to add a layer of myth and mysterious legend. Otherwise, it seems, there is not enough to highlight his sublimity and his greatness. Now that the twentieth century is here and scientific knowledge has spread everywhere, all traditional ideas must be judged anew, and even sacred inviolable religions cannot avoid this tendency of the times. Accordingly, if religions are based on myths and legends, they cannot be accepted by the widespread modern consciousness. It is preferable to study the life of the founder of a religion from a humanistic standpoint and investigate how he discovered the truth about the universe and human life, how he sublimated his human qualities, transcended ordinary life, and entered sagehood. An account of a religious teacher's life from this point of view is easy for people to believe and does not detract from the standing of the religion itself. But in introducing the life of the founder of a religion in an era when the old and new ideas are just replacing each other, we cannot stick rigidly to the old accounts throughout, nor can we altogether reject the old and adhere only to the new. All we can do is make an eclectic mix of elements from both, do all we can to arrive at relatively objective facts, and await the appraisal of the knowledgeable.

SHAKYAMUNI'S LINEAGE

As for the course of the life of Shakyamuni Buddha, the founder of Buddhism, as the whole world knows, he was born to the Indian nobility. The high standing of his family is clearly and reliably established. There was no need for Buddhist hagiographers to embellish on this any further: Shakyamuni was already born at the pinnacle of glory in the human world. His father was a king and he himself was the crown prince. This is something that everyone has known here in China in the two thousand years since Buddhism entered our country.

A Great Man Who Refused to be King

India, at the time when Shakyamuni was born, was quite similar to our own Spring and Autumn period. At that time in China, the 8th to 5th century B.C., the Zhou dynasty emperor held the highest position in the nation, but real power was held by the various feudal lords who had divided the country into rival territories. Furthermore, neighboring states encroached on each other. This was the period in Chinese history when the decentralized feudal system was rapidly heading for collapse. At that time, in the five regions of India, there was no central power with the strength to impose its rule and no common monarch. India was still experiencing a situation of small states led by chiefs holding local power. In fact, India as a whole was divided into two or three hundred states.

According to the traditional Chinese historical account, Shakyamuni's father was by no means an overall monarch or emperor who united all of India. He was only the king of a small local state. By lineage, he belonged to the class of *kshatriyas* who held military power and he possessed the authority of the hereditary nobility.

Among the ranks of all the founders of the world's great religion, Shakyamuni, with his royal lineage and his illustrious station, was by no means one of those who raised himself up above the dusts of conventional life because he had experienced the sadness of human life through hardships and suffering. On the contrary, he was born into circumstances of comfort, wealth, and honor. Nevertheless, he had an awakening and he vowed to seek the path of eternal liberation, not only for himself, but at the same time for all sentient beings. He boldly and decisively renounced his royal vocation and refused to be a king. With great vows of compassion to save sentient beings, with responsive teachings of enlightening practice addressed to all beings, he ended up founding the great religion of Buddhism, which represents the ultimate truth. This sagely spirit of his was really praiseworthy and deserves our acclaim and our respect.

The Dates of Shakyamuni's Birth and Death

In studying the life history of Shakyamuni, there is one difficult issue that should be confronted at the outset, even though there is no way to resolve it. All along, the Indians have lacked a concept of historical tradition and the idea of an accurate standard of historical time. In the past, when the Indians themselves spoke of history, they relied on the mythical epics of the brahmanical religion, and these always lacked a strict division between the past and the present generation. The history that Indians learn nowadays has been determined and compiled anew based on the researches of both Easterners and Westerners since the 18th century. Moreover, the classical Indian calendrical systems used years and months of different lengths from the modern calendar. The five regions of India—east, west, south, north, and center—differ in their local climates and their cold and warm seasons, and so they also had slight differences in their calendrical reckonings of the days, months, years, and seasons.

Therefore, ascertaining the dates of Shakyamuni's birth and death has become a disputed issue among Chinese and foreign scholars. Modern people believe in scientific methods and sometimes, when they displace old ideas with new ones, it is impossible to avoid shocking conventional opinion. When we try to ascertain anew something that took place thousands of years ago, if we cannot be careful and search for proof, bold hypotheses will always tend to be idiosyncratic or arbitrary and we can hardly accept this. Here, the best thing to do is be ready to compromise, rely on objective certainties, and thus seek a factual conclusion.

First, let us mention our sources. Texts bearing on the date of Shakyamuni's death include *Fa Xian Zhuan (Account of the Manifestation of the Dharma), Lidai San Bao Ji (Record of the Three Jewels Through the Generations), Po Xie Lun (Refutation of Heresies), Xiyu Ji (Record of Western Regions), Shijia Fangzhi (Gazetteer on Shakyamuni), Jiuling Shengxian Lu (Record of the Sages of Vulture Peak), Seng Shilue (Brief History of the Sangha),* and *Fanyi Mingyi Ji (Collection of Translation Terms)*, among others. From these records that have circulated in Tibet, Burma, Sri Lanka, and other countries, and from the works of European scholars, the theory that places the earliest date of Shakyamuni's death says that he died in 422 B.C. The latest date given is from 330–320 B.C. With these two opinions on the date of his death so far apart, this really seems to be an ancient historical fact worth investigating and unearthing.

But based on Western history and the data of world history, we can ascertain the date of the most glorious event in India at that time by the historical fact of the invasion of India by the king of Macedonia, Alexander the Great. Alexander's hitherto invincible army encountered the stubborn resistance of the soldiers of India and the arguments of the Indian philosophers. The time when Alexander the Great invaded India was precisely the time when King Ashoka, the great protector of Buddhism, had appeared in India. Now we can take as the point of reference the dates of King Ashoka, which all the world knows, and from them trace back his deeds and count back to the date when Shakyamuni Buddha died.

When we attempt, this we discover two facts. Most of the Buddhist texts of the northern transmission say that the rise of Ashoka and the death of Shakyamuni were separated by a hundred or more years. The Buddhist texts of the southern transmission say they were two hundred and eighteen years apart. The discrepancy of more than a hundred years might be due to the variations in the calendrical reckoning of dates in southern and northern India.

The date for Shakyamuni's death given by the Buddhist texts of the southern transmission accords with the date given in "Records of the Many Sages" in the *Lidai San Bao Ji*, written by Fei Changfang in the Eastern Han dynasty. The dates recorded in the *Da Tang Nei Dian Lu (The Inner Record of the Great Tang)*, the *Kaiyuan Shijiao Lu (The Kaiyuan Period Record of Buddhism)* and the *Zhenyuan Shijiao Lu (The Zhenyuan Period Record of Buddhism)* are all also close to this.

Tracing back from these Chinese sources, one can ascertain the date of Shakyamuni's death to be the thirty-fourth year of the reign of King Jing of the Zhou dynasty (486 B.C.). Tracing back another eighty years, the date of Shakyamuni's birth becomes the seventh year of King Ling of the Zhou dynasty, that is, 565 B.C. As for the month and day of his birth, by tradition in China, it is said to have been the eighth day of the fourth month. However, this is the date according to the Chinese lunar calendar, not the contemporary Indian calendar in use in those days.

In the final analysis, it is very difficult to say to what date on the contemporary calendar or lunar calendar Shakyamuni's birthday corresponds. Nevertheless, according to traditional practice in China, it is the eighth day of the fourth lunar month. This already has a history of over two thousand years behind it, and it does not seem necessary to keep arguing about this.

The Clan Tradition

As we have already indicated, we have determined the date of Shakyamuni Buddha's birth to have corresponded to the eighth day of the fourth month of the seventh year of the reign of King Ling of the Zhou dynasty in China (565 B.C.). Shakyamuni was born in the town of Kapilavastu in north-central India. In terms of Indian geography, this place was northeast of Benares and northwest of Patna, near Gorakhpur, on the southern border of Nepal in the valley of the Kohana River, known in ancient times as the Rohini, a branch of the Ganges. Shakyamuni Buddha's birthplace was in the Lumbini Garden to the east of Kapilavastu.

"Shakya" was his family name. It is translated into Chinese as "capable of true humanity." "Muni" was his sobriquet. It is translated into Chinese as "solitary." In addition, he had four other clan names: Gautama, Ikshvaku, Suryavamsa, and Sakya. His was a clan that belonged to the warrior class, the *kshatriyas*. According to the researches of later scholars of the humanities, this clan had originally migrated from Central Asia and had settled along the Indus River on the western side of the central plain of India. They passed their high position in the nobility down through the generations. The Shakya clan were the rulers of the Kapilavastu region: following the ancient Indian practice, they could be called kings of that country. At that time, Kapilavastu was located on the west side of the Rohini River. On the east side of the river was the town of Koli, which belonged to another *kshatriya* clan. These two clans intermarried in order to maintain close bonds of consanguinity.

When the worthy king of Kapilavastu, Suddhodana, was over fifty, Buddha's mother, Queen Maya, who was already over forty-five, became pregnant. She was fond of pure and quiet places and she liked to go for walks in the natural scenery of the gardens around the town. One day, when Spring was at an end and Summer was just beginning, on the eighth day of the fourth lunar month when the wind was mild and the Sun was shining and the birds were singing and the flowers were blooming, she was wandering in the Lumbini Garden. She saw a pure, shady Ashoka tree that was growing luxuriantly. As she raised her hands to break off a branch, unexpectedly Shakyamuni spontaneously came forth from her right side and there were all sorts of auspicious signs. The whole country rejoiced. This is the famous story of Shakyamuni's birth. The story goes that, when Shakyamuni was seven days old, his mother, Queen Maya, unfortunately passed away. Shakyamuni was therefore nurtured and raised by his aunt, Queen Mahaprajapati, whose name is translated into Chinese as "path of great love." He received the love and protection of his aunt, who cared for him as a mother would.

In most cases, the historical records of world-famous personages (for example, those that deal with the births of the founders of religions and the founders of empires), follow legendary accounts and are always full of supernatural omens like crimson lightning winding around a central pillar, or red lights filling a room. These kinds of things show that these are births of special consequence: their purpose is to provide the individual with a supernatural embellishment or cast them in the mold of an icon. This practice gives much food for thought.

The story of Shakyamuni's birth that we cited above surely belongs in the category of the supernatural, and strains our credulity. But in this story, there are several points worth noting. First, Suddhodana had his son late in life, and he was concerned with the continuity of his line and passing down the throne. It goes without saying that this was a fervent wish. Shakyamuni was born into a noble lineage, in opulent surroundings, but after he had grown up and become an adult, he boldly abandoned his royal position and left home to cultivate the Path. What kind of boldness of spirit was this? What kind of heart was this?

In addition, Buddha's mother gave birth to him through her side. This is indeed incredible to the ordinary person. But according to the legend that she died seven days after the birth, it is possible to imagine it as some kind of birth by Caesarean section, or perhaps some special kind of birth. This is almost beyond a doubt.

Finally, Queen Mahaprajapati, who raised Shakyamuni to maturity, was another of King Suddhodana's noble consorts. Later on, she followed Shakyamuni Buddha, left home to study the Path, and became a nun. From this it is obvious that she was both a great woman whose compassion will shine forever, and a venerable protector of the Dharma who was a woman of wisdom. When we think about this, we see that this was no chance occurrence, and she deserves our respect and reverence.

Legends of Shakyamuni's Innate Spiritual Uniqueness

According to what Buddhism says and the words of the classic Buddhist scriptures, we know that what is called the buddha-world is not only in this world. We know that this period and the presently existing time and space was inaugurated by the hand of Shakyamuni Buddha. It is said that this world on which we depend for our existence has passed through innumerable cycles of formation, abiding, and destruction. On the smallest scale, an example is that the earth has already had several ice ages and several periods of being inundated. It is truly the case that the sea has become dry land and the dry land has become the sea many times, but the existence of the Buddha Dharma has continued forever without being cut off.

According to Buddhist cosmology, we are now in the "eon of worthy sages." This term means that, in this universe over a period of billions of years, many worthy sages will continue to be born. By cultivating the bodhisattva path of Mahayana Buddhism, they have already realized the perfect enlightenment that is the fruit of the tenth-stages bodhisattvas. When their present lives end, they are reborn among the multitude of devas as devas of the Tushita Heaven, or devas of the inner court of the Tushita Heaven. They are called "auxiliary bodhisattvas." They wait until another eon arrives in this world and human history changes, and Buddhism in the world is declining toward extinction. Then these auxiliary bodhisattvas again enter into the human plane of existence to be born, leave home, and finally become buddhas. Then the Buddha Dharma flourishes greatly again and, because of them, the Buddha Dharma abides in the world. The auxiliary bodhisattva of the present is Maitreya, who is also the prospective buddha of the future.

Some accounts in the Buddhist scriptures say that Shakyamuni had been dwelling in another world, and he had long since become a buddha. He was born here in our world Saha to serve in his turn as the eighth buddha in the "eon of the worthy sages" of this world. (Some say he was the fourth buddha.) Before this buddha, there had already been seven other buddhas who had lived in our world.

The accounts in the various Buddhist scriptures relate five or six hundred stories of Shakyamuni's past lives and his virtuous conduct and myriad merits. In general, all of these are wondrous, superlative achievements of unexcelled meritorious deeds, and there is no need to explain them in detail one by one. But to sum up his whole life in the world, we generally speak of the eight special marks shown by Shakyamuni Buddha. These express the achievements of his lifetime, which can be divided into eight phases. The inner meanings of the eight special marks are as follows:

His descent from the Tushita Heaven to be born in our world: First Shakyamuni dwelt in the Tushita Heaven and, when he saw that the moment was ripe, he descended into the human world.

Going into his mother's womb: Riding to Earth on a white elephant with six tusks, Shakyamuni sent his spirit into his mother's womb.

His birth: On the eighth day of the fourth month, Shakyamuni was born from the right side of Queen Maya in the Lumbini Garden.

Leaving home: When Shakyamuni was 19, he saw that the world is impermanent, so he left the royal palace and went into the mountains to study the Path.

The descent of Mara to torment Shakyamuni when he was on the verge of enlightenment: After six years practicing austerities, sitting under the bodhi tree, Shakyamuni vanquished the armies of Mara, the demon of delusion.

Consummating the Path, attaining enlightenment: On the eighth day of the twelfth month, as he saw the morning star appear, Shakyamuni emptied out and was enlightened.

Turning the Wheel of the Dharma: After his enlightenment, Shakyamuni spent forty-nine years preaching the Dharma and saving living beings.

Entering final nirvana: After living in the world for eighty years, Shakyamuni entered final nirvana under the twin pala trees.

Besides these, the best thing to pay attention to in investigating the meaning of Buddhism and studying the biography of Shakyamuni is the following story, which is recorded in the scriptures. Soon after Shakyamuni Buddha was born, he could already walk. He took seven steps and said: "After countless eons, this is my last birth. Among all the devas and humans, I am the most honorable and the most excellent. In this lifetime I will benefit devas and humans. I vow to bring universal salvation to all sentient beings." After Buddhism was transmitted to China, this statement of Shakyamuni's was expressed as the saying: "In Heaven and on Earth, I alone am the honored one."

Stimulated by this, we must pay careful attention to investigating the following two points. First, if we look at this statement only from the religious standpoint, what Shakyamuni said at that time was meant to make people feel that this was a unique sign of possessing, to the highest degree, authority as the founder of a religion. People either feel absolute faith in this, or great repugnance.

Second, if we investigate it thoroughly, the statement "In Heaven and on Earth, I alone am the honored one," is where the essential meaning of Buddhism lies, because this statement explains the true value of human life and reveals the dignity of true human nature. We must have the spirit to develop ourselves and become the best possible human beings between heaven and Earth. We must have the courage to arouse ourselves and become the best possible beings between heaven and Earth. This is the best extension of the traditional idea in Chinese culture of "Heaven and humankind joining as one." Whether we proceed from being humans to being reborn as devas and becoming buddhas, thus becoming spiritual and sovereign, or whether we descend from being humans

and sink down, it all depends on ourselves and our choices of good
or evil. When Shakyamuni said, "In Heaven and on Earth, I alone
am the honored one," this "I" is not just the self of Shakyamuni
alone. It is just like the meaning of the Confucian saying: "What
kind of a man was [the sage] Shun? What kind of a man am I?" In
other words, self and others are of one enlightened suchness. So
such phrases refer to the inherently enlightened true self of human
nature.

Shakyamuni, the founder of the religion, was able to talk at
birth, developed quickly, grew up, and became a sage. But the
spirit of his lifetime of teachings is all in this statement he was able
to say shortly after his birth. By saying "In Heaven and on Earth, I
alone am the honored one," he had already revealed his message.
On the other hand, if we understand this purely from an emotional
viewpoint and see it as boasting, we are gravely slandering the
words of the Buddha.

A Special Youth of Many Talents

After Shakyamuni was born, his father, the king, invited many famous brahman scholars to perform the naming ceremony. Everyone knew that his birth had been accompanied by all sorts of auspicious signs, so they named him Siddhartha. This name means
"accomplishing all truths and possessed of lucky omens." His special marks and adornments were particularly beautiful.

At that time, among the Indian brahmans was a wise man of
the highest authority, Asita Rshi. He lived on Fragrant Mountain
cultivating the Path, far removed from any attachments, always in a
state of meditative concentration. Knowing that Shakyamuni had
been born, he came to offer salutations. Asita Rshi said to King
Suddhodana: "I see that the prince has the thirty-two marks and
the eighty good points of an enlightened sage. With these marks
and good points, if he stays in worldly life, at the age of nineteen
he will become a Cakravartin, a Wheel-Turning Sage King. If he
leaves home, he will achieve omniscience and bring salvation on a
wide scale to devas and humans. Your Majesty, I observe that your
son the prince will surely study the Path, attain true enlightenment, turn the wheel of the Great Dharma, benefit devas and humans, and open the eyes of the world."

King Suddhodana had had his son late in life and he most earnestly hoped that his son would be able to succeed to the throne and extend the power of the country. When he heard that his son might follow the road of leaving home to study the path, he was very worried. So he became even more intent on protecting Shakyamuni and devised ways to take precautions against his son leaving home. King Suddhodana made plans to have brought to the royal compound whatever would delight the senses and hoped to keep his son lingering among the pleasures of the sounds and colors of beautiful scenery and the enjoyments of the human world. He intended to make sure the prince would not think of leaving home, thus preventing the fulfillment of Asita Rshi's prediction.

When Shakyamuni was 7 years old, he began to receive instruction in the palace. King Suddhodana sought everywhere for noted teachers for him and ordered them to come and impart their learning to him. First, he invited a brahman named Visvamitra (the name means "chosen friend"), who was especially excellent in the cultivation of literary studies, to instruct Shakyamuni in literature. One day, Shakyamuni mentioned the fact that there were more than sixty-four writing systems in use in India at the time. He asked which one of them should be considered as the standard. This made Visvamitra feel extremely embarrassed. Moreover, the boy Shakyamuni was able to pick out the defective characters in books and ask his teacher about them. In the end, this made Visvamitra praise Shakyamuni and filled him with admiration. He felt ashamed of his own limited knowledge and withdrew from the position of Shakyamuni's tutor.

At the same time, King Suddhodana also invited a famous expert on the military arts from the Shakya clan called Kshantideva (the name means "god of patience"). He taught the boy Shakyamuni about military exercises and training and methods of using weapons, along with twenty-nine martial arts exercises. Thus by the time he was 14 or 15, Shakyamuni was able to tame a great elephant. With one hand, he could hurl an elephant over the city wall, then immediately pick the elephant up off the ground. The great elephant let him do this and did not injure him. When Shakyamuni bent his bow and shot arrows, they would pass right through a huge drum and still have enough force to penetrate the seven-layer iron boss on the target.

Shakyamuni started his studies when he was 7, and, over the course of the next seven years, he studied deeply and thoroughly mastered astronomy, geography, the classics, the commentaries, sacrifices, divining, philology, mathematics, music and dance, literary composition, painting, and all the contemporary arts and techniques.

To summarize, because he was the heir to a royal throne, Shakyamuni received an excellent education in the palace, and to this was added his innate intelligence and good qualities. So, by the time he was 15, he had already completed his learning in all branches of cultural and military knowledge. Thereupon, King Suddhodana set the eighth day of the second month of that year for the great ceremony anointing Shakyamuni and investing him with the position of crown prince. King Suddhodana invited the kings, great ministers, and brahmans of all the neighboring states to come view the ceremony. Shakyamuni was anointed with waters from the four seas, given the seal of office, and made heir apparent.

Shakyamuni's Compassionate Temperament

Due to his innate intelligence and his birth in a royal palace, Shakyamuni had thoroughly mastered all worldly learned knowledge and had naturally developed a level of wisdom surpassing that of ordinary people. Precisely because of this wisdom beyond that of other people, all his life he had delved into the universe and life, and he had doubts about worldly affairs and human life. Hence, in the end, there was no way he could rest content with apparent reality. Added to this, in contemporary India there was the constant fighting among rival lords and their domains and the vast inequality between the classes because of their lot in life. All these things struck his eye and agitated his mind. Because of this, with his great compassion for the uncontrollable pain of impermanence which the multitudes of the world's sentient beings always have with them, he used his compassionate heart to seek for the total release of all people from the sufferings and afflictions of the world. He wanted to enable human nature to rise to a higher level, and human life to attain liberation. For this reason, Shakyamuni was continually sunk in deep contemplation and silent concentration.

One day, while out for an excursion, he was resting beneath a large tree and saw a peasant working in the fields. The fierce Sun was beating down on the peasant, and he was covered with sweat as he struggled over his work. The plow oxen were pulling a double plow, being driven along with blows of a whip, and enduring cruel treatment. All in all, both man and beast were suffering, driven on by hunger and thirst. Shakyamuni also saw that, when the earth was turned over as the field was being plowed, the insects that lived under the ground had no way to hide. A swarm of insects crawled out, as if they already had sensed that a great disaster was imminent and were looking for someplace where they would be safe. As things turned out, a flock of birds gathered and ate them up, and Shakyamuni saw that not a single one escaped. These characteristics of worldly existence—the strong eating the weak, the troubles of a multitude of sufferings, the cruelty and heartlessness—all plunged Shakyamuni into even greater confusion and even deeper pain. What is human life for? Why does such a cruel world exist? What is the ultimate meaning of life in the universe? With this, Shakyamuni sat down under a tree and his mind felt an aversion to the world. He pondered the issues of worldly life and transcending the world, and again fell into a state of deep contemplation and silent concentration for a long time.

Thus, Shakyamuni's life in his early years was not one of joy and happiness because of the security and wealth and renown of his family. On the contrary, he was always looking for liberation from the afflictions and sufferings of the human world and passed his days in solitary contemplation. This made King Suddhodana remember Asita Rshi's prediction. He became afraid that Shakyamuni would leave home to study the Path, and he wept disconsolately.

Thus, when Shakyamuni was 17, King Suddhodana arranged for him to take as his consorts two beautiful girls named Yashodhara and Gopika. He also had palaces for the three seasons built for Shakyamuni. (North-central India does not get very cold, so he only built palaces for the three seasons.) This gave Shakyamuni an extremely comfortable and appropriate dwelling place for each of the three seasons, Spring, Summer, and Autumn. But Shakyamuni was not at all delighted by his beautiful consorts or the pleasures of his magnificent palaces. He did not desire these things or care about them at all. According to the accounts in the Buddhist scriptures, Shakyamuni never had conjugal relations with his two consorts, and this made them suspect that he was a man in appearance only. He understood their doubts, so one night while he was sleeping, he deliberately left his male parts showing so they could be sure that it was not that he was unable, but that it was his special excellence to refrain from sexual intercourse.

In order to resolve the question of human life and search for the ultimate truth of the universe, Shakyamuni wanted with all his heart to leave home and study the Path. This made his father, the king, and the whole royal family feel more and more burdened with sorrow, so the king ordered that Shakyamuni be prohibited from leaving the palace, lest even greater compassion for the world be aroused in him. Moreover, the king selected a famous brahmanical philosopher of deep learning named Udayin to be Shakyamuni's constant companion and become his friend, in the hope that Udayin would be able to guide and influence him to change his mind and become more interested in the world of apparent reality and mundane human life. But in the end, this too failed.

Shakyamuni was constantly requesting that his father let him travel outside the palace compound. He had understood that human life is impermanent and that no one can avoid the encroachments of birth, old age, sickness, and death. He understood that no one can escape from the trap of birth, old age, sickness, and death. He wondered whether or not there is an ultimate order over this impermanent life and whether or not ultimately there is a real self.

Shakyamuni thought along these lines: If there is no ruler, then the meaning of life is basically worthless and without a purpose. This is similar to the materialist viewpoint and later, in Buddhism, this is called the "annihilationist view." It is absolutely wrong. If there is a ruler and a real self does exist, then what form do they take? If we say it transcends humanity and myriad things, but still can control them, this is just something formed by the speculations or concepts of human psychology. Moreover, if a ruler had the power to control things, then why would it have to make this world and human life in so miserable a form? Later in Buddhism, this is called the "eternalist view." In reality, apart from mind, when we observe the worldly and the world-transcending, all phenomena are impermanent and there is nothing that exists eternally.

Thus Shakyamuni's intention to leave home and seek the Path became more and more urgent. He formally raised this request with his father, the king. King Suddhodana told him that, if Shakyamuni's consort Yashodhara were to get pregnant and bear a son, so that the royal succession would not be cut off, he would reconsider the matter. According to the account in the Buddhist scriptures, Shakyamuni then pointed to Yashodhara's belly with his right hand and caused her to feel pregnant immediately.

Like the story of Shakyamuni being able to walk when he was seven days old, this incident is easy to relate, but it is the same kind of extraordinary miracle and, in the same way, it is hard for people to believe. Nevertheless, for Shakyamuni to produce a son for his father's sake before leaving home, because his father was worried about the lack of an heir was an excellent fulfillment of the filial path, and stands to reason. Moreover, because he had fulfilled his duty as a son, afterward he was single-minded in his practice of the Path that transcends the world of humans and devas. This serves to show even more how admirable and great and rare and excellent his special qualities were. So, the tales of miraculous events are just superfluous: we can keep them without discussing them.

LEAVING HOME AND AWAKENING TO THE PATH

Because there are no credible historical accounts that we can use as evidence for the date when Shakyamuni left home, all we can do is follow the traditional account and say that he left home on the eighth day of the second lunar month of the year he turned nineteen. He judged that the circumstances were ripe, so, in the middle of the night when his wives and guards were sleeping soundly, he arose and summoned his groom, Chandaka, to saddle a swift horse, telling him that they would go together outside the city walls to drink the sweet dew and the spring water. Chandaka already knew what his intention was: he urged Shakyamuni not to go, but could not hold him back. All he could do was hold on to the horse's tail with all his might. Shakyamuni could not open the palace gate, so he boldly urged on his horse and, dragging Chandaka along with them, horse and rider leaped over the north wall and galloped off.

The way this scene unfolded was the beginning of Shakyamuni's lifetime of great courage and great compassion. We can compare this with the all-powerful commanding heroes who have gone to war a hundred times and won every battle, who

have plunged ahead into the torrent. This act of Shakyamuni
vaulting over the wall on his horse in order to leave home to
cultivate the Path was poles apart from the spirit of the home-
leavers we see before us nowadays. It is the business of heroes to
conquer the world, but it is extremely hard for humans to conquer themselves. Shakyamuni alone was the exception: with his
great fearless spirit, he conquered himself. He smashed the rebel-
lious mind in formlessness and cast aside temporal power like a
worn-out shoe. Thus he was able to transform the ordinary into
the wise, and he was worthy to be the teacher and model for humans and devas.

The Young Prince Who Fled the World to Seek Enlightenment

Once Shakyamuni and Chandaka had gotten past the north wall of
the city, they galloped off toward the east, moving so fast they
seemed to be flying. They came to the forest where the ascetic
Bhargava practiced austerities. The night had already passed and
the Sun was in their eyes.

Shakyamuni had his mind made up that he would enter Bhargava's retreat to ask about the Path, and so he ordered Chandaka
to return to the palace. He took off the pearl in his topknot for
Chandaka to take back to the king and removed his necklace, to
offer to his aunt. As to his other ornaments, he told Chandaka to
give them to Yashodhara. After he had given away all his finery, he
took his sword and cut off his beard and hair. He changed his
clothes and put on an ascetic's robe to show his resolve to go forward to cultivate the Path. At the same time, he took an oath: "If I
do not finish with birth and death, I will never return to the
palace. If I do not consummate the Path of enlightenment, I will
never return to see my father, the king. If I do not exhaust my sen-
timental feelings of gratitude and love, I will never return to see
my aunt and my two wives."

All this made Chandaka distraught and he was crying with
sadness, to the point that he passed out. When he revived, all he
could do was return to the palace and report that the crown prince
had left home. This filled the whole city with sorrow, even as they
sighed in admiration for Shakyamuni's bold resolve.

Shakyamuni Studies the Various Schools for Six Years

After this, Shakyamuni drifted like the clouds, going everywhere to study and learn. He saw the place where Bhargava and his followers cultivated their practices. He saw many people who cultivated the Path through austerities, people who had detached from sensory experience and cut their ties with the conventional world. Some wore clothes of grass, some wore clothes of bark. They all ate wild fruits to satisfy their hunger. Some ate only a single meal a day, some a single meal every two or three days. Their plan was to complete the Path through the practice of austerities. They treated the myriad beings with respect. Some worshipped water or fire, or made offerings to the Sun and Moon. Some lay in the mire or slept in thickets of thorns. Some stayed close by fire or water for years, enduring the sufferings of being scorched or soaked.

Such things were the traditional forms of religious life and methods of cultivating the Path within Indian culture. Around the time that Shakyamuni left home, they were obviously in widespread practice in Indian religion, no matter whether it was the religion of the brahmans or among the practitioners of the arts of yoga. Such practices have been handed down with undiminished currency even to the present.

At the time Shakyamuni observed these phenomena, he exchanged views with Bhargava and conducted serious discussions. He asked what the ultimate purpose of all these kinds of austerities was. Bhargava answered that, by inflicting pain on one's body, one could thereby gain the blessings of ascending to heaven. Shakyamuni, on the other hand, thought that pain and pleasure were relative to each other, that wrongdoings and merits were interdependent, and that, by performing austerities, one would still be going around and around within the confines of cyclical existence and would never be able to be liberated from birth and death. He said that austerities can indeed cleanse the mind and will, and lead to detachment from entanglements, but that they did not necessarily lead to liberation from birth and death, or the consummation of the Supreme Path. Accordingly, Shakyamuni spent one night at Bhargava's place, then departed.

Subsequently, Shakyamuni also learned the well-known contemporary Indian methods of meditative concentration and he cultivated the *samadhi* without thought for more than three years. The meditation work of what is called "*samadhi* without thought" had as its highest method obliterating thought. In the course of three years, Shakyamuni really reached the point of having no thoughts, but finally he recognized that this too was not the true Path, so he abandoned it. He reached this conclusion because this kind of experiential realm (having no thoughts) is also a creation of one's own mind. In the end, he still did not know what to do about the basic root of the ruler of this mind.

So Shakyamuni then went to Aratakalama's place, to learn the *samadhi* that is neither thought nor no thought. When it is said that this *samadhi* is not thought, "thought" in this context means the thinking and false thoughts of ordinary mental activity. When it is said that this *samadhi* is not no thought, "no thought" means the stage reached when, even though there is no ordinary false thought and thinking, one is still able to be aware of everything. Many people think that, when meditation work reaches this stage, this is already in the category of what is too lofty to attain, but in reality, this amounts to falling into the subtle afflictions of the confusions of perceptions and thoughts.

After three years of this, Shakyamuni raised several questions. In this *samadhi* that is neither thought nor no thought, is there a self or is there no self? If one says there is no self, it should not be called neither thought nor no thought. If one says there is a self, then it is not liberation. It is precisely because sentient beings think they have selves that all the forms of suffering arise. In the *samadhi* that is neither thought nor no thought, even though one can temporarily cause the coarser forms of false thought and affliction to stop, the subtler forms of affliction are still there as before. If one cannot abandon the form of self and the concept of self, how can one reach genuine liberation? For these reasons, Shakyamuni also abandoned this practice and left.

Shakyamuni Practices Six Years of Austerities

During the six years' time that Shakyamuni had been cultivating practice in the mountains, he had already visited all the famous men of the Path. But he had found no genuine enlightened teacher, so he had not gotten any results. He had already cultivated and practiced all the various contemporary methods of cultivating the Path, no matter how difficult or painful they were to carry out, and he had pursued them to a high point of refinement and mastery.

During this period, Shakyamuni's father, King Suddhodana, had made inquiries into his whereabouts and had sent his officials to urge him to return to the palace. But Shakyamuni was not moved by any of this and all the king could do was to secretly dispatch five of the sons of his high ministers to accompany the prince in his practice and try to protect him clandestinely. These five men later became, among all Shakyamuni's disciples, the famous five great disciples of the early period. Chief among them was Kaundinya.

At this time, having traveled all over calling on teachers without finding the path to ultimate liberation, Shakyamuni stopped his journeying for a while and stayed on Pandava Mountain. He often went into the nearby city of Rajagrha for the day to beg for food. The lord of the city, King Bimbisara, soon found out of his whereabouts and came in person to entreat Shakyamuni to return to worldly life. King Bimbisara even vowed to cede his own throne to Shakyamuni, but he declined politely yet firmly.

Finally, all King Bimbisara could do was to make a pact with Shakyamuni: "When you complete the Path, I hope you will come to deliver me first." Later on, when Shakyamuni had consummated the Path, he often stayed in Rajagrha, spreading his teaching widely there.

After this, Shakyamuni traveled on until he was in the vicinity of the Nairanjana River. In the snowy mountains near the southern end of Gajashirsha Mountain (the name means "Elephant Head") was Uruvilva Forest, where there were congregations of ascetics. Shakyamuni practiced quiet sitting and contemplation and cultivated the practice of austerities. Sometimes he ate only a single sesame seed or a single grain of rice for his daily meal. Sometimes he ate only a single sesame seed or grain of rice every other day, or just once in seven days. He sat cross-legged without getting up to walk around, his eyes unblinking, his mind free of fear. After a while, he became so emaciated from his austerities that he looked like a skeleton. His hair and beard grew as tangled and matted as brush weed: birds mistook this for thickets of grass and built their nests there. The reeds grew up all around him and wound around his knees. At this time, Shakyamuni was very weak. As he sat there dignified and erect, he looked like a man so feeble that he was on the brink of death.

Shakyamuni cultivated this type of difficult austere practice for six years. Afterward, it suddenly occurred to him that there was no difference between this and the common way of doing things that assumed that cultivating the body through austerities was the true Path. So he abandoned this too and went off alone toward the south.

Shakyamuni Opens Through in Sudden Enlightenment and Achieves Buddhahood

For the six years, Shakyamuni had taken great pains to practice meditation and contemplation. Without a doubt, it was because he had not had proper nutrition that he had become unbearably weak and enfeebled. Yet so adamant was his faith and so firm his spirit that even the great ministers sent by King Suddhodana to find him had been greatly moved, and all of them felt great respect for him. Thus Kaundinya and the other four grandees' sons all wished to remain there with him and accompany Shakyamuni in learning the Path and looked for places nearby to concentrate on their cultivation.

At this time, Shakyamuni was in his years of full vigor—about 30 years old. After he realized that this kind of practice was not the correct path, he went off alone, leaving behind the forest where the ascetics practiced austerities. He accepted an offering of rice gruel made with milk from a herd girl named Nandapala and recovered the physical strength proper to a youthful mature man. When Kaundinya and the others saw this, they thought that Shakyamuni had been unable to sustain the test of austerities. This made their aspiration for the Path waver and they became very disconsolate. As a result, they left Shakyamuni and went off to the Deer Park in the land of Varanasi (modern Benares) to continue to practice austerities on their own.

Having already recovered his physical strength, Shakyamuni went into the Nairanjana River to bathe. After he had washed off all the grime that had accumulated in the course of his laborious austerities, his body and mind felt extraordinarily happy. He went alone to sit under a pipala tree about three miles from the Nairanjana River. (After his enlightenment, the name was changed to the bodhi tree.) He spread out a mat of lucky grass and sat down cross-legged. He took an oath, saying: "I will not arise from this seat until I do experience bodhi." (The Sanskrit word *bodhi* means "inherent true enlightenment.")

Because Shakyamuni had in the past studied all kinds of meditative concentrations, his meditative power was already profound. After sitting for forty-eight days, he entered deeply into a wondrous realm of meditative contemplation.

On the evening of the seventh day of the twelfth lunar month, as he was sitting in meditation, all sorts of demonic realms of delusion appeared before him to torment him: such things as sensory pleasures and desire for wealth, and fear of birth and death. He was not deluded by any of them. In the end, all the so-called armies of delusion, including female demons and all the rest, were vanquished by his power of concentration.

In the course of this night, Shakyamuni experienced various spiritual powers one by one: the power of the knowledge of the realm of the spirits (the power to travel anywhere instantly); the power of the knowledge of supernatural vision (the power to see things no matter how distant); the power of the knowledge of supernatural hearing (the power to hear things no matter how distant); the power of knowing the minds of others (the power to read minds); the power to know at will past abodes (the power to know past lives); and the power of stainless wisdom (the power to end all leaks and defilements). When he reached the realm of the six spiritual powers, his body and mind spontaneously emitted a great light.

On the morning of the next day, Shakyamuni suddenly saw a bright star appear. (This must have been the Sun, since the customary term in Indian astronomy for the Sun was "the bright star.") At this, he emptied through in great enlightenment and experienced *anuttarasamyaksambodhi:* supreme, perfect, complete enlightenment. Then he joyfully exclaimed: "How strange! All sentient beings are equipped with the characteristics of the wisdom of the tathagatas, but because of the clingings of false thought, they cannot realize them."[1]

---

[1] There are slight variations in this statement made by Shakyamuni when he was first enlightened in the various Chinese translations of the Buddhist sutras. Here we are using as the standard the version that has been handed down through the generations in the Zen school. We select the version above because it is comparatively clearer and easier to understand.

Let us retrace the circumstances of this great affair. After leaving home to study the Path at 19, Shakyamuni spent twelve years traveling all over to study and experienced an ample measure of hardships and sufferings. When he was about 30, he finally realized the realm of various spiritual powers and got a penetrating view of the incomparable wondrous function latent in the minds and bodies of human beings, and of the basis of life. At the same time, he was enlightened upon seeing a bright star and completely comprehended the real truth of the universe and of human life. He felt refreshed and at peace, realizing that it was actually like this.

At that point, Shakyamuni wanted to enter nirvana (peaceful extinction and perfect illumination) immediately. He was not inclined to preach the Dharma. This aroused the devas, who came in great numbers to entreat him to keep his physical body, remain in the world, and teach sentient beings on a wide scale. He said to the devas: "Stop, stop. My Dharma is so wondrous it is inconceivable."

By saying this, Shakyamuni Buddha let us know where the mystic meaning of the Buddha Dharma is and what kind of thing it ultimately is: as he said, it is inconceivable. People generally think because of this that the Buddha Dharma cannot be learned, that it cannot be touched, that it cannot be seen. They do not realize that "inconceivable," just like the statement that "My Dharma is so wondrous it is inconceivable," is only a manner of speaking. This is because, according to the general custom, all religions and philosophies are approached by people using thinking and inference, or are believed in and discussed on the basis of emotional feelings. Drawing inferences by thinking is just conceptual thought, and rendering belief and holding discussion based on emotion is just opinion. If you just proceed from conceptual thought and emotional opinions to try to find the real truth about the universe and human life, that is the same as turning your back on the Path and running off in the other direction. The Path really has the sense of being so wondrous that it is inconceivable. Saying the Path is so wondrous that it is inconceivable just points out the methodological error ordinary people make. It does not mean that the Path is impossible to think about! All we have to do is put our bodies and minds to work to really experience it, not try to make inferences about it with conceptual thinking and opinions. Then we will be able to arrive at the realm of buddhahood, the realm of the true awakening with which our inherent nature is fundamentally endowed.

THE FOUNDING OF THE TEACHING

After his enlightenment, because he was earnestly asked to do so by the devas, Shakyamuni Buddha resolved to disseminate the teaching and bring salvation to the world. The first thing he did was go to the Deer Park, which had been a holy ground since ancient times, to find the five men who had found him in the forests of the snowy mountains in years gone by, and who were now concentrating on the practice of austerities. He preached to them the four noble truths of suffering, the formation of suffering, the extinction of suffering, and the path to the extinction of suffering. One after another, the five men understood and they began to cultivate the Path according to the Buddha's teaching. They were called *bhikshus*. (*Bhikshu* means beggar: above they beg for the teaching from Buddha and below they beg for food from sentient beings.) This was the start of Shakyamuni Buddha's teaching activities. In Buddhist terms, it is called the initial turning of the Wheel of the Dharma. It was also the beginning of what in Buddhism are called the Three Jewels: the jewel of the Buddha, the enlightened one, the jewel of the Dharma, the enlightening teaching, and the jewel of the Sangha, the community of those seeking enlightenment.

Shakyamuni's Teaching and His Original Disciples

At this time, in the city of Varanasi, was a man named Yashas who was the son of a prominent man. Because he felt the suffering of human life, he began to believe in the true Dharma and, hearing of Buddha's reputation, he left home, went to the Deer Park, and took refuge with him. He brought with him his companions, some fifty sons of prominent men, who all became disciples of Shakyamuni Buddha. The parents of Yashas and his wife also came along and put their faith in Buddha. They became householders who cultivated practice, called in Sanskrit *upasakas* and *upasikas*.

During his first stay of three months in the Deer Park, Shakyamuni Buddha had already accepted fifty-six faithful disciples. He sent them out in all directions to propagate the teaching. He himself went alone to the city of Rajagrha in the land of Magadha beside the Nairanjana River and displayed his spiritual powers in order to convert those followers of outside paths who worshipped fire. At the time, the three chief teachers of orthodox brahmanism were the three brothers Uruvilva-kashyapa, Nadi-kashyapa, and Gaya-kashyapa. They came leading their thousand disciples to sincerely take refuge with Shakyamuni Buddha and become his followers. Next, Buddha won over the scholars Shariputra and Maudgalyayana, who were famous among the brahman communities for their intelligence and wisdom. These two also brought along a hundred disciples, and all of them became followers of Buddhism.

Thus, while in his 30s, Shakyamuni Buddha began to assemble the twelve hundred and fifty home-leavers who were to be his basic disciples. They traveled everywhere teaching and converting people. They heard Buddha expounding the Dharma and were his constant companions. In the Buddhist scriptures that were assembled later, they often mention "twelve hundred and fifty bhikshus." This refers to this group of worthy disciples of long experience and deep capacity.

Later on, there was another man of outstanding intelligence, talent, and virtue named Mahakashyapa who also became a follower of Shakyamuni Buddha. He was the First Patriarch of the Zen school passed down through the subsequent generations.

In fact, at that time, Shariputra and the three Kashyapa brothers were a good deal older than Shakyamuni and, when they first went out to spread the teaching, many people who did not know them assumed at first that the relatively young Shakyamuni was one of their disciples. In the context of the contemporary Indian religious sects, it was quite astounding the way Shakyamuni Buddha had gathered over a thousand disciples as soon as he emerged from the mountains and exerted such a powerful influence.

Subsequently, Shakyamuni Buddha expounded the Dharma and spread the teaching for more than forty years. Among the disciples who had taken refuge with him, both home-leavers and householders, there were people of all castes, high and low, men and women, young and old. In name and in fact, they formed the "four congregations" of Buddha's disciples. Male home-leavers were called *bhikshus*. Female home-leavers were called *bhikshunis*. Male householders were call *upasakas*. Female householders were called *upasikas*.

From then on, all those whose minds were set on the realm of buddhahood though their bodies might abide in the world of the dusts, those who adopted the Buddhist way of thinking and conduct in detaching from the dusts of sensory experience and the conventional world, and those who made the great vow to work endlessly for the salvation of sentient beings, unlimited by time or space—no matter whether they were householders or home-leavers, no matter whether they were male or female, or young or old—all such people were called Great Vehicle bodhisattvas. A bodhisattva is a person who possesses the supreme wondrous truth of enlightening oneself and enlightening others, of benefiting oneself and benefiting others.

At that time, among the bhikshus who were the disciples of Buddha there were ten great disciples, each acclaimed for his own special ability: Shariputra, foremost in knowledge; Maudgalyayana, foremost in spiritual powers; Mahakashyapa, foremost in asceticism; Aniruddha, foremost in supernatural vision; Subhuti, foremost in understanding emptiness; Purna, foremost in preaching the Dharma; Katyayana, foremost in discoursing on meanings; Upali, foremost in upholding the precepts; Rahula (Buddha's only son), foremost in esoteric practices; and Ananda (Buddha's cousin), foremost in listening and remembering. These were the ten great and outstanding disciples who had received the transmission directly from Buddha and achieved special excellence.

Preaching the Dharma

Leading a band of his disciples, followers of the newly arisen religion, Shakyamuni Buddha traveled from place to place teaching. He came by stages to Rajagrha, the royal city of King Bimbisara. Previously, when he had first abandoned his noble status and entered the mountains to cultivate the Path, Shakyamuni had made a pact with King Bimbisara that, after he consummated the Path, he would go first to save him. Thus, as he had promised, Shakyamuni Buddha came to him, and stayed in a retreat King Bimbisara had had specially constructed for him called the Venuvana Vihara, the "Bamboo Grove Retreat." People of all ranks, from the king above to the common people below, all looked up to Buddha with sincere respect. This place became the first Buddhist temple in India.

Not long after this, a man of wealth and renown named Sudatta, who lived under the rule of King Prasenajit in the land of Shravasti and who enjoyed doing good works and distributing charity, came to believe in Shakyamuni Buddha's teaching. Spreading the ground with gold leaf to arrive at the price, he purchased for Shakyamuni the Jetavana Grove, which had been the property of the Crown Prince Kosala. The Crown Prince was moved by this and joined in extending patronage to Shakyamuni. All the people of the land, high and low, were united in their faith in Buddha. So they built a Jetavana Garden Vihara in Rajagrha especially for Buddha; it was also called the Almsgiver's Garden. It got this name because Sudatta liked to do good works and distribute alms, to succor the widows and orphans, and help the poor and suffering. This vihara was built with twelve stupas, seventy-two lecture halls, three hundred and sixty monastic cells, and five hundred storied towers. The vihara offered support and accommodations for both monastic and lay disciples of Buddhism. This could be said to be India's first Buddhist college.

From then on, as Shakyamuni Buddha constantly traveled back and forth, he stayed at the Venuvana Vihara in Rajagrha in the land of Magadha, or else at the Almsgiver's Jetavana Vihara in the land of Shravasti. These became two centers from which he often disseminated the teaching.

In the India of those days, the land of Magadha was a peaceful and happy country whose political order was secure and whose economy was flourishing. Thus the life of the people there was passed very comfortably. By repute, it was a country of feasting and music, where the entertainments were always happy and the revelry went on day and night. After Shakyamuni Buddha began to stay there and spread his teachings, it became silent and still day and night in the city of Rajagrha, with only the quiet sound of chanting to be heard. The people forsook their worldly pleasures and became abstemious, disciplined, and studious. They gave their allegiance to the Three Jewels and honored only Buddha. At the same time, the atmosphere in the land of Shravasti became one of devotion to good works because the people there honored and served Buddhism. The neighboring lands looked to these examples and the teaching spread greatly.

From these developments, we can see the educational power of Shakyamuni Buddha's teaching and its power to purify and transform people's lives and entire states. Its great influence and its broad effectiveness flourished mightily at that time. The fact that, by appearing in person to preach the Dharma, Shakyamuni achieved such success in a little more than ten years is really enough to make people feel attracted to him!

During the period from Shakyamuni's enlightenment till the time when he began to disseminate his teachings, his father, King Suddhodana, longing to see him again, had sent word asking him to return to his homeland. Shakyamuni sent one of his disciples ahead, who returned there and displayed spiritual powers. After that, Shakyamuni himself returned and expounded the Dharma for his father to enable his mind to attain realization. At the same time, he converted his aunt Mahaprajapati to whom he owed a debt of gratitude for rearing him, and his wife Yashodhara, so that later they both left home and followed his teaching. At the same time, he also converted his kinsmen Ananda, Devadatta, and Aho-rudra, and also his own son, Rahula. There were also members of the sudra caste (the debased hereditary groups in the view of the Indian caste system), like Upali, who came one after another to take refuge with Buddha and leave home.

When Shakyamuni was in his homeland, he still followed the Buddhist system: he went out personally as usual to beg for food. This made his father the king very uneasy, but in the end, Shakyamuni persuaded his father that he must still abide by the ordinary regulations for home-leavers and practice begging.

Later on, probably during the five or six years when Shakyamuni first started spreading the teaching, his father became gravely ill due to old age and was on the brink of death. He very much wanted to see Shakyamuni again, so Shakyamuni led Ananda and Rahula and the others back to their homeland and personally performed the ceremonies to honor his father's passing. He was at his father's side as he was about to die and rubbed his father's heart with his hand, to enable him to depart peacefully. Following the prescribed ritual form, Shakyamuni and his kinsmen stood solemnly in proper order at the head and foot of the corpse of the king and offered their respects to his spirit. When his father was carried out in his coffin to the gravesite, Shakyamuni carried it personally to demonstrate his grief. Finally, the king was cremated in his coffin on Spirit Peak in Rajagrha, where Shakyamuni himself had lived, carrying out his pure cultivation and teaching. A stupa was built there for the ashes. Everything was done according to the prescribed ritual forms, to teach that a child must properly fulfill the path of caring for parents while they are alive and seeing them off when they die. This was a demonstration of a perfectly developed sense of propriety and duty.

In the forty-five years from Shakyamuni's enlightenment to his death, Magadha and Shravasti were always the northern and southern centers of his teaching. As the occasion arose, he also carried on his teaching in the various lands along the Ganges River. Shakyamuni Buddha made no categorical distinctions between monks and nuns and laypeople, between high-ranking and low-ranking, between rich and poor, between male and female, between young and old. He explained the teaching to all alike, according to their mentalities. All who came in contact with his great, perfectly developed character and heard the lofty, profound, and subtle principles of his teaching were won over by him.

There is no way to accurately calculate how many people ultimately took refuge with him and became his followers. Through his decades of teaching, the number of people in his congregation of disciples increased. He took in and nurtured both the wise and the stupid, both the worthy and the unworthy. In the course of a lifetime of teaching and guiding people in this spirit and engaging in collective educational work, inevitably there were many things that came up concerning the relationships between individuals and the group, between the outer world and the inner circle, and within the congregation itself. Because of this development over time and the lessons of experience, and in addition to the teachings on basic moral character (the prohibitions on killing, stealing, sexual excess, and lying), there also were gradually established many rules and regulations. Later these became the Buddhist code of discipline.

When Shakyamuni was about 80 years old, that is, forty-eight or forty-nine years after his enlightenment, on a summer day as he was passing the rainy season in the village of Beluvana near the city of Vaishali, he let it be known that he would soon enter nirvana. Then he set off toward the north on his last journey, to the city of Kushinagara. Under the twin sala trees in the sala grove where he had been born, Shakyamuni preached the Dharma to the elderly brahman Subhadra and when he had finished, he accepted him as his last disciple. Then he appeared to be sick and did not get up. He lay down on his right side and entered nirvana.

The date of Shakyamuni's death in Western terms was about 490–480 B.C. He died at midnight on the fifteenth day of the second lunar month. His disciple Mahakashyapa hastened there from Spirit Peak and took charge of the funeral rites. As Buddha lay in his golden coffin, he unexpectedly showed his spiritual powers: he extended his foot to put Mahakashyapa's mind at rest, then he entered into a profound stillness.

When Buddha was about to die, his disciples asked him what would happen to them after his demise. He then instructed them very earnestly that, after he was gone, they should take the precepts of discipline as their teacher. This is why Buddhists ever since have looked upon the precepts of discipline with the same respect they give to the scriptural teachings that he imparted, and have followed them faithfully.

The Compilation of the Buddhist Scriptures

Once Shakyamuni Buddha had entered nirvana, his disciples felt that their teacher and guide was gone and they felt confused because they had no one on whom to rely. They all discussed the matter and decided that the most important task facing them was to gather together Buddha's explanations of the Dharma and compile them into scriptures. Gathering together Buddha's teachings meant reciting them from memory and collecting and compiling them. At that point, under the leadership of Mahakashyapa (one of the ten great disciples), they chose people who had personally received teachings spoken by Buddha and who had genuinely realized the fruit of the Buddha Dharma's Middle Path, and had them recite the teachings they had heard Buddha impart over the many years that he was in the world. These were recorded in writing and established as the canonical scriptures. At the time there were, altogether, five hundred people who had already attained the fruit of arhatship. (*Arhat* means "one who has slain the robbers," "one who has totally eliminated the afflictions that are the mind's robbers.") They gathered together at a cave beneath Seven Leaf Crag outside of Rajagrha. On the second day of the second month of the first rainy season after Buddha's demise, which was the seventeenth day of the sixth lunar month, they began the work of assembling Buddha's teachings. Mahakashyapa was elected as the chief of this assembly.

First they proceeded to put together the *Vinaya*. (The word *Vinaya* means "the precepts of discipline used to subdue the afflictions of the mind and body.") They proceeded by having Mahakashyapa bring up each item in the code of discipline and then inquiring of Upali, who was the foremost among Buddha's disciples in upholding discipline. Upali answered by proceeding one by one to recite aloud when each precept was instituted, where it was instituted, the reasons why this precept was created, the occasion for which it was prescribed (for what person or what event the precept had been defined), the precept's regulations (defining the exact rules that must be observed), the violations of the precept (defining what would be called a violation), and so on. After this, the precepts of discipline that had been recorded were read aloud. Then they were adopted by having the great assembly of five hundred bhikshus recite them together, thus defining them in perpetuity as the Buddha's regulations. Only then was the work of assembling the *Vinaya* considered completed.

After this, Buddha's disciple Ananda recited the *Dharma*. (The word *Dharma* means "treasury of teachings.") After he had recited this, Mahakashyapa asked him questions and Ananda answered, telling him when each teaching was given, where it was given, the reason it was given, the occasion or person to whom it was addressed, the method by which it was given, and the degree to which it was comprehended by the audience who heard it at the time. Again, this account was adopted by being recited by the whole assembly together and accepted as an error-free version of the Dharma spoken by Buddha. Only then was the assembling of the scriptural teachings considered completed.

This was the first conclave held to assemble the teachings after the Buddha's nirvana, so it is called "the first collection of the teachings," or "the collection of Rajagrha." The criterion for selecting the people who participated in this conclave to assemble the teachings took as the standard the five hundred arhats who had already realized the fruit of enlightenment.

But there were several hundred to a thousand of Buddha's disciples who did not participate in this conclave, so they held one of their own. With Vashpa, one of Buddha's first five disciples, presiding at a site not very far to the west of the conclave of the five hundred arhats, they made their own collection of Buddhist scriptures. Later, this was called "the collection of the great congregation," or "the collection from outside the circle of the arhats," or "the Great Vehicle collection."

There are some who say that, in the Buddhist teachings assembled at that time, there were the *tripitaka* (three baskets) of the *sutras* (spoken by Buddha), the *vinaya* (the code of discipline), and the *shastras* (analytical commentaries). Some even add to this the miscellaneous collections and the mantras, to make five baskets in all.

In summary, in his lifetime of teaching the Dharma, Shakyamuni Buddha only taught by personal example and by the spoken word. Even though he was a master of the written language and well able to develop his teachings in that way, he never composed any written works or left anything at all in writing. He did not want to construct a monument to his mission and perpetuate his fame in later generations; that's a fact. The fact that Shakyamuni left no writings has given later people great inspiration, and is rich with the true spirit of philosophical teaching.

Moreover, we can see that most of the founders of religions and wise men revered by the people of the world left no written works. In China, though the ancient sage Laozi is reputed to have written the five thousand characters of the *Dao De Jing,* if we investigate how much of it came from his own writing brush, that is very difficult to determine. But has it ever been any cause for regret that he could not be moved to discard the pristine for the contrived? Confucius was a perfect sage; he edited the *Classic of Poetry* and *Classic of History,* and defined the proper rites and music. But he also said of himself: "I do not compose any writings. I have faith in and fondness for the ancient ways." Isn't this a very good example?

The teachings spoken by Shakyamuni Buddha were subsequently made into scriptural texts. This was due to the efforts of Buddhist disciples with a high level of cultivation and virtue who were good at literary composition. They devoted themselves wholeheartedly to the work of gathering and compiling Buddha's verbal teachings. Whatever they had personally heard from him they gathered together and recorded in writing, using a rich and beautiful literary style and a consummate sense of its principles and meaning. Because of this, the propagation of Buddhism developed greatly. Of this we can say: "He originally had no intention of becoming the founder of a religion. Who knew that the role would be pressed on him?" Still, we feel a deep allegiance to him as our teacher and know he is worthy of respect and admiration. All we can do is lower our heads and bow in homage.

The Buddhist canon was defined by the Rajagrha collection for about a hundred years. After that, a controversy arose because some people thought that the ten rules being practiced by the Sangha (the community of Buddhist monks) in eastern India were not in accordance with the Dharma and the Vinaya. So a new conclave was convened in the city of Vaishali under the leadership of the bhikshu Yashas, who was the leading elder of the Sangha in western India. About ten thousand monks, young and old, attended this gathering, which lasted more than eight months. At the conclave, the orthodox Dharma and Vinaya were reiterated.

Because of the large number of participants, in later generations this assembly was called *Mahasangika,* "sect of the great congregation" and its doctrine was called "the standard teachers' doctrine" (meaning the doctrine of the learned ones qualified to be teachers). But among the orthodox *bhikshus,* the majority were leading elders who would not defer to the conclusions of this assembly. This became the source of the sectarian divisions that arose in Indian Buddhism at that time. In later generations, the orthodox congregations in the east were called *Sthavira,* "the sect of the elders," meaning virtuous ones.

More than a hundred years after this conclave, King Ashoka, the great protector of Buddhism and grandson of the first great unifier of India, was in power. He was a sincere believer in Buddhism. Eighteen years after coming to the throne, he chose one thousand sagacious monks noted for their learning and their virtue and put the monk Moggaliputta Tissa in charge. Another conclave was held at the imperial capital, Pataliputra, also known as Kusumapura, to recompile the Buddhist scriptures. This is recorded in the Buddhist scriptures of the southern transmission, but the scriptures themselves that this conclave defined are not extant.

Later on, during the reign of King Kanishka (second century A.D.), another conclave to compile the scriptures was held. Five hundred wise monks were chosen and convened at Circle Grove Temple in Kashmir, with Vasumitra presiding. For the Buddhist scriptures they collected together, they first composed a hundred thousand verses of *upadesha* to explicate the sutras. Then they composed a hundred thousand verses of *vinaya-vibhasha* to explicate the vinaya, the codes of discipline. Finally, they composed a hundred thousand verses of *abhidharma-vibhasha* to explicate the shastras. This work took twelve years to complete and then the conclave was finished. In the Chinese Buddhist canon, a translation of the *Abhidharma-vibhasha shastra* mentioned above still survives.

According to Tibetan Buddhist accounts, in the time of King Kanishka, five hundred arhats, five hundred bodhisattvas, and five hundred savants were called together at Jalandhara Temple in Punjab and ordered to reassemble the tripitaka (the sutras, vinaya, and shastras). Because Buddhism had divided into eighteen sects over the past hundred years, each with its own views, fierce debates continued at this conclave for sixty-three years. At this conclave, the different views of the eighteen sects were acknowledged as true Buddhism. The conclave also collected and recorded tripitaka scriptures that had never been recorded before, and re-edited those that had already been recorded.

The scriptures assembled by Buddhist disciples, the tripitaka, or three baskets, consisting of sutras, vinaya, and shastras, became the comprehensive collection and repository for the teachings of Buddhism. Besides this, the scriptures of the tripitaka in fact also include a great part of the thought system of classical Indian philosophy and learning. If we think that the Buddhist canon is made up of purely Buddhist teachings or purely Buddhist philosophy, we are inevitably taking too narrow a view.

No matter what debates there are in Buddhist history regarding the compilation of the Buddhist scriptures, we can at least be certain of the following. Beginning about a hundred years after the demise of the Buddha and continuing for four centuries, sectarian divisions gradually developed within Buddhism. These were due to differences in the doctrines held by disciples of the teachings Buddha had imparted, and differences in views they learned from their teachers. Starting with the division into *Mahasangika* and *Sthavira*, in an evolution lasting three or four centuries, the various Indian Buddhist sects formed. In all, these are usually classified into anywhere from eighteen to more than thirty sects. The derivation and names of the traditional eighteen sects are given on page 66.

In the Buddhist canon there is a *Treatise on the Different Sects (Yibuzong Lun)* which contains a more detailed explanation

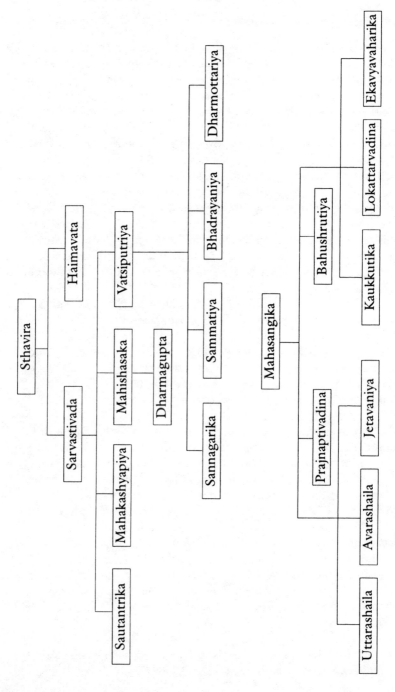

The derivation and names of the eighteen traditional Indian Buddhist sects.

of them. But the Buddhism of these sects has traditionally been designated as falling within the scope of Hinayana Buddhism. The great teacher Fazang summed them up by dividing them into six schools of thought. Later, there were sometimes more sects and sometimes fewer sects; they waxed and waned one after another. We cannot deny that the division of Chinese Buddhism into different schools was subject, whether directly or indirectly, to the influence of the doctrines of the various Indian Buddhist sects. This was inevitable.

Besides these divisions, Buddhist doctrine is also divided into Mahayana and Hinayana and into exoteric and esoteric. Those who advocate Hinayana consider that Mahayana is not the teaching of the Buddha. Those who champion Mahayana equate Hinayana with the outside paths. Those who honor the exoteric teachings think that the esoteric teachings are delusions. Those who emphasize the esoteric teachings say that the exoteric teachings are not the ultimate truth. In addition, the followers of Madhyamika emphasize *prajna,* transcendent wisdom, while the followers of Yogacara emphasize an analysis of the characteristics of perceived phenomena.

Within Buddhism, schools of thought differ, as do lines of transmission, to the point that the situation is too complex to be clarified and disputes constantly arise. The phenomenon can be compared to sunspots: they move periodically across the Sun without damaging its original light, but in the end it comes back to the lingering regret felt when there is a flaw in an otherwise perfect thing.

Buddhism arose and flourished in India, but by the middle years of the eighth century A.D., Buddhism in central India had already begun to decline. It was still being passed on only in northern and southern India. By this time, East Asian Buddhism was already flourishing in China: a firm foundation had been laid, and almost all of the Buddhist scriptures had already been translated into Chinese.

The decline of Indian Buddhism certainly gave the original brahmanical religion an opportunity to rise again. Other non-Buddhist teachings also seem to have sprouted anew. With the Muslim invasions of the 12th century A.D., many Buddhist temples and monasteries were destroyed and many followers of the religion fled to such places as southern India and Tibet. Thus Buddhism was totally cut off in its original homeland, and all that remains in India are a few scattered historical traces for later people to visit and reflect upon.

As for Indian Buddhism as it exists today, since the 18th and 19th centuries, a tiny portion of the Buddhist culture that was exported to other lands has been flowing back into India. Naturally, this is not the authentic Indian Buddhism of the old days. Moreover, this reimported Buddhism does not distinguish been Buddhism and spirit worship and is mixed with many misguided teachings. In the middle years of the 20th century, after World War I, there were Chinese monks who went to India for the purpose of establishing Buddhist temples, and this left some mark.

In its modern history before independence, the national fate of India was to meet with the aggression of the imperialist powers. This had nothing whatsoever to do with Buddhism. I only mention this incidentally, for the sake of argument. Some people attribute the imperialist conquest of India to the supposed debilitating effect of Buddhism. This is a misapprehension of history that is utterly ridiculous.

CHAPTER SUMMARY

When worldly people speak of religious philosophy and the history of religion, it is common knowledge that Buddhism was founded by Shakyamuni Buddha. From the religious standpoint, he was, of course, the founder of a religion. But from the viewpoint of philosophy or learning in general, many people recognize that Shakyamuni was not just the founder of a religion in the narrow sense: he was someone who came to save the world, a great philosopher, and a great educator.

The commonly held views that Buddhism is a kind of atheism or a kind of pantheism, along with various other opinions, are very interesting for the contradictions they contain. Here we need not discuss them. Based on the standpoint of Buddhism itself, the Sanskrit word *buddha* means "enlightened one." This word holds many meanings: someone who is himself enlightened, who has attained the self-benefiting path of great wisdom and liberation; someone who enlightens others, who brings enlightenment to the world and opens the way for people and thus benefits others; someone whose enlightening practices are complete, who has perfected the merits of saving himself and saving others. Because of this, we cannot just use a literal semantic translation and translate *buddha* as "enlightened one." In order to encompass the whole meaning, we keep the original word *buddha*.

In the Buddhist scriptures, the Buddha has many epithets: "World-Honored One," "Tathagata," "Teacher of Devas and Humans," "Omniscient One," and so forth. Commonly, ten or even more different appellations are used. Except for "World-Honored One," most of the appellations for Buddha convey his great compassion in saving the world and his dignity as a teacher and guide. Indeed, there is little of the idea that Buddha is the sole lord of myriad things.

The foregoing introduction has already conveyed some general knowledge of the Indian cultural background and the history of Shakyamuni Buddha's achievements in the world. In this chapter, I have tried to give an objective study of such matters as the circumstances of his times, his character and thought, his cultivation of the Path, and his work in spreading the teaching. Two conclusions can be drawn from the discussion.

First, if we observe human history, we see that, whenever there are persons who possess intelligence and wisdom and a great deal of human fellow-feeling and courage, there are only two paths in life that they choose from: they either become heroes or they become sages. The heroes are the ones who achieve splendid deeds in their lives and whose fame reaches through the ages. The mission of a hero is at best to manage to restore proper order to a world in chaos, to bring the people relief, and to give human society a brief period of peace and security or raise its level of justice. Thus, a hero is one who becomes a political leader in order to bring perfect order to the contemporary world. But history has many examples in the rise and decline of societies and the succession of regimes where the so-called kingly mission has left a legacy of endless harm. This is because the transfer of power can seem like a lively opening act of a play, but can really turn out to be the last scene of a tragedy, where the ruler misleads his people and misleads himself at every turn, so that in the end not a single thing is correct.

In contrast to this, even though the sage may be in solitude throughout his life, his work can give humankind down through the ages peace and security in body and mind. Given all the intricacies and complexities of human issues, if we seek stability and order and justice only by means of political power, this is only the conventional point of view and a naive way of thinking. This is because it seems to be a rule of history that the good and evil of the human mind and the associated political flourishing and decline follow a pattern of periods of good order and periods of chaos coming one after another in a cycle: there is never an ultimate answer.

Besides the level of concern reflected in the saying, "The people and I are from the same womb," there is also concern for the whole universe of sentient beings reflected in the saying, "All creatures are my companions." Their problems too must be totally solved.

Therefore, from a philosophical standpoint, we must take upon ourselves the work of the Tathagata and seek the final destination of absolute truth in order to find a comprehensive solution to the whole issue of human life in society. We must completely comprehend the absolute truth of life in the universe. This alone is the fundamental work of bringing salvation to ten thousand generations and giving shelter to all sentient beings universally.

In India at the time of Shakyamuni, due to the confusion of culture and thought, the instability of politics and social structure, and the disturbances of war, the grief and sadness of the human world struck the eye and alarmed the heart wherever he looked. With his innate intelligence and courageous character, it would have been very possible for him to succeed to the throne, extend his realm, and become the heroic ruler of the age. But he saw clearly where the key problem of human nature was located and that to deal with it and resolve it was not a matter of relying on external accomplishments, but rather a matter of the moral work of teaching and transforming people.

Thus Shakyamuni boldly abandoned his royal status and left behind the conventional world of sensory pleasures. He took up the Path and sought the Real, and became the teacher of sentient beings, replete with all the glories of human existence. By renouncing the petty, private self, he perfected the greater self's spirit of saving the world and revealed himself to preach the Dharma. He loudly proclaimed that all sentient beings are equal and that we share the same suchness with the enlightened ones, thus forcefully breaking with the rigid Indian caste system and the self-centered egotistical viewpoint of humankind. What a noble intention, what a generous spirit!

But all through his lifetime of spreading the teaching and explaining the Dharma, what Shakyamuni was seeking was for sentient beings to save themselves by their own inherent nature. He was by no means fond of the role of teacher, nor did he intend to win honor for himself by founding a religion. Yet what he did not desire, other people all gave him. After his demise, his many disciples ended up honoring him as their guide and teacher and serving him as the founder of their religion. This really had nothing to do with his original selfless intent. It's a case of "when the reality is there, the name is applied." The sages have no constant mind: they take the mind of the common people as their mind. Because Shakyamuni only gave and never avidly sought anything, the descendants of his life of wisdom will be there forever, for ten thousand generations, with no limits of time or space, wherever the Sun and Moon shine, endlessly paying homage to him. Given the circumstances of his birth, on the border between heroes and sages, he will always be a prophetic pioneer.

In addition, we can conclude that, taking up the duties of the teachers' path, Shakyamuni showed that all sentient beings have buddha-nature. Proceeding from the religious standpoint, the accounts in the Buddhist scriptures tell how Shakyamuni cultivated practice for countless eons and how he was adorned with myriad virtuous qualities in order to become a buddha. The scriptures are full of all sorts of miracles and wonders vividly portrayed, and there are indeed things there that are inconceivable. If we look on such miraculous elements from the viewpoint of the present or future centuries, they can only circumscribe Buddhism within the confines of religion and provide people with things to worship. They block the way for modern-day people to advance onto the great highway of Buddhism and inevitably present all sorts of obstacles.

When we study Buddha's life, we realize he was a man, not a god. Starting as a human, he transcended ordinary humanity and became a buddha. But this was the completion of a process of education and cultivation involving a sequence of many causes and effects. It was not that he was a sage with innate knowledge who didn't have to learn in order to develop his capacities. Moreover, though he cut his ties with his loved ones and abandoned his princely rank in order to seek the Path, he did have the ordinary human experiences of getting married and having a child. Toward his parents, he carried out the path of filial duty that a child must fulfill. He considered this so important that he declared that filial service to one's parents is equal to making offerings to the buddhas. In Chinese Buddhism, even more emphasis is placed on "repaying the four forms of benevolence," which means to repay the benevolence of one's parents, the benevolence of the nation, the benevolence of sentient beings (the benevolence of society as a whole), and the benevolence of the enlightened ones (one's teachers).

Shakyamuni took upon himself the responsibilities of the teachers' path. He taught that, to elevate human nature and transcend ordinary humanity, to enter into sagehood and become a buddha and an enlightened teacher, we must proceed from our fundamental position as human beings. If our moral character and behavior as human beings is not complete, yet we hope to be able to attain the Path and realize the fruit of enlightenment as soon as we enter the gate of the buddhas and become a teacher of devas and humans, then we are either stupid or crazy. This is definitely not the reality of Buddhism.

Shakyamuni taught that all sentient beings possess buddha-nature. If people are deluded, then they are ordinary humans; if they awaken, then they become sages. Sagehood depends on our own awakening: it is not attained from others. Thus it is necessary to use our completely enlightened, awakened, true nature to seek to experience the fundamental true thusness. After this, we can share in the still quiet of the source of life, the source of the universe, the source of mind and all things. When we reach this point, we can finish with birth and death; we can equalize self and others. This is the supreme, wondrous, excellent realm of the buddhas, the tathagatas, the enlightened ones who come forth from thusness.

CHAPTER 3

The Transmission of Buddhism to China

THE FIRST PERIOD OF THE TRANSMISSION

When we put aside the purely religious accounts in the Buddhist scriptures and try to find historical answers by making logical assessments and judgments, it is very difficult to ascertain the actual situation of the spread of Buddhism and the extent of its power or what territories and how many people had been reached by Buddhist influences in the period following the founding of Buddhism by Shakyamuni. We can surmise that, probably while Shakyamuni was in the world and in the one or two centuries after his demise, the territory to which Buddhism had been disseminated probably extended from the foothills of the Himalayas in the north, regions like Nepal, to the Vindhya Range in the south, and from Mathura in the west to the land of Anga in the south. In other words, Buddhism had still not spread beyond the Ganges Valley in north-central and northeastern India. But, given that probably less than a hundred thousand people had been taught in person by Shakyamuni, given the size of the population of ancient India, it could be said that Buddhism had already acquired great momentum and was capable of making an impact on the times.

Beyond the efforts of Buddha's disciples to spread the teaching, the real large-scale dissemination of Buddhism still had to depend on political power. Two centuries after the demise of Buddha, India produced a king famed in history. His heroic exploits could be matched with those of Alexander the Great. This was the world-famous King Ashoka. At the same time, he was also a fervent Buddhist, one who, in the technical language of Buddhism, is called a "great Dharma-protector." Under the aegis of his formidable power, following the expansion of his military forces, the teaching of Buddhism naturally extended everywhere throughout his empire, which covered all but the southern reaches of the Indian subcontinent.

Indian Buddhism in the Time of King Ashoka

During the reign of King Ashoka, an assembly of a thousand bhik-shus was convened at Kukkutarama Temple in Kusumapura, the imperial capital. With Moggaliputta Tissa presiding, the conclave made a new collection of the Buddhist scriptures. This was the "Kusumapura collection," which is famous in the history of Buddhist culture.

The story goes that Ashoka also built many stupas to house the relics of Buddha. There are even legends saying that some of the stupas built by King Ashoka were later dismantled and sent to China and rebuilt there: for example, the great stupas in several temples in such places as Zhejiang and Sichuan. Even today, legends still adhere to these stupas, claiming that they are "stupas of King Ashoka" that flew here from India. This is, of course, a figment of the religious imagination, so we need not investigate it any more deeply.

As evidence of historical fact, in the text of the thirteenth of the royal edicts which King Ashoka had carved on cliff faces throughout his realm, the following is recorded: "In the ninth year of King Ashoka's reign, he conducted a punitive expedition against the Kalingas. . . . After his conquest of the Kalingas, he became a sincere protector of the True Dharma, and gave his allegiance to the True Dharma, and undertook to spread the teaching of the True Dharma. . . . " It also says: "The King felt pity for the barbarians who lived in the mountain forests of his territory, and his wish was that they would give their allegiance to the True Dharma . . . so that all sentient beings would be peaceful and happy. The supreme victory is the victory of the True Dharma. The victory of the True Dharma had already been achieved throughout the King's realm, and had extended to the neighboring countries for a distance of six hundred yojanas, into the lands of the Yavana (Hellenistic) kings Antiochos, Ptolemy, Antigonas, and Magas and Alexander. . . . This was all due to King Ashoka disseminating and following the True Dharma."

According to what is recorded in this edict, it is obvious that Buddhism was already flourishing in the age of King Ashoka and had spread beyond India to the Hellenistic kingdoms of the Middle East. For example, the Antiochos mentioned in the text was Antiochos II (Theos), king of Syria; Ptolemy was Ptolemy II

(Philadelphos), king of Egypt; Antigonas was Antigonas II (Gonatos), king of Macedonia; Magas (of Cyrene) and Alexander (of Epiros) were other Hellenistic rulers. The later part of the edict records that King Ashoka had sent out Buddhist teachers to spread the religion in Syria, Egypt, Macedonia, and Central Asia. The wide extent of his efforts to spread Buddhism are obvious from this.

Furthermore, according to what is recorded in the second of Ashoka's rock edicts, the regions to which King Ashoka sent out missionaries included Kashmir and Gandhara in the northwest, the Yavana regions of the Hellenistic kingdom of Bactria (modern Afghanistan), the Himalaya region, the Aparantaka region in western Punjab, Maharashtra, Mahisamandala (the region of modern Mysore), Vanavasi in southern India, the lands of the Cholas, Pandyas, and Kerala, Suvarnabhumi (the coast of Burma and possibly Cambodia), and Lanka (modern Sri Lanka).

In the three or four centuries after King Ashoka (who reigned 264–227 B.C.), Buddhism gradually became widespread in countries like China, Afghanistan, and Sri Lanka, while in India itself, its homeland, it declined little by little. In the second century B.C., the brahman general Pushamitra usurped the throne of the Maurya dynasty, of which Ashoka had been the third emperor, and launched a great persecution of Buddhism in central India, burning temples and massacring monks and nuns. The damage and destruction was considerable. But Buddhism in northern India continued to flourish as before. Before long, thanks to the efforts of the monks and nuns who had survived the persecution, Buddhism in central India revived to some extent. But there were internal divisions that produced sectarian disputes, and more than eighteen sects formed.

The development of Buddhism in Sri Lanka began in the time of King Ashoka. Subsequently, due to a succession of enlightened monarchs, it became the state religion there. King Dutta-Gamani (r. 101–77 B.C.) began to build Buddhist stupas, and King Vatta-Gamani (r. 43–17 B.C.) erected the vihara at Anuradhapura, the capital, and also had the oral Pali canon committed to writing. The succeeding kings all performed many services for Buddhism.

Long after King Ashoka, around the second century A.D., King Kanishka rose to power in India and Buddhism enjoyed another flourishing period. King Kanishka was a descendent of the

Central Asian Kushans, who had gradually taken over northwestern India and parts of central India. After King Kanishka became a Buddhist, he vowed to invite the learned bodhisattvas Vasumitra, Ashvagosha, and Parshva to an assembly at the capital city, Kashimira, to assemble the Buddhist canon. This work took twelve years to complete. The sutras, vinaya, and shastras which the Tang dynasty teacher Xuanzang brought back from his study trip to India and transmitted in China belong mostly to the version of the canon compiled at this assembly.

Still later, in the second or third century A.D., the bodhisattva Nagarjuna rose to prominence in southern India and spread Buddhism widely. In the fourth century, the brothers Asanga and Vasubandhu spread the learning of the bodhisattva Maitreya, and developed Yogacara philosophy. They were very famous at the time.

The Chinese monk Faxian, who had journeyed to India to study Buddhism and collect texts, also made his contributions, and he reached India in A.D. 411, long before Fazang.

In the sixth century, great shastra masters like Dinnaga, Dharmapala, and Bhavaviveka propagated Yogacara and Madhyamika Buddhist philosophy. In the early Tang period, the great teacher Fazang arrived in India. These teachers were dead, so Fazang studied with the Dharma teacher Silabhadra and his disciple Jnanaprabha, and with the Buddhist layman Prasenajit. Fazang plumbed the depths of Yogacara and Madhyamika theory.

During the same period, many famous Indian monks like Bodhiruci, Bodhidharma, Paramartha, Dharmagupta, and the Central Asian monk known in Chinese as Xianshou Fazang all came to China to transmit Buddhism and translate the scriptures.

Late in the seventh century, the Chinese Dharma master Yijing traveled to India to study and spend time in the various countries of Southeast Asia. He wrote many works on Buddhism when he returned to China.

In the eighth century, Indian Buddhism was gradually declining. In this period, Indian adepts like Shubhakarasimha, Vajramati, and Amoghavajra came to China and spread the teachings of Tantric Buddhism.

In the 12th century, after Islam entered India, many followers of Buddhism fled to places like southern Indian and Tibet. From this point on, Buddhism declined continuously in India, its original homeland.

The Initial Transmission of Buddhism to China in the Late Han and Three Kingdoms Periods

There are already traces of interaction between the cultures of India and China as early as the Qin dynasty and the beginning of the Han dynasty (c. 220–200 B.C.). In Buddhist annals, there is a story that, in the time of Emperor Qin Shihuang, eighteen foreign *shramanas* were imprisoned, but in the middle of the night a sixteen-foot tall figure made of diamond smashed into the prison and set them free. After researching the evidence for this, the general opinion of scholars is that this story is unreliable. In fact, in ancient India, the term *shramana* was not limited to Buddhist bhikshus. It is very probable that these men could have been followers of the brahmanical religion or of yoga.

It is probable that, in the Qin and Han periods, there had already been some intercommunication between techniques of the Taoist adepts and brahmanism and yoga. Thus, we have some proof that the cultural interchange between India and China had probably commenced far earlier than the introduction of Buddhism into China. Of course, at this initial period, contact between the two cultures was extremely sparse.

The older histories all place the beginning of the transmission of Buddhism into China in the period of the Emperor Han Mingdi (r. A.D. 58–75). Due to a dream he had of a golden man, Mingdi sent eighteen emissaries, Cai Yin among them, to travel west to the Central Asian Buddhist city-states in search of Buddhist scriptures. In the land of the Yuezhi, they encountered the two Dharma teachers Kashyapa-Matanga and Dharmaraksha. The two teachers were invited back to the Han imperial capital, Luoyang, and installed in White Horse Temple there. Working together, they translated the *Sutra in Forty-two Chapters*. This was placed in a stone chamber at Lantai. This was the start of the introduction of Buddhism into China.

On the basis of their researches into this matter, modern scholars all have their own accounts: they think that the previous story is unreliable and doubtful. The most trustworthy records and reliable historical sources come from the late Han and the Three Kingdoms periods.

During the time of Emperor Han Huandi (r. A.D. 147–167), a Buddhist monk from Parthia named An Shigao came to China, and a Buddhist monk from the land of the Yuezhi named Zhichan came to Luoyang. Each of them translated several dozen Buddhist scriptures, amounting to one or two hundred fascicles altogether.

During the reign of Emperor Han Lingdi (r. A.D. 168–189), an Indian monk known in China as Zhu Folang also came to Luoyang, where he did his utmost to promote Buddhism. The famous work, *Mouzi Lihuo Lun,* which proposes a synthesis of Buddhism and Chinese culture was written in this period.

Later on, early in the third century A.D., we find the Sogdian Buddhist monk Kang Senghui and the three famous Yuezhi Buddhist laymen Zhiqian, Zhichan, and Zhiliang. All of them were very learned and honored both at court and throughout the country. They devoted themselves to spreading Buddhist doctrines. They came to live in eastern China in the kingdom of Wu, where they were honored guests of the government of Sun Quan, the founder of the kingdom of Wu. They all mastered literary Chinese and contributed as much as they could to the work of translating the Buddhist scriptures.

In the Jiaping years (249–253), in the Wei kingdom, due to the initiative of the noted Indian monks Dharmakara and Dharmagupta, a system of procedures for Chinese Buddhism was first established, including the regulations for leavers of home to receive the precepts. This at last was the beginning of the formal introduction of Buddhism into China.

In the period of the late Han dynasty and the Three Kingdoms (c. A.D. 190–265), Buddhist scriptures and Buddhism in its initial phase were continuously coming into China, and there was obviously a sharp struggle with the way of thinking of the original culture of the country and the doctrines of Confucianism and Taoism. In the history of Chinese thought, this was a great uproar brought about by the encounter with the stimulus of a way of thinking coming from outside the country. Nevertheless, among the common people acting freely on their own, belief in Buddhism was constantly increasing. Over the course of almost a hundred years, the intelligentsia also gradually came to accept the Buddhist way of thinking. This led to the formation of the abstruse philosophical style of the high culture of the period of the Western and Eastern Jin dynasties (A.D. 265–420).

For almost two centuries during the period of the Northern and Southern dynasties (A.D. 420–580), China's culture and politics went through a period of internal contradictions and fragmentation. From the point of view of historical development, the character of this period was certainly not brought about due to the influence of Buddhism on the land. In reality, the dramatic political changes, in conjunction with the influences of warfare, made Buddhism a timely gift to the people during this period.

There were two hidden major factors underlying this, both for the common people and for the intelligentsia (including the courtiers and the landed gentry). First, faith in Buddhism among the common people was the result of a prolonged period of warfare which had left the people's livelihood precarious. Human effort offered no solution to a life of starvation and misery. The Way of Heaven offered nothing on which to rely; life was insecure and filled with fear, pessimism, and world-weary feelings. At just this time, Buddhist thought surged into China. Its teachings on the force of good and evil karma bringing about karmic retribution through a process of cause and effect extending through past, present, and future lives, and its accounts of heaven and hell and cyclical existence in the six planes enabled people to be more certain that the arrangement of their fate was created by the force of karma from past lives. Thus, in a worldly situation of disorder and chaos, Buddhist concepts spread very quickly. By believing in them, people could soothe their bodies and console their minds. They took the original Buddhist concepts of buddhas and bodhisattvas and transformed them to resemble their traditional faith in spirits.

As for the allegiances of the intelligentsia, ever since the factional struggles among the Eastern Han dynasty elite starting in the second half of the second century A.D., the influence of political and social trends had made it impossible for people to be satisfied with or fully believe in the traditional doctrines of the early Han dynasty Confucians. In the Wei-Jin period (third to fourth centuries A.D.), the intellectuals among the social elite had all been searching in a variety of ways for a new direction in thought. They pursued the study of the signs of fate and delved into the area of philosophy. Very open-minded in their thinking and valuing individual freedom, they entered the realm of abstruse discourse.

It was just at this time that the thought of the so-called three mystic doctrines contained in the *Book of Changes, Laozi,* and

Zhuangzi, encountered the imported Buddhist theories of *prajna* and *shunyata* (transcendent wisdom and inherent emptiness). From this, there was an increased tendency among the intelligentsia to combine the indigenous mystic doctrines with borrowed Buddhist ideas. This became the style, so prevalent among the landed gentry stratum and the famous scholars among the so-called intelligentsia, of fleeing from worldly life into Buddhism.

Based on the two factors just mentioned, Buddhism spread throughout China and began its development there. But what really enabled Buddhism to lay a foundation in China were the efforts of many people, among them the famous monks from Kucha in Central Asia, Fotudeng, who was active in the Northern Dynasties in the time of Shi Le, barbarian emperor of the Later Zhao dynasty (r. 330–349), and Kumarajiva (d. 413), the Central Asian master translator who worked under the Later Qin dynasty ruled by the Yao family. Also playing key roles were the eminent Chinese monks Dao An (312–385) and his disciple Huiyuan (344–416), and Kumarajiva's disciple Sengzhao (374–414). Only the strength of people like these enabled Buddhism to establish a foundation in China that could not be uprooted.

Buddhism in the Wei, Jin, and Northern and Southern Dynasties

When we look at the development of history, we see that, whenever there is a period of decline and the world is in disorder and people are demoralized, the result is either a turn toward immediate reality and a life of extravagant excess, or else a flight from immediate reality and the pursuit of higher realms.

When we try to observe China in the period of the Wei and Jin dynasties and the Northern and Southern dynasties, we see that the turmoil of the political situation was bringing about certain trends in society. For example, things like the invasions of alien tribes and the subsequent transformations in ways of thinking, were everywhere stimulating people's minds and sending them on the road of either positive activity or withdrawn passivity.

In A.D. 330, the tribal chieftain Shi Le, who was bloodthirsty, avaricious, and barbaric by nature, proclaimed himself monarch in northern China. But at precisely the same time, the eminent monk, Fotudeng, from Central Asia had come to China and was spreading the compassionate teachings of Buddhism within the territory of Shi Le's Later Zhao state. Besides disseminating the principles of Buddhism, Fotudeng also demonstrated many spiritual powers. This not only made Shi Le believe in him, which reduced the barbarian monarch's ferocity, but at the same time it induced many people to have faith in Buddhism.

In addition to these activities, Fotudeng also taught Buddhist techniques for cultivating realization. He promoted the method of meditative concentration that uses counting breaths *(anapana)* to focus the mind (becoming peaceful and quiet and tempering the breath, in order to focus the mind and enter a state of concentration). This enabled people not only to have faith in Buddhist theories, but also to have a genuine method of cultivating practice that they could follow. We can say that these Buddhist techniques and the Chinese Taoist techniques of nurturing life complemented each other; they accomplished the same results by different methods. Besides all its theoretical accounts of emptiness and existence, Buddhism also offered methods for genuine realization of spiritual powers and meditative concentration that could be relied on in actual fact. This is the major reason that Buddhism began to develop so vigorously in China with Fotudeng. Later on, his Chinese disciple, Dharma teacher Dao An, was also very learned and a master of worldly affairs, whose virtuous qualities impressed the scholars of the time. The founding patriarch of Chinese Pure Land Buddhism, the great teacher Huiyuan, was one of Dao An's favorite disciples.

The Founding of Pure Land Buddhism

The great teacher Huiyuan was a son of the Jia family of Yanmen in Shanxi in northern China. As a youth he studied Confucianism and accumulated a lot of book learning. He had a particularly profound understanding of the three mystic studies, the *Book of Changes, Laozi,* and *Zhuangzi,* and he also practiced the arts of Taoism. Later, in order to avoid the political chaos, he went to southern China and became a monk and a follower of Dharma teacher Dao An.

Since he was fond of the scenery on Mount Lu, Huiyuan sent out invitations to the famous scholars of the time, such as Tao Yuanming and Liu Yimin, and they formed the White Lotus

Society there on the mountain. As their guiding standard, they adopted the *Amitabha Sutra* and the *Sutra of Infinite Life* from among the Buddhist scriptures. They devoted themselves to advocating the practice of invoking the buddha-name by chanting "Hail to Amitabha Buddha," in order to seek rebirth in Amitabha Buddha's pure land, the land of ultimate bliss. Thus Huiyuan became the first patriarch of the later Pure Land school of Chinese Buddhism. One could say that the establishment of the Pure Land school by Huiyuan was the real beginning of Chinese Buddhism. It was also one of the most obvious aspects of the rich religious spirit of Buddhism. There were perhaps two basic causes leading to the creation of the White Lotus Society on Mount Lu and Pure Land Buddhism: the trend of the times and the choice of methods of nurturing life.

Now, as to the trend of the times, the transformation of thought—underway since the Wei and Jin dynasties—and the rise of abstruse discourse, had already gone as far as it could, but it had left those seeking knowledge with no way to satisfy themselves. The contemporary style of free and broad-minded thought had influenced the minds of people in society, and they had gone from a dejected, demoralized state to one of complete excess and abandon. This had made politics even more chaotic and society even harder to stabilize and pacify. As a result, the intellectual trend of fleeing from the world was ever increasing. This was everywhere the case with the representatives of the intelligentsia—men like Tao Yuanming and Xie Lingyun. Feeling compassion for these people, the great teacher Huiyuan invited famous contemporary literati to form the White Lotus Society.

The tendency toward eremitic retreat was also an inevitable trend of the times. An example is this sad statement from a letter by Liu Yimin in response to an invitation to come to Mount Lu: "The Jin royal house does not have the solidity of a stone chime, the feelings of living creatures are as precarious as a pile of eggs." In this we can see the general state of mind of the literati of the period, and their desire to flee the world and take refuge in Buddhism.

Ever since the Western and Eastern Han dynasties, and through the Wei and Jin dynasties, besides the abstruse discourse at the level of philosophy, the theories of the Taoist adepts on nurturing life had also been very popular in the world. The fashion for techniques of "refining the elixir" in order to seek to become a spirit immortal, and live forever without growing old was already widespread throughout the country. Dharma master Huiyuan had himself studied these Taoist arts, but he finally came to feel that they were vague and unreliable and were not the ultimate method, and so it was still necessary to search within oneself and return to the One Mind to attain the Tao. Thus, he came to a deep comprehension of the Buddhist principle of perceiving inherent emptiness via cultivating transcendent wisdom.

Having received the theories and techniques that were the bequest of the illustrious adepts Fotudeng and Dao An and as their direct successor, Huiyuan had a deep knowledge of the difficulties that would confront future people in seeking genuine realization. Thus he advocated the method of reciting the buddha-name as a way of elevating and sublimating the spirit, as a method of cultivating practice that included people of all capacities and levels of consciousness. Even if people did not finish with birth and death in this lifetime, this method could still enable their souls to reach a transcendent realm.

The founding of the Pure Land school established the religious spirit and style of Buddhism in China. In the present day, more than a thousand years later, the phrase "Amitabha Buddha" has become a popular expression in Chinese society. No matter whether it is recited as practice to refine the mind or uttered as a casual expression, wherever we go we can hear "Amitabha Buddha" being said by Chinese people.

Kumarajiva and Sengzhao

In the period of the Later Qin dynasty in northwest China, the famous monk Kumarajiva came to China from Central Asia. His great mission was to translate the Buddhist scriptures and to disseminate the Buddhist teaching of *prajna,* transcendent wisdom. This was a key event in opening a channel between Chinese and Indian culture and thought, and in developing Buddhist civilization.

Among Kumarajiva's disciples were men like Sengrui and Sengzhao, who were both figures of outstanding learning and talent in contemporary China. The deep learning and dignified bearing of this teacher and his disciples deeply influenced the learned world of the Northern and Southern dynasties, and they were held in the highest esteem by their contemporaries. Especially influential was the treatise written by Sengzhao which synthesized the thought of Laozi, Zhuangzi, and Confucius with Buddhism. Sengzhao's other works, such as the treatises titled "Transcendent Wisdom is not Ordinary Knowledge" and "Nirvana Has No Name," also proved to be famous works whose special reputation has endured through the ages in the history of Chinese philosophy and literature. The Buddhist works of Dao An and his disciple Huiyuan were also very much influenced by Kumarajiva.

Kumarajiva's coming to China was a special event in the history of Chinese culture. But the circumstances of his coming to China were very painful and bitter. Because he admired Kumarajiva's learning, Fu Jian, the lord of the Former Qin dynasty, did not shrink from sending to the west a great army under the leadership of his general Lu Guang to attack Kucha, a Central Asian city-state which was Kumarajiva's home. Later, Lu Guang heard the news that Fu Jian's army had been defeated and he took advantage of this temporary reverse in 386 to proclaim the state of Liang with himself as the monarch. Kumarajiva was then captured by Lu Guang. During the time of the Later Qin dynasty, ruled by the Yao family, which was founded in 394 when Yao Chang overthrew his former lord Fu Jian, Kumarajiva was brought to the great city of Chang'an in China's Central Plain after Lu Guang's son, Lu Long, surrendered to the Later Qin in 403. Yao Chang's son and heir, Yao Xing, invited Kumarajiva to live at Xiaoyao Garden in 405 and made him the National Teacher.

Kumarajiva and his team translated over three hundred volumes of Buddhist scriptures. About three thousand people took part in the translation work, all supported by the Yao government. Many famous monks emerged from this project, and the reputation of Buddhism grew.

We can draw four conclusions from the circumstances of Kumarajiva's coming to China to translate Buddhist texts. First, the warlords of the time were not averse to sending out armies to conquer other states and engage in repeated conflicts, all for the sake of a single scholar. This is a highly unusual event in history. Looking at the good side, it shows they held deep respect for learning and the glory of a particular teacher. From another aspect, it is also true that this only could have been done by men of a low cultural level, because this was an act of coercion through military force. Nevertheless, down through the ages, most intellectuals have tended to look down on themselves and each other. The ones that have truly honored the intellectuals and been able to appreciate their talents have been, in general, the so-called nonintellectuals. This is almost a rule of history.

Second, Kumarajiva's work of translating Buddhist scriptures was under the control of a political power and only this enabled it to have such great success. The project had a foreigner who had mastered written Chinese as its chief translator, and he worked with the help of talented Chinese scholars. Because of this, their translations of the Buddhist scriptures not only gave Chinese Buddhist texts their special characteristics, but also added another look to Chinese literary style, the look of Buddhist scriptural literature. The language of these scriptures was the vernacular language created at that time; it is only when modern-day people read it that it seems ancient.

Third, before Kumarajiva, the dissemination of Buddhism had often depended on demonstrations of the teaching through the display of spiritual powers. Only when Kumarajiva came to China was Buddhist philosophy put on a par with Confucianism and Taoism. Only then did it become a major stream in Chinese culture and learning. Only after Kumarajiva did the learning of the three schools of thought, Confucianism, Buddhism, and Taoism, come to form the totality of Chinese civilization.

Finally, because of the influence of Kumarajiva, the number of people leaving home to become Buddhist monks and nuns increased. They varied in quality and many were unruly. This impelled the Later Qin government to establish monk-officials to oversee the congregations of monks. Later, this was taken as a precedent for the system of monk-officials instituted by the Sui and Tang dynasties and continued down through the ages in China.

Daosheng, Nirvana, and Buddha-nature

In this period, Buddhism had been transmitted into China from the northwest, via the Buddhist city-states of Central Asia. The center of Chinese civilization was still in the zone north and south of the Yellow River. Learning and thought in southern China still remained within the confines of Laozi and Zhuangzi, Confucius and Mencius. Moreover, all the Buddhist scriptures had still not been translated. For example, at this time, only half of the *Nirvana Sutra* had been translated.

Many contemporary Chinese adherents of Buddhism had the idea that sentient beings, with their extreme evil and serious wrongdoings, could not become buddhas. At that time the Dharma teacher Daosheng (d. 424) had studied Buddhist philosophy deeply and he thought that this idea was due to an incomplete knowledge of Buddhist principles and that it was not the complete teaching of Buddhism. He proclaimed that, even with their extremely evil and serious wrongdoings, sentient beings still possess buddha-nature and that, when they repented of their sins and renewed themselves, they could become buddhas. He was the first advocate of the idea of "becoming a buddha through sudden enlightenment."

Because of these ideas, Daosheng was attacked by most of the followers of Buddhism. He could not remain in the north, so he went to southern China and lived in hiding on Huqiu Mountain, preaching the Dharma to the rocks. The expression, "When Master Daosheng preached the Dharma, the rocks nodded their heads," refers to the story of Dharma teacher Daosheng explaining the sutras while alone in the mountains. Later, when a full translation of the *Nirvana Sutra* was completed, there was at last proof that what Daosheng had said about all sentient beings having buddha-nature was not wrong.

The source of Daosheng's thought was really still inspired by the three mystic studies of the *Book of Changes, Laozi*, and *Zhuangzi*. This also makes it obvious that, at that time, Buddhist thought and Chinese culture were drawing on each other's discoveries and that they had already reached a state of interpenetration.

THE HEYDAY OF CHINESE BUDDHISM

From the late Han dynasty, through the Wei and Jin dynasties, and into the Northern and Southern dynasties period, the fashion in learned thought turned away from the simplicity of the Han dynasty philosophy and everywhere tended toward metaphysical pursuits. Thus in this period, both Buddhist and Taoist religious learning developed more and more. Confucianism vacillated between Buddhist and Taoist influences. Moreover, because of the elevation of monarchical authority in the Northern and Southern dynasties and the fact that many of the rulers of those dynasties patronized Buddhism, Buddhism came to be held in high esteem both at court and throughout the countryside, a high esteem that could scarcely have been added to.

Nevertheless, from the time of the Western and Eastern Jin dynasties (A.D. 265–420), into the Sui and Tang period (A.D. 580–900), though Chinese Buddhism still mostly followed the patterns of Indian Buddhism, it was being subjected to the influences of Chinese civilization and was in the midst of a process of gradual transformation.

The Sui and Tang Periods

In the time of Liang Wudi (Emperor Wu of the Liang dynasty who reigned over southern China from 502 to 549), Buddhism was particularly flourishing, thanks to that monarch's religious beliefs. Liang Wudi believed in both Buddhism and Taoism, but he was particularly fond of Buddhism. These Buddhist temples and monasteries sprang up in great numbers all over southern China. Buddhist temples were built at most of the famous mountains and scenic places.

Thus we read, in the Tang dynasty poet Tu Mu's verse on Spring in Jiangnan, the famous lines:

> Four hundred and eighty temples in the South
> So many towers and platforms in the mist and rain.

Even so, this passage is only referring to the Buddhist temples in the region around the Yangzi River; it does not include the Buddhist buildings in the Yellow River Valley. Rather than characterize the culture and thought of the Northern and Southern dynasties period according to the usual term "Dark Learning" (that is, abstruse metaphysics), it would be more accurate to say that this was a period of religious culture and thought.

In the time of Emperor Wu of the Liang dynasty and Emperor Xuanwu of the Northern Wei dynasty (r. 499–515), the Indian monk, Bodhidharma, arrived by sea in Guangdong. Bodhidharma was the Twenty-Eighth Patriarch of Indian Buddhism's special transmission outside the scriptural teachings: the Zen school. Having come east to China, Bodhidharma had an interview with Liang

Wudi, but the two did not reach accord. So Bodhidharma crossed the Yangzi River and traveled to northern China. He lived in seclusion in Shaolin Temple on Mount Song and sat for nine years facing a wall. This was the beginning of the transmission of Zen into China.

From the early Tang onward (seventh century A.D.), the Zen school flourished greatly, transforming Buddhism in China into a purely Chinese form of Buddhism. We can say that the great teacher Huiyuan's founding of the Pure Land school and Bodhidharma's transmitting of the Zen school were two great events in the history of Chinese Buddhism.

The interaction of political factors and their impact on learning and philosophical thought had plunged China's historical culture into an extremely confused situation during the Northern and Southern dynasties period. Against this background, Wang Tong, in his lectures in northern China, had propounded a system of thought that brought together Confucianism, Buddhism, and Taoism and established the basis for Tang culture from the early Tang period on.

In this same period, the great teacher Zhiyi (538–597) formally established the Tiantai school of Chinese Buddhism. He used meditative cessation and contemplation as the methods of genuine Buddhist realization. Using the systematic categories of three kinds of cessation and three kinds of contemplation, correlated with the three meditation perspectives of emptiness, provisional existence, and the mean between them, Zhiyi brought together the whole of Buddhist theory. He started the practice of categorizing and classifying the scriptural teachings and gave the first critical treatment of the Buddhist legacy of teachings. Zhiyi composed the book *Moho Zhiguan, The Great Cessation and Contemplation*. This great work is surely the first comprehensive guide to Buddhism written in China. The second such great comprehensive guide was the *Zong Jing Lu, The Source Mirror Record*, written later by Zen master Yongming Yanshou (d. 975) during the Song dynasty.

The Founding of the Tang Dynasty

The Tang dynasty was founded by the heroism and strategic brilliance of Tang Taizong, assisted by his ministers and generals at the beginning of the dynasty. Most of them were talented men of broad knowledge who had, in addition, absorbed the political experience and painful lessons of the preceding Six Dynasties period.

The attitude of the founders of the dynasty toward religion was one of uniform tolerance, no matter whether toward Buddhism, Taoism, or even Nestorian Christianity and spirit cults. They allowed everyone in the country, from high to low, freedom of religious belief. In the government's system to oversee religion, there was an officer called the *seng-zheng* for the Buddhist clergy and an officer called the *dao-lu* for the Taoist clergy. These were the Tang dynasty equivalents of the specialized oversight departments previously established for each religion.

The single greatest event in Chinese cultural history and the history of Chinese Buddhism in this period was the great teacher Xuanzang's pilgrimage to India and his return to China. Tang Taizong established a translation institute for him and gathered together several thousand learned monks and noted literati to take part in the work of translating the Buddhist texts which Xuanzang had brought back with him from India.

On one hand, Tang Taizong did his utmost to promote Taoism as a religion whose founder was a member of his own clan. (Taoists revered Laozi as the founder of their religion. Laozi's surname was Li, the same as the Tang royal family; Tang Taizong's personal name was Li Shimin.) On the other hand, Tang Taizong also had sincere faith in the message of Buddhism. He greatly respected the great teacher Xuanzang and many times urged him to return to lay life so he could serve as an imperial minister, but Xuanzang always declined. The great teacher Xuanzang's work of spreading Yogacara philosophy on a wide scale caused a great dissemination of later Indian Buddhist philosophy and the Mahayana and Hinayana scriptures throughout Chinese Buddhism and Chinese culture.

At the same time, the Indian teacher known in Chinese as Xianshou Fazang reached China, and the teachings of the Huayan school were established within Chinese Buddhism and flourished greatly. Coming after the Tiantai school's categorization of the Buddhist teachings, a second classification of the totality of Buddhist principles was carried out based on the viewpoint of the Huayan school.

Soon after this, Dharma teacher Daoxuan energetically promoted the Vinaya school, and this established and strengthened

the foundation of the codes of discipline and the system of regulations for Chinese Buddhism.

Following upon these developments, various Buddhist schools
sprang to life, like the school based on the three Mahdyamika treatises, the school based on the *Abhidharma-kosha*, and the school
based on the *Satyasiddhi Shastra*. These all vied with each other,
producing many wondrous offshoots, each giving rise to its own
theoretical system. Thus the ten schools of Tang Buddhism took
shape, as shown on the following list.

PURE LAND SCHOOL

Indian founders: The bodhisattvas Ashvagosha, Nagarjuna, Vasubandhu, and others.

Chinese founder: Huiyuan.

Date of founding: Eastern Jin period (c. A.D. 400).

Principal scriptures: *Infinite Life Sutra, Contemplation of Amitabha
  Sutra, Amitabha Sutra, Treatise on Birth in the Pure Land,
  Treatise on the Awakening of Faith in Mahayana.*

Main teaching: Its method of cultivating realization is to focus the
  mind on buddha-remembrance through reciting the buddha-
  name, and thus be reborn in Amitabha's land of ultimate bliss
  in the West.

VINAYA SCHOOL

Indian founders: The main focus is the vinaya section of the teachings spoken by Buddha, so the first patriarch of the school is
  considered to be the Venerable Upali, who was the foremost
  of Buddha's disciples in upholding the vinaya, the precepts of
  discipline.

Teachers in China: The start of the practice of accepting the precepts in China was when Chinese monks accepted the Dharma
  from the Indian monk Dharmakala (Chinese: Fashi).

Date of founding: Second year of the Jiaping era of the Wei dynasty (A.D. 250).

Principal scriptures: The *Four-part Vinaya*, the *Five-part Vinaya*,
  the *Ten Verses on the Vinaya*, etc.

Main teaching: To realize sagehood by upholding the precepts
  of discipline using the vinaya studies of both Hinayana and
  Mahayana.

TIANTAI SCHOOL

Chinese founders: Founded by Huiwen and his disciple Zhiyi.

Date of founding: The period of the Northern Qi and Sui dynasties (late sixth century A.D.).

Principal scriptures: *Lotus Sutra* as the main basis, *The Great Perfection of Wisdom Shastra* as the guide, the *Nirvana Sutra* as the support, and *The Greater Perfection of Wisdom Sutra* for methods of contemplation.

Main teaching: The One Vehicle, the vehicle of attaining buddhahood, as the main principle; the three forms of cessation and contemplation correlated with the meditation perspectives of emptiness, provisional existence, and the mean as the method of cultivating realization.

SATYASIDDHI SCHOOL

Indian founder: Harivarman.

Teacher in China: Dharma founder Kumarajiva spread it.

Date of founding: Thirteenth year of the Hongshi era of the Later Qin.

Principal scriptures: It made use of the best of the Hinayana scriptures and the *Satyasiddhi Shastra* written by Harivarman.

Main teaching: With the *Satyasiddhi Shastra* furnishing the guiding principles, it taught a progression of steps of cultivating realization through twenty-seven stations.

THREE TREATISES SCHOOL (SAN-LUN)

Indian founder: The bodhisattva Nagarjuna.

Chinese founder: Kumarajiva.

Date of founding: Later Qin period (384–417).

Principal scriptures: *Madhyamika Shastra, Shata Shastra,* and *The Dvadashanikaya Shastra* by the bodhisattva Deva.

Main teaching: Refutes clinging to the absolute and conventional truths, and reveals the truths of emptiness, existence, and non-abiding.

ABHIDHARMAKOSHA SCHOOL

Indian founders: The bodhisattva Vasubandhu and the shastra master Sthiramati.

Teachers in China: Paramartha Tripitaka and Xuanzang.

Date of founding: In the fourth year of the Tianjia period of Emperor Wen of the Chen dynasty (A.D. 563) Paramartha translated the old edition of the *Abhidharmakosha*; in the seventh year of the Zhenguan era of Emperor Taizong of the Tang dynasty (633) Xuanzang translated the new edition of the *Abhidharmakosha*.

Principal scriptures: The four *Agama-sutras* as the main texts, *The Abhidharmakosha Shastra* as the correct basis, and in addition, such treatises as the *Vibhasha Shastra*, the *Abhidharma Mind Shastra*, the *Abhidharma Mind Shastra with Interpolated Commentary*, and so on.

Main teaching: The main teaching was based on the *Abhidharmakosha Shastra* by the bodhisattva Vasubandhu, translated by Xuanzang, It posited seventy-five basic dharmas to encompass the principles of such phenomena as mind and form and so on.

ZEN SCHOOL

Indian founders: (Buddha's disciple) the Venerable Mahakashyapa.

Chinese founder: Bodhidharma.

Date of founding: In the period of the Liang and Sui dynasties (sixth century A.D.).

Principal scriptures: *Lankavatara Sutra,* and *Diamond Sutra.*

Main teaching: The Zen teaching was a separate transmission outside the scriptural teachings that did not posit any written texts as sacred; Zen pointed directly to the human mind to enable people to see their real nature and become buddhas.

HUAYAN / AVATAMSAKA SCHOOL

Chinese founders: Founded by master Dushun, it was spread by the great teacher Xianshou Fazang, so it was also called the Xianshou School.

Date of founding: In the period of the Chen and Sui dynasties (second half of the sixth century A.D.).

Principal scriptures: *Huayan / Avatamsaka Sutra.*

Main teaching: The teaching of the school was based on the four realms of reality and the ten mysterious gates set forth in the *Huayan Sutra.*

FAXIANG / YOGACARA SCHOOL

Indian founders: The bodhisattvas Maitreya and Asanga.

Chinese founders: Dharma teacher Xuanzang caused it to flourish in China.

Date of founding: In the reign of Tang Taizong (627–649).

Principal scriptures: Its main texts were six sutras and eleven shastras. The six sutras were: the *Avatamsaka Sutra, Sandhinirmocana Sutra, Sutra of the Tathagata's Manifestation of Meritorious Qualities and Adornments, Abhidharma Sutra, Lankavatara Sutra,* and *Sutra of the Pure Land of Vairocana Buddha.*

Main teaching: To explain the subtle truth that all perceived phenomena are only the representations of consciousness.

TANTRA / ESOTERIC SCHOOL

Indian founder: The bodhisattva Nagarjuna.

Founders in China: In the Tang period Subhakarasimha, Vajrajnana, and Amogha Tripitaka came to China to propagate it.

Esoteric Buddhism is also divided into an Eastern branch transmitted to Japan from China in the Tang period, and a Tibetan branch, which was propagated by the great teacher Padmasambhava who entered Tibet from India.

Date of founding: Early Tang period (seventh century A.D.).

Principal scriptures: The basic scriptures are the *Vairocana Sutra* and *Diamond Crown Sutra.*

Main teaching: It is also called the True Word school (because of its use of mantras). It posits ten stations of stabilizing the mind to include its various teachings, and sets up mandalas, and the three esoteric correspondences of body, mouth, and mind (with dharmakaya buddha by means of mudras, mantras, and contemplation of truth), by which practitioners can move from the state of ordinary humans to enter sagehood.

The Zen School's Change of System

Due to the breadth and vigor of culture and thought in the early Tang period, many famous monks who were Buddhist scholars appeared. They all had the talent to achieve great things, and they set to work on the task of propagating Buddhism on a wide scale. The credit for really making Chinese Buddhism develop must be given to these Tang dynasty figures. By the time of Emperor Tang Gao-zong (r. 650–683) and Empress Wu Zetian (r. 684–704), just when learned Buddhist monks were reaching an impasse in their work of composing learned commentaries on the Buddhist scriptures, many noted Buddhist scholars were developing purely theoretical accounts of Buddhism and were leading each other into a labyrinth of Yogacara studies.

At that moment, the Zen school suddenly rose to prominence, taking as its standard the special transmission outside the verbal teachings, which did not establish any written texts, but instead directly pointed to the human mind to enable people to see their true nature and become buddhas. This corresponded exceedingly well to the direct simplicity of the Chinese people and to the need for genuineness and honesty in Tang dynasty thought and learning. Against a background where scholarly Buddhists were to be found everywhere, the Zen school brought forth a great adept who was an unlettered man, Huineng, the Sixth Patriarch. At Caoqi in Guangdong Province, he vigorously propagated the message of seeing true nature and becoming enlightened without setting up texts as sacred to the society of the common people.

At the same time, his fellow student Shenxiu was at Empress Wu Zetian's court, in the honored position of National Teacher, spreading the Zen school's Buddha Dharma among the social elite. Shenxiu's scholarly attainments were very good. He made gradual cultivation the main principle of his Zen teaching. Because of the high esteem he received from the Tang courtiers and grandees, the study of Zen became very widespread among the intellectuals who were part of the government.

Huineng's branch of Zen took sudden enlightenment as its main principle. Because Huineng was born among the common people and did not rely on written texts, he always used common colloquial speech when he explained the Dharma. Buddhist doctrine, which is so lofty and profound and hard to understand, he stripped totally of its pedantic trappings, transforming it into a purely popular philosophy of the common people. By this means, he enabled the influence of the Zen school to spread far and wide, with the transformative power described in the Chinese saying, "When the wind moves, the grasses bend down."

The influence of the two brother teachers, Shenxiu and Huineng, at the imperial court, and throughout the countryside, formed two immense criss-crossing currents running up and down China through the north and south during the early Tang period. They spontaneously gave impetus to the transformation in learned thought in their own time and achieved splendid success breaking fresh ground.

The branch of Zen that came through the great teacher Huineng later became popular throughout the whole country. We can only say emphatically, quoting the famous verse:

> Look at the territory of the house of Tang
> The whole of it is the realm of the Zen school.

In the third generation of the transmission after Huineng, there was Zen master Mazu Daoyi and his disciple, Zen master Baizhang. These two men boldly changed the prevailing monastic system and transformed the guidelines that had been in force ever since Buddhism entered China. Thus they created a truly Chinese style monastic system. At the time, Baizhang and his disciples were reviled by other followers of Buddhism as monks who had broken the precepts of discipline, and they were bitterly slandered and criticized. Little did their opponents know that it was because of the system devised by Baizhang that Buddhism was able to be transmitted for such a long time thereafter. This system of guidelines has been handed down through time to the present and is followed by Buddhist temples and monasteries both within China and abroad. Moreover, this system influenced later Chinese society and its political system, and played a very great role in both.

There are four special characteristics of the Zen monastic system:

1. It transformed the Buddhist sangha from a dependent community that lived by begging, to a self-sufficient economic system of collective agricultural production.

2. It focused on the cultivation of practice and used a system of teachers to lead and guide students so that they worked on a Buddhism of genuine realization in which knowledge and practice were unified.

3. It eliminated stiff and inflexible superstitious religious formal-
   ism. Its goal was a collective process of teaching and learning,
   using real practice with body and mind to seek realization in
   order to achieve the equality of mind and buddha and complete
   both human nature and buddha-nature.

4. It replaced the Indianized forms of discipline with a set of rules,
   the *Pure Rules of Baizhang*, which suited Chinese culture and
   Chinese conditions and set moral standards for both collective
   and individual conduct.

Thus the great Song dynasty Confucian, Cheng Yi, acclaimed
Baizhang's *Pure Rules*, saying: "The rites and music of the Three
Dynasties [which Confucians consider the paradigm of correct cul-
ture] are all in this." The general opinion is that the rise of
Huineng's school of Zen was a revolution in Buddhism. In reality,
the honor of a truly revolutionary event in Buddhist history must
be assigned to Zen master Baizhang's changing of the monastic
system.

The Rise of Esoteric Buddhism

The rise of the Zen school made Tang-period Buddhism become a
purely rationalistic religion and changed it into a mighty current
within Chinese civilization. But beyond this, in the early Tang period, Esoteric Buddhism, that is, Tantric Buddhism, was transmitted from northern India into Tibet. In the middle Tang period,
Esoteric Buddhism was transmitted to China from southern and
central India. This too represented a major change in Chinese
Buddhist history.

     Based on comparatively reliable historical facts, the rise of
Tantra within Indian Buddhism was really a teaching that belonged
to the late period of Buddhism there. It synthesized the Mad-
hayamika school's contemplation of the mean between emptiness
and provisional existence by means of *prajna* (transcendent wisdom), with the theories of Yogacara Buddhism, and fused this with
the techniques of cultivating practice of Brahmanism and Yoga that
were already present in India. The religious sect that was formed in
this way, by combining ancient and modern methods of cultivating
realization, was very different from the method of cultivating real-

ization that Shakyamuni Buddha had taught when he was in the world.

The development of Tantric Buddhism is an extremely complex and intricate issue that is impossible to address fully in a few words. The development of Tantra in Tibet can be summarized as follows. In the period when Tang Taizong was founding the Tang dynasty, the king of Tibet, Srongtsen Gampo (617–698), wanted to spread civilization within his territory. Due to a momentary lapse in judgment by Tang Taizong's state minister, Fang Xuanling, the Tibetan king's request for instruction in Chinese culture was not granted. Other than the few Buddhist scriptures and images that the Chinese Princess Wencheng brought with her when she was sent to marry the Tibetan king, and the several Taoist priests and others who accompanied her to Tibet, the Chinese never gave the Tibetans any instructions in their civilization.

A political measure is not only a "grand strategy for a hundred years." Policy makers must at the same time take note of the effect their decisions will have down through the ages. Only then can they make an objective judgment of the results in terms of success or failure that historians and the readers of history in later generations will see from their policies.

Due to this decision by the Tang government not to instruct Tibet in Chinese culture, Tibet turned toward India and asked the Indians to spread their civilization to Tibet. First, the Tibetan king invited several famous Indian monks to come to Tibet. They began to spread Buddhist civilization and devised a system for writing Tibetan based on Sanskrit. After this, the great Tantric teacher Padmasambhava (eighth century) came to Tibet and propagated the teachings of Tantric Buddhism there. Thus, from the Tang period onward, Tibet became a totally Tantric Buddhist land. It also developed into a special country where politics and religion were joined together.

Through the Song, Yuan, Ming, and Qing periods in China (10th to 19th centuries), the transmission of Tantric Buddhism in Tibet never declined. Although in all this time, there were inevitably sectarian divisions within Tibetan Buddhism, nevertheless its wholly Tantric form was never altered very much. This high plateau north of the Himalaya Mountains thus became Buddhist civilization's Shangrila for more than fourteen hundred years. This must be considered a unique event in the history of the East.

Tantric Buddhism in Tibet started with the Nyingmapa, the Red Hat School. Later it split into the Kagyudpa and the Sakyapa sects. Around the turn of the 14th century, Tsongkhapa (1357–1419) appeared. He was a native of the northern area of the Tibetan world, known in Chinese as Qinghai. In his youth, he became a monk in Tibet and, after he completed his studies, he founded the Gelugpa, the Yellow Hat School. Later, his four great disciples and their reincarnated successors down through the generations were active in the various regions of Mongolia and Tibet and spread their teaching there. The Dalai Lama and the Panchen Lama both became Dharma Kings, who combined both religious and political authority and guided the government in Tibet with religious teachings. In Inner and Outer Mongolia, the reincarnated lamas known as the Jangjia and the Jebtsundampa continued the same Dharma tradition through the generations by the system of succession through reincarnation. But they also received titles from the Chinese imperial house down through the generations and were honored as *khutughtu*, which has the meaning of great teacher and living buddha.

Now let us turn toward the development of Tantric Buddhism in China itself. During the time of Tang Xuanzong (r. 713–755), the Indian Tantric teachers Subhakarasimha, Vajrajnana, and Amogha Tripitaka brought the Tantric teaching to China. Through the ages, they have been called the three mahasattvas of the Kaiyuan period (Xuanzong's reign period). They all had certain spiritual powers which aided them in spreading the teaching. At that time, apart from the Zen school, esoteric Tantric Buddhism was the richest in mystical coloration and the most novel and stimulating form of the teaching. Therefore, both at the capital and in the countryside, people eagerly practiced it and, before long, it had become popular in the various regions of China.

Khubilai Khan (r. 1277–1294), of the Yuan dynasty, the Mongol dynasty that ruled China, revered as the National Teacher Phagspa (1235–1280), a great Tantric Buddhist teacher of the Tibetan Sakyapa sect. At the time, Phagspa was only a youth of fifteen. Not only was he very learned, but he also worked many striking miracles. Based on the Tibetan script, he devised a writing system for the Mongolian language. When Khubilai ruled China, he made Tantric Buddhism the national religion. This went so far that all the Yuan dynasty emperors after Khubilai had to undergo a rite of being initiated by Tibetan lamas before their coronation.

Given the imperial Mongol patronage of Tibetan lamas, corrupt forms of Tantra became popular at court and among the people, and spread everywhere. Both the Zen school and the other sects of Buddhism in China were greatly influenced by this. It was for this reason that the famous Zen master of the late Song dynasty, Gaofeng Miao, publicly announced that he was going into seclusion until his death and would never set foot again outside his mountain retreat. During the Yongle period (1403–1424) at the beginning of the Ming dynasty, which had overthrown the Mongol Yuan dynasty, the Chinese government decided that esoteric Tantric Buddhism was not an orthodox path and adopted the policy of expelling all Tibetan lamas from the court.

The Tantric teaching that the three mahasattvas of the Kaiyuan period had brought to China was then spread to Japan. In China, this is usually called "Eastern Tantra." The Japanese term for esoteric Buddhism is *Mikkyo*. Because of the reform of Tibetan Tantra carried out by the great teacher Tsongkhapa, the guidelines of the Yellow Hat School were established throughout Tibet. The original form of the Tantric teaching was still widespread only in the border region between Xikang and Tibet. In China, this is usually called "Tibetan Tantra."

The Song, Yuan, Ming, and Qing Periods

In the period from the middle Tang to the Five Dynasties (c. 750–960), Chinese philosophical thought, literary style, arts, and Chinese life itself, were all molded by the pattern and flavor of the Zen school.

As for the Zen school itself, in the middle and late Tang and the Five Dynasties periods, the Five Houses of Zen were established, each with its own method of teaching. The Five Houses were the Linji school, the Caotong school, the Yunmen school, the Guiyang school, and the Fayan school.

During this period, the Zen school's spirit of learning and the influence of its thought was on a par with that of the Dark Learning philosophy of the Northern and Southern Dynasties period. Many of the most talented people went into Zen and studied

Buddhism. Naturally, there was a background of many political and social factors that produced this trend at that time.

When the Song Confucian savant Ouyang Xiu was passing judgment on the Five Dynasties period (c. 900–960), his opinion was that there were no men of talent at that time. Ouyang Xiu's contemporary, the great reformer Wang Anshi, on the other hand, thought that Ouyang Xiu's viewpoint was incorrect. He said that the talented people of the Five Dynasties period had all become enmeshed in Zen. This is closer to the truth.

Given this background, during the period of the founding and consolidation of the Song dynasty late in the 10th and early 11th centuries, Confucianism underwent a major transformation. This was promoted by such figures as Zhao Kuangyin, the founder of the dynasty known to history as Song Taizu, and his state minister Zhao Pu, and later by men such as the noted scholar-official Fan Zhongyan. The 11th century witnessed the rise of such men as the five great Neo-Confucian philosophers Zhou Dunyi, Zhang Zai, Shao Yong, Cheng Hao, and Cheng Yi. All this signified the reversal of a long-standing accumulation of defects in a tradition of culture and thought.

The Confucianized Buddhism of the Song Period

The Song dynasty Neo-Confucians had been inspired by such figures as Han Yu and Li Ao in the Tang dynasty, and been guided by Ouyang Xiu and others. They emerged suddenly, claiming to be the direct heirs of the essential teachings on mind of Confucius and Mencius after an interval of more than a thousand years. They raised their own standard apart from the Confucianism that had existed from the Han through the Tang periods. We need not hesitate to state that the Song Confucians had been subjected to the influences of the Zen school and had absorbed a portion of the thought of Laozi and Zhuangzi: only in this way could the new face of Song-dynasty Confucianism have been created.

To put the matter another way, Song-period Buddhism had already entered Confucianism via Zen. To produce Neo-Confucianism, known in Chinese as *Li-xue,* "the Study of the Inner Design," on the basis of Zen, was a necessary development in the history of Chinese culture and the result of the fusion between Buddhist civilization and Chinese civilization. Although Buddhism had already become Chinese Buddhism over the centuries from the late Han period, through the Wei, Jin, Northern and Southern dynasties, Sui, Tang, and Five Dynasties, nevertheless, throughout this historical process, there had been ceaseless competition among Confucianism, Buddhism, and Taoism for position in the learned world and a continuous development of the way of thinking that recognized that all three teachings had a common source. By the late Southern Song period (13th century), the great teachers of the Zen school often discussed Confucian principles, and the signs of the Confucianization of Buddhism and the Buddhization of Confucianism were already extremely obvious. Thus we can say that the creation of Song-dynasty Neo-Confucianism had already been coming for a long time. Its inauguration by the five great Confucian philosophers of the 11th century was only its formal beginning.

Tantric Buddhism in the Yuan Dynasty

The influence of Tibetan Tantric Buddhism was extended by the military and political power of the Yuan dynasty, and it penetrated everywhere throughout China. Possessing special powers over religion, the Tibetan lamas, patronized by the Mongol nobility, dreamed of a situation where politics and religion were merged. All the other sects of Buddhism in China were greatly demoralized by this. From this point on, the various sects of Buddhism lost much of their original energy and were almost unable to recover. Only the Zen school, under the aegis of its monastic system, was still able to keep an enfeebled version of its traditional succession going.

Buddhism in the Ming Dynasty

The Ming dynasty inherited the remnants of the Yuan dynasty system in many areas: military, political, and religious. In the Yongle period (1403–1424), the Emperor ordered the expulsion of the Tibetan lamas and their version of Tantric Buddhism. But ever since the Song dynasty, Neo-Confucianism had entered deeply into the intellectual stratum. Moreover, the Ming dynasty political authorities promoted Confucianism and the anti-Buddhist Song Confucian philosopher Zhu Xi's commentaries on the Confucian classics, and made this the route of advancement for the gentry, via the official examinations. During the three centuries of the Ming dynasty, it was hard for the Zen school, which was the only form of Buddhism with any authority and prestige, to compete with Neo-Confucianism on even terms. The Zen school stayed complacent in its old ways and its traditions remained unbroken. In the later years of the Ming dynasty, the Wang Yangming school of Neo-Confucianism became very popular. Buddhism was weak in talented people and the Buddhist sangha was of uneven quality. Thus, it was impossible for Buddhism to regain the prestige it had had in the Tang and Song periods.

Then in the Wanli years (1573–1619), four illustrious Buddhist monks appeared one after another: Hanshan, Zibo, Zhuhong, and Ouyi. In Buddhist circles, these men are known as the four great teachers of the late Ming. All of them were deeply versed in Confucian learning. The Buddhist thought that they promoted stressed the joint study of Confucianism and Buddhism as teachings that mutually reinforced each other.

The great teacher Hanshan became too eminent and got dragged into the controversy within the imperial family over the installation of the crown prince. He was defrocked and sent into exile in Chaozhou, on Hainan Island. His disciples collected what he had written over his lifetime and made an edition of his complete works, entitled *The Dream Wanderings Collection*. In it, there are things like Buddhist commentaries on Confucian classics such as *The Great Learning* and *The Doctrine of The Mean*, and on Taoist classics like *Laozi* and *Zhuangzi*.

The great teachers Zhuhong and Ouyi devoted themselves to propagating Pure Land Buddhism. Among Ouyi's works, there are also Buddhist commentaries on Confucian classics like *The Analects* and the *Book of Changes*. As to the monk, Zibo, he was implicated in the factional conflict that arose over the issue of installing the crown prince and died in prison.

The fate of Buddhism in the late Ming period was that of continual decline, which went along with the decline of the imperial house. In the transition between the Ming and Qing (in the mid-17th century), there was a monk named Cangxue who was a famous poet. He became a secret friend outside official circles to many of the Ming loyalists at the end of the dynasty who refused to switch allegiance to the new masters, the Manchu founders of the Qing dynasty, and secretly aided their movement to reorder and restore the Ming ruling house.

The Decline of Buddhism in the Qing Period

When the Manchu founders of the Qing dynasty first entered China proper, the patriarch of the Yellow Hat Sect of Tibetan Tantra, the Fifth Dalai Lama, had already made a secret pact with them. In order to immobilize the Mongols and unite the power of the Mongols with their own, the Manchus had already professed their adherence to the Jangjia Khutughtu, one of the principal leaders of Mongol Buddhism. Thus, when the Manchus came into China, from 1644 on, they enfeoffed both the Dalai Lama and the Panchen Lama and venerated the Fourteenth Jangjia as their National Teacher. The first two Qing dynasty emperors, the Shunzhi Emperor and the Kangxi Emperor who reigned from 1644 to 1722, both had close links with the Tantric Buddhism of Mongolia and Tibet. Though the Shunzhi Emperor also studied Zen from the National Teacher Yulin, this did not make him change his policy of maintaining close ties with the lamas and venerating Tantric Buddhism. Regardless of whether it was out of political necessity or religious conviction, the early Qing rulers were inclined toward Tantric Buddhism.

When the third Qing emperor, the Yongzheng Emperor (r. 1723–1735), was in the border regions, before he ascended the throne, he had had contact with Zen master Jialing Xingyin and others, and he had intently studied Zen for quite a while. Thinking that he was already greatly enlightened, the future emperor decided that Xingyin's Zen was not good enough and he transferred his allegiance to the Fourteenth Jangjia, the National Teacher. He said that Jangjia was a man who had seen the Path, a man who had true wisdom and clear perception.

When he came to the throne, the Yongzheng Emperor used his venerated status as imperial monarch to lead Buddhist monks and Taoist priests to study Zen inside the imperial palace. The Emperor gave himself the sobriquet of "Buddhist Layman of Perfect Illumination" and acted as the great Zen teacher of the age. Several times, he issued edicts to promote the Linji school of Zen, and he ordered the abolition of the Dharma line of Zen master Hanyue Cang, which was an offshoot of the lineage of Zen master Miyun Wu of the late Ming. The Yongzheng Emperor issued a command stating that all the Zen teachers in the empire could freely seek him out to discuss the Zen path, and that he would not rely on his imperial status in his dealings with them. At the same time, he sent down another edict stating that Buddhist monks should not study literary composition or poetry, and that their duty was to devote themselves wholeheartedly to cultivating the Path.

The story goes that it was the Yongzheng Emperor who instituted the practice by which Chinese Buddhist monks burned a scar to symbolize discipline on the top of their heads when they accepted the precepts. Because the Yongzheng Emperor believed in Buddhism, he exercised his compassion and permitted anyone in the empire, whether gentry or commoner, to leave home at will to become a monk. But he was afraid that people still loyal to the Ming dynasty would hide in the Buddhist sangha and inevitably persist in their efforts to revive the fallen Ming dynasty. So he instituted the practice of having would-be monks burn a scar on their heads, so monks could truly be recognized as such, and so to prevent people from entering the sangha under false pretenses, thus bringing confusion to the source. Whether this was deliberate or not is hard to determine at present from the textual evidence. But this lifted the strict early Qing prohibition on Buddhists leaving home to become monks, so at least it can be said that the Yongzheng Emperor was being strict with the sangha out of his love for it.

In the Qianlong period (1736–1795), continuing the traditional practice of the Qing imperial house, the Emperor sincerely believed in Buddhism and specialized in cultivating the techniques of Tantric Buddhism. When he abdicated the throne and went into retirement, his zeal for Tantra increased even more and he kept on chanting mantras right up until his death.

During the Jiaqing period (1796–1820), with the gradual spread of European influences in East Asia, Western culture, thought, and religious groups all arrived together. Under the impact of the trends of the times, the fate of Buddhism was greatly transformed.

CHAPTER SUMMARY

The three centuries after Buddhism entered China, from the late Han dynasty through the Wei and Jin dynasties and the period of the Northern and Southern dynasties, can be called a time when Chinese learned thought began to flow in new channels. It could also be said that this caused Chinese learned thought to undergo a rather long period of dissension and dispute. But throughout Chinese history, Buddhism never functioned as a direct influence on politics.

During the Sui-Tang period, there were many disputes over the learned standing and dignity of Buddhist teachers. The outcome was that it was acknowledged by the imperial political authorities that Buddhist monks, by virtue of their religious status, would always be treated with the etiquette due to teachers, so that, in audiences with the emperor, they could present their salutations and carry on dialogues without kneeling and bowing down. This tradition continued until the end of the Qing dynasty in the early 20th century.

In the early period of Buddhism in China, many talented people came forth from the Buddhist ranks. This was especially true in the Sui, Tang, Five Dynasties, and Song periods, when, generation after generation, the eminent monks were all outstanding figures with broad learning and deep comprehension. At the height of the Tang dynasty, there were several times when official examinations were held on the Buddhist sutras and shastra in order to select monks. The historical records that tell how such and such a monk was ordained because of his success in examinations on the scriptures reflect this system. Thus, the Buddhist sangha was of comparatively excellent quality.

But during the time of Empress Wu Zetian (r. 684–704) and Emperor Xuanzong (r. 713–755), the imperial government resorted to the sale of ordination certificates (credentials that gave permission to become monks and nuns) to supplement its finances and meet expenses. This was like the granting of official rank in return for "contributions" during the late Qing dynasty.

To sum up the role of Buddhism in Chinese political history, because the eminent monks emphasized their work of religious teaching, they never meddled in politics. Thus they were always honored and respected and the government allowed the people freedom of religious belief.

Although four brief but intense government campaigns against Buddhism occurred in Chinese Buddhist history, during the Northern and Southern dynasties and the Tang dynasty, if we carefully study their history and assess them in all fairness, these were not due to the political considerations of the monarchs who launched them, nor were they purely religious conflicts. Rather, there were indeed many problems among the Buddhists themselves at the times when these persecutions occurred. For example, the famous Tang dynasty Confucian Han Yu attacked Buddhism. But if we carefully investigate the historical facts and the thoughts expressed in the essays he left behind, rather than say that Han Yu's idea was to rigorously eliminate Buddhism, it would be better to say that his anti-Buddhist feelings had been aroused by the way in which the Buddhists themselves were acting. Of course, this misconduct by Buddhists was one of the major factors behind the political measures he advocated. But Han Yu had friendships with famous Buddhist monks like Zen master Dadian and others. This, too, is a fact. It is obvious that, in assessing events and people, it is very hard to pass judgment lightly, and we cannot be in a hurry to follow received opinions.

On the other hand, when Emperor Huizong of the Song dynasty persecuted Buddhism in 1119, this was indeed entirely due to the influence exercised over him by certain Taoists. But apart from this, throughout Chinese history, Buddhism, Confucianism, and Taoism waxed and waned in complementary cycles, with one rising as the other two declined in vigor. Together they formed the mighty current of Chinese culture and thought, which included all three teachings.

As for Buddhist thought, it was the style of the Zen school above all that made the greatest contribution and had the greatest influence on Chinese civilization. Its achievements were too numerous to count and its beauties were utterly dazzling. In politics, in social organization, in philosophy, in literature, in architecture, in painting and sculpture, and even in the art of living of the Chinese people, the traces of Zen Buddhism are everywhere. The influence of Zen in Japan was even greater.

Let us mention a few of the contributions of Buddhism to learning and literature in China:

During the Wei dynasty, ruled by the Cao family, in the third century A.D., Cao Zijian heard the sounds of Sanskrit and this caused him to write *Yushan Fanchang,* a work that broke fresh ground in the Chinese study of phonology and music.

The Buddhist translator Kumarajiva's Chinese disciples, early in the fifth century, created the Chinese Buddhist literary style.

In the period of the Northern and Southern dynasties (fifth and sixth centuries), eminent Buddhist monks engaged in the task of translating the Buddhist scriptures invented the *fan-qie* method of indicating the sounds of Chinese characters by combining the initial sound of one already known character with the final sound of another already known character. This was the start of Chinese phonology, and the *fan-qie* method continued in use for over a thousand years. The present method of phonetic transcription for Chinese developed from this.

In the Liang dynasty (early sixth century), the phonological studies prepared by Shen Yue and Liu Xie's great contributions to literary criticism and his work on literary theory, *Wenxin Diaolong,* both had their source in Buddhist influences.

The Classic of Tea, by the Tang dynasty scholar Lu Yu, the great Tang dynasty teacher Yixing's *Yinyang Shushu,* and the Song dynasty Confucian philosopher Cheng Yi's *Taiji Tu,* all have great affinities with Buddhism.

The martial arts developed by Buddhist monks at the Shaolin Temple aided the founder of the Song dynasty, Song Taizu, in pacifying the empire. In the Yuan dynasty, the Buddhist adept and statesman Yelu Chucai contributed to medical science. Liu Bingzhong worked behind the scenes to influence the Mongol rulers to implement humane policies and avoid slaughter. In the Ming dynasty, Yao Guangxiao counseled the Yongle Emperor against tyranny. All these were historical contributions.

As for Buddhist contributions to Chinese art, to mention only the most glorious ones, there are the Yungang caves, the Dunhuang wall paintings, and so on. All these are world famous.

In sum, because of the outstanding level of learning and cultivation of its leading exponents down through the ages, Buddhist thought was able to exercise a great influence on Chinese learning and culture. If we try to observe China's literary people and scholars down through the generations, we see that there were very few indeed who had no relations with Buddhist monks, or who had not absorbed a little bit of Buddhist thought. As the Qing period poetess Cai Jiyu wrote in a famous verse:

> Slaying the whale barehanded, a deed that will be famous
> for a thousand years
> Returning to Buddha when old, the intent of a lifetime.

This verse reveals what the intellectuals of old China in general wanted, the most lofty orientation of their thought, and the ultimate realm of human life: naturally, it is filled with the echoes of Zen Buddhism. This is an authoritative representation of the significance of Buddhism in Chinese cultural history.

CHAPTER 4

Buddhism in Other Countries

BUDDHISM IN ASIA

Let us consider the dissemination of Buddhism through the various countries of the world. In the Western world, Buddhism in Europe and America has been indirectly influenced by Chinese Buddhism. In southern Asia, Hinayana Buddhism had already entered the territories of the modern nations of Burma and Thailand long ago, in the time of the Indian King, Ashoka. In the third century B.C. Buddhism was transmitted to the countries of East Asia, like Korea, Japan, the Philippines, Singapore, and Vietnam, through their connection with China.

From an historical point of view, Korea was the earliest country Buddhism entered from China; the next was Japan. Here we will give a simple account of the sequence of events in the dissemination of Buddhism to these two countries.

Korea

Modern-day Korea includes the three ancient kingdoms that were known in history as Koguryo, Silla, and Paekche. Buddhism entered these three kingdoms at different times.

Koguryo, in the northern and central portions of the Korean peninsula, was the earliest of the three to receive Buddhist teachers. In the fourth century A.D., during the period of the Jin dynasty in China, Fu Jian, the barbarian monarch of the so-called Former Qin dynasty, in power in north China, dispatched the Buddhist monk Shundao to Korea along with a load of Buddhist images and scriptural texts. The king of Korguryo, Sosurim (r. 371–385), received Shundao and came to believe in Buddhism. He founded Songmun Temple, where he installed Shundao as his teacher in the Dharma. This was the first transmission of Buddhism to Koguryo and the first time a Buddhist temple was built there.

Twelve years later, the Indian Buddhist monk Marananta came from China to Paekche, in the southeastern portion of the Korean peninsula, bringing Buddhism along with him. The king of Paekche, Ch'imnyu, received him with full honors and had a Buddhist temple erected. The king allowed men to be ordained as Buddhist monks and officially became a Buddhist.

Fifty years later, the Koguryo monk Mukhoja brought Buddhism to the kingdom of Silla, in the southwest region of the Korean peninsula, but Buddhism did not become widespread there. It was not until a century later, during the time of King Pophung (r. 514–540), that Buddhism was propagated widely in Silla. Buddhist temples were thereafter built, and Buddhism began to flourish in Silla.

During the 660s and 670s, King Munmu of Silla defeated Koguryo and Paekche and unified the whole of Korea under the rule of Silla. During that time, eminent monks like Wonhyo (617–688) propagated the teaching of the *Huayan Sutra* widely throughout the country. Famous monks of high quality appeared in great numbers and Buddhism flourished greatly.

Early in the tenth century, after Silla had disintegrated and split up into three kingdoms, Wang Kon rose to power and established the new unified state called Koryo. This was the time of the Five Dynasties in China, a time of militarization and political turmoil, when Chinese Buddhism was being weakened by political influences. But in Koryo, the new regime inherited the remaining traditions of the previous dynasty and Buddhist studies were flourishing there. Many Chinese Buddhist works, for example Tiantai treatises and Huayan commentaries, which had been lost during the chaos in China, had to be reintroduced into China from Koryo, in order that these schools of Buddhism could be revived in China.

In the early years of the Song dynasty, which was founded in 960, a party of more than thirty Buddhist monks from Koryo came to Yongming Temple to study with Zen master Zhijue, from whom they received the *Zong Jing Lu,* the Source Mirror Record. They brought this great encyclopedic synthesis of Zen and scriptural Buddhism back with them to Koryo and made use of it as they became teachers in various parts of Koryo. This was the beginning of the transmission of Zen to Korea.

Later on, the Koryo king sent ambassadors to the Song court to get the official Song edition of the Buddhist canon. This was compared with the two previous Korean editions of the canon, and the Khitan version of the canon, to prepare a new edition of the Buddhist canon. The Khitan were a people northeast of China who were the ruling group of the Liao dynasty in the tenth to twelfth centuries. This became the famous Koryo Canon acclaimed by later generations and recognized as an excellent version of the canon for the study of the Buddhist scriptures. Korean Buddhism was at the height of its glory in this period.

In the late 14th century, Yi Song-gye put an end to the Koryo dynasty, which had continued in power as vassals of the Mongol Yuan dynasty, and changed the name of the country to Chosen. During this period, Taoist thought and Neo-Confucian doctrines became very popular in Korea and Buddhism went into decline and did not again equal its early level.

In sum, Korean Buddhism was the result of the transmission of Buddhism from China and did not establish any distinctive sects of its own. The school that specialized in Huayan Buddhism was particularly prominent in Korea, as was an offshoot of the Fayan House of Zen. Apart from this, one stream of Korean Buddhism stressed gradual cultivation and advocated upholding the precepts of discipline, chanting sutras, and other practices aimed at planting a good karmic basis. This was called the school of the scriptural teachings. There was another stream of Korean Buddhism, oriented toward sudden enlightenment, that advocated single-mindedly reciting the buddha-name and rebirth in the Pure Land. This was called the school of mind. These were the two main tendencies.

Around 1910, Korea fell victim to annexation by Japan and Japanese Buddhism invaded the country on the heels of Japanese political and military power. Due to this, the true Buddhist spirit of Korea went into decline. Korean Buddhism in the 20th century was substantially altered by the Japanese occupation. But now that Korea has regained its independence, many outstanding people are doing their utmost to restore and renew the original Korean Buddhism.

Japan

The formal transmission of Buddhism into Japan took place in the middle of the sixth century A.D., during the thirteenth year of the reign of the Japanese Emperor Kimmei (A.D. 551). At that time, the king of Paekche sent an emissary to Japan with gifts of Buddhist images and scriptures. From this point on, there was a gradual tendency toward belief in Buddhism at the Japanese imperial court.

Several decades later, in the seventh century, with the rise of Prince Shotoku, Buddhism got the chance to develop further. Prince Shotoku was both the political and religious ruler of Japan. He founded temples and spread the Dharma and did all he could to promote Buddhism. Prince Shotoku also promulgated a constitution, which became the legal charter of the Japanese imperial house down through the ages. He himself composed commentaries on the *Queen Shrimala Sutra*, the *Vimalakirti Sutra*, and the *Lotus Sutra*, which became a model for later Japanese Buddhists. Because of these achievements, Prince Shotoku has always been revered as an enlightened monarch.

Over the course of the next century, during the Nara period (646–794), there was a trend toward unification of politics and religion. Buddhist groups devoted to the study of the *Vimalakirti Sutra*, the *Benevolent King Sutra*, and the *Diamond Light Sutra* were established, and various schools derived from the Tang dynasty schools of Buddhist philosophy arose in Japan: the Sanron (Madhyamika Three Treatises) School, the Hosso (Yogacara) School, the Kegon (Avatamsaka) School, the Ritsu (Vinaya) School, the Jojitsu (Sattyasiddi) School, and the Kosha (Abhidharmakosha) School. These were the famous six schools of Nara period Japanese Buddhism.

In the Nara period, many eminent monks appeared in Japan and Buddhism became popular. The Three Treatises School was introduced by the Koguryo monk Huiguan. Later it split into two sects, the Genko and Dai-an. The Sattyasiddhi School in Japan was dependent on the Three Treatises School. The Yogacara School was brought to Japan from Tang China by the monk Xuanfang. Later this school split into northern and southern branches which contended for preeminence. The Abhidharmakosha School in Japan was dependent on the Yogacara School. The Vinaya teacher Daorui transmitted the Avatamsaka School to Japan, and master Jianzhen brought the Vinaya School there. All these schools had their source in the Buddhism of Tang China.

More than a century passed, the capital was relocated, and Japan entered the Heian Period (794–1185). The early Heian period witnessed the rise of Saicho (767–822), the transmitter of the Tiantai school to Japan, where it became the Tendai school, and Kukai, known as Kobo Daishi (774–835), the propagator of Tantric Buddhism, known in Japanese as Shingon.

The great teacher Saicho began propagating Buddhism at Mount Hiei and won many believers from among the royal family. Later, he went to Tang China to seek the Dharma. He returned to Japan after receiving the transmission of the Tiantai, Vinaya, Zen, and Tantric schools. On the basis of this, he greatly extended his teaching activities on Mount Hiei and propounded teachings that included these four schools. He did all he could to disseminate the teachings of the Tiantai school, and he became the most famous Buddhist teacher of his time in Japan.

The great teacher Kukai came to China soon after Saicho, seeking to learn more about Buddhism. Kukai learned Tantric Buddhism from the Buddhist monk Huiguo (746–805). After Kukai returned to Japan, he established Toji Temple and worked energetically to propagate the rites associated with the Diamond and Womb mandalas. He became very famous and influential and laid the basis for the long-enduring esoteric Buddhist center on Mount Koya.

By the time Saicho and Kukai had done their work, Japanese Buddhism was dominated by the Tendai school and the Shingon school. The Tendai school, transmitted by the great teacher Saicho, contained within it elements of both exoteric and esoteric Buddhism, so it is sometimes called a blend of Tendai and Tantra. Later, his disciples Ennin (794–864) and Enchin (814–891) also went to Tang China to study Buddhism. Their school of esotericized Tendai flourished even more, and stood in opposition to the so-called esoteric teaching founded by the great teacher Kukai at Toji. Subsequently, due to disharmony among the followers, it split into two sects called Sanmon and Jimon. From this point on, sectarian differences multiplied, each with its own line of transmission.

In sum, the influence of esoteric Buddhism at that time was all-pervasive, and all the sects of Japanese Buddhism bore an esoteric coloration. The believers all put their emphasis on offering prayers and getting supernatural results. Thus, Buddhism was changed into a secret supernatural teaching of miracles and marvels, and became a major force in all strata of Japanese society. Because of this, many abuses appeared that went against the genuine original intent of Buddhism.

During the later Heian period, Japan's political order became chaotic and insecure, and this exerted an influence on the general psychology and made people world-weary. In this era, the Buddhist teacher Kuya (903–972) worked hard to promote the Pure Land method of reciting the buddha-name (in Japanese: *nembutsu*). The Buddhist teacher Ryonin (1072–1132) followed after him and founded the Yuzunembutsu sect, advocating the principle of reciting the buddha-name while adapting to circumstances. In Japanese history, the late 12th century was the time of the civil war between the Minamoto and Taira factions. Their deadly struggles left the people with nothing on which to depend. For this reason, the method of reciting the buddha-name and relying totally on the power of Amitabha Buddha, which was advocated by Honen and Shinran, became popular around that time.

In the Kamakura period (1185–1382), the period of the rule of the Minamoto shoguns, whose headquarters was the town of Kamakura, several sects of Buddhism rose to prominence in response to the trend of the times: Jodo (Pure Land), Shingon (Tantra), Ji (the Time sect), Zen, and the Nichiren sect. Many eminent monks appeared to make Buddhism flourish and spread its influence.

The Jodo school was started by Honen and became an independent sect. Honen (1133–1212) had originally studied on Mount Hiei. Later, because he venerated the teachings of China's great Pure Land teacher, Shandao, he advocated the Pure Land method of reciting the buddha-name. Among his direct disciples were many outstanding talents, so many later streams of Pure Land practice in Japan were handed down from him. Shinran (1173–1262) was his favorite pupil, and he inherited Honen's message. A special point of Shinran's teaching was that monks could marry and eat meat. He thought that, by developing faith and taking vows, anyone could certainly receive the protection of Amitabha's power and attain rebirth in the Western Paradise. The principles he taught were simple and easy to practice, so they exerted a deep attraction on people's minds. Shinran's teaching became a sect in its own right, called the Jodo Shinshu. Its influence extended widely and has continued undiminished up to the present day. Another example of a sect descended from the great teacher Honen's disciples is the Jishu, the Time sect, founded by Ippen (1239–1289), who traveled around holding meetings to recite the buddha-name.

The methods of the Zen school had already been transmitted to Japan earlier, but not until Eisai (1141–1215) and Dogen (1200–1253) did Zen become a distinctive school of Japanese Buddhism. Both Eisai and Dogen had been to Song China to study Buddhism. They transmitted to Japan the Linji (in Japanese: *Rinzai*) and Caodong (in Japanese: *Soto*) schools of Zen. The call of pointing directly to the human mind to enable people to see their inherent nature and become buddhas fitted very well with the needs of the people of the time, and so Zen spread all over Japan. The Zen idea of being liberated from birth and death influenced the fearless spirit of the later Japanese warriors' code of Bushido. All the Japanese arts benefited greatly from Zen: gardening, poetry, painting. The call of Zen was felt everywhere.

The famous Nichiren sect arose as a transformation of the Japanese Tendai school. It was founded by the Buddhist teacher Nichiren (1222–1282). He advocated the practice of reciting the title of the Lotus Sutra, (in Japanese, *Myohorengekyo*) as a way to see inherent nature and become buddha. Nichiren had a very bold and adamant personality. He used his heroic qualities to carry out compassionate Buddhist teaching activities. He was full of energy and devoted his life to the role of "saving self and saving others," so his teachings became very popular. Nichiren was truly an outstanding figure in the history of Japanese monks. He had many able disciples and they expanded the sect even further.

During the Kamakura period, new Buddhist sects rose to prominence one after another. This stimulated the older established sects dating from the Nara and Heian periods to re-energize themselves. Thus, the Kamakura period became the most flourishing period for Buddhism in Japan.

Later on, during the Yoshino (1336–1392) and the Muramachi (c. 1392–1482) periods, the Rinzai school of Zen was the most flourishing branch of Japanese Buddhism. In the area around the capital of Kyoto in the west, and in the Kanto region, the eastern plain around modern Tokyo, there was a network of major

Rinzai Zen temples and affiliated branch temples called the Five Mountains (Gozan) system. The Soto Zen school barely managed to survive in the northeast. The Nichiren sect had first been propagated by Nichiren around Kyoto, but later it became popular throughout Japan and branched into many streams. Two subsects arose within the Jodo sect: the Shirahata sect and the Myoetsu sect. In the Jodo Shinshu sect, there was the revival movement of Rennyo (1415–1499).

After this came the chaos of the Warring States period in Japan's history (1482–1558). The various sects of Buddhism were brought to the brink of ruin by the political decline of the country. The Warring States period culminated in the reunification of Japan under the Tokugawa shogunate early in the 17th century. After the Tokugawa regime had unified the country, they wanted to use the power of religion to win the allegiance of the people. Thus, they did everything they could to promote Buddhism. Thus Buddhism regained its influence and authority, and various Buddhist schools and academies were started.

The transformation in Buddhist learned thought that took place in Japan in this period can be compared to what happened in the Jin dynasty with the Dark Learning philosophy and in the Tang dynasty with the proliferation of Buddhist commentaries. Let us mention a few examples. The Buddhist teacher Hodan put forth a new account of the Avatamsaka (in Japanese: *Kegon*) philosophy. In Rinzai Zen, there was the influential teaching of Zen master Hakuin. In the Tendai school, the Anrakuritsu code of discipline became very popular. The Shingon school put into practice its Shoboritsu code of discipline. This was the period when the East and West Honganji Temples of the Shingon school were founded. In the Nichiren sect, there were doctrinal controversies. At this time, the Chinese Zen teacher Yinyuan came to Japan and founded the Obaku sect. Soto Zen also revived in this period. With all these developments, Buddhist learning and Buddhist thought prospered in the Tokugawa period. The philosophy of the Abhidharmakosha and the Yogacara treatises became the common basis for study and cultivation. The Japanese call this Buddhism's "age of commentaries."

After 1867, with the Meiji Restoration, Japan undertook a vigorous policy that involved accepting new ideas from the West. All the Meiji trends in political thought, in learning, and in education show a great reorientation from traditional Asian influences toward new Western models. Because of this, even though Buddhism retained its old dignity as the national religion, the philosophy of the divine origin of imperial rule and the old spirit of Japanese Shinto rose to prominence.

Due to these developments, Japanese Buddhism again broke fresh ground and began to evolve in two directions. First, sects proliferated throughout the country that advocated a nationalistic society where Buddhism and Shinto were not separated. These sects were closely linked to the militaristic nationalism of the warlords. Next, the Japanese intelligentsia learned Western methods and renewed the study of Buddhist thought, delving into the question of how religious belief had evolved into philosophy. They also pursued textual studies on the Buddhist scriptures with a skeptical attitude.

Nevertheless, in the realm of learned thought, Buddhist studies flourished in Japan because of these developments. Over the course of several decades, into the 20th century, Japanese Buddhist studies exerted a very powerful influence on Chinese Buddhist circles. As for the Japanese Buddhist monks, they too were subject to the impetus of the trend of the times, and they established various Buddhist academies and universities. They edited the Buddhist canon and worked hard at the task of spreading the Dharma throughout society and developing it further.

After World War II, militarism in Japan went into decline and the power of the militarists in the government was eliminated. Japan repented its past mistakes and began to renew itself. Many Japanese went overseas to America and other Western countries, and they brought Buddhist culture along with them.

Thus Buddhism entered a new continent, North America. Nowadays in America, there are Buddhist temples and the beginnings of a Buddhist sangha. Much of this is due to the efforts of Japanese since the war. Japanese scholars who have devoted themselves to propagating Zen studies in the West, like Suzuki Daisetsu, have spread the style of Japanese Zen studies throughout the world in twenty or thirty years. Now the Japanese government has certified Dr. Suzuki as a "National Treasure."

Thus it has come to pass that many people in these Western countries only know of Zen in Japan; they are unaware that the source of the Zen transmission was actually in China. Though the people in these countries have only been influenced slightly by Zen, many of them have begun to expound on Zen. Studying without the benefit of genuine teachers from whom to learn, relying on their own intuition, they cannot understand Zen correctly. We feel boundless regret and deep sadness over this state of affairs.

In sum, when we want to study Buddhism as a world religion, even though Japanese Buddhism was transmitted from China over the course of more than a thousand years, it has genuinely become a citadel of Buddhism that represents the religion on a world scale. Thus Japanese Buddhism has a very important position.

If we trace it back through history, Japanese Buddhist thought, although it originated with transmissions from China, has over the course of its history, gradually and in a hidden way, changed its principles. Since the Meiji Restoration and onward up through today, Japanese Buddhism changed into another distinct system of philosophy, perhaps because of its connections with national politics, and by no means retains its original aspect. It goes without saying that we must be concerned with this when we study the history of Buddhism in Japan.

For example, before the outbreak of the Second World War, when Japanese Buddhists explained Vairocana, the Great Sun Buddha, their explanations had a latent tinge of militarism, tacitly making the Great Sun Buddha a symbol for the Empire of Japan, traditionally the Land of the Rising Sun.

Before 1935, in front of the office of the Japanese chargé d'affaires in Hangzhou in China, there was a large signboard inscribed with the words "Great Sun Buddha." I witnessed this with my own eyes. This was the use to which Buddhist thought was put by the Japanese at that time.

At present, the whole world takes Japanese Buddhist studies as the standard for the field. This has gone so far that even the majority of Chinese Buddhists think this way. All I can do is quote the Buddhist term and say that this is "inconceivable." As for Japanese Zen studies (whether or not this can be called Zen itself), it is even harder to pass judgment.

As for present-day Japanese Buddhism, since the Second World War, there has been a vast proliferation of sects within Japan. There are sects combining Buddhism and Shinto, sects combining Buddhism and Taoism, and even some with secret-society links. These sects have cropped up like sprouts after a spring rain: there are at least three to four hundred of them. They are constantly changing, and these are not changes in name only. An example is the rise of the Sokka Gakkai movement, affiliated with the Nichiren sect, which takes part in politics under the canopy of Buddhism. It is hard to judge whether or not Sokka Gakkai will have any other ambitions as it develops in the future.

As we look upon Japanese Buddhism as it takes shape at the close of the 20th century, all we can do is send our salutations from afar and wish it a great future. May the true Dharma and the destiny of the nation both flourish!

Burma

Buddhism entered the territory of modern Burma by direct transmission from India in the third century B.C. through the missionaries sent out by King Ashoka. In this early period, it was the Hinayana form of Buddhism that was transmitted to Burma, and this planted deep roots in the country. Later on, Mahayana thought gradually entered the country and the controversies between Mahayana and Hinayana were very sharp. In the end, the Mahayana form of Buddhist thought lost all influence in Burma and, up through the present day, it is Hinayana Buddhism that holds complete sway in the country. Moreover, Burma is a purely Buddhist country.

Burma is dotted with Buddhist temples, and in their temples the Buddhist monks devote themselves to educational work. In general the people send their sons to the temples to receive a Buddhist education, and over 60 percent of the people can read and write. Usually boys over the age of seven are sent to the temples to receive a general education. Those who excel at their studies of Pali Buddhist textbooks are sent on to higher-level academies, where they receive a higher-level education and eventually become monks.

In the recent history of Buddhist studies, since Burma is one of the remaining homelands of Indian Buddhism, when Europeans first began to feel the influence of Buddhist thought, Burma was a center of its transmission. Many of the Europeans who have become Buddhist monks were ordained in Burma. They have started various English-language journals about Buddhist studies, and many noteworthy essays have appeared in these journals.

Nevertheless, it is a cause for worry that, in the last years of the 20th century, Burma relies totally on Hinayana thought in its politics and in its efforts to resist the mad ambitions of Communist philosophy to dominate the world. Not only is this worrisome, but it is probably something that the average person does not think about. This is something that must be criticized.

Thailand

Thailand was called Siam in the past. Early on, Buddhism was brought from Cambodia to the region that is now Thailand. In those days, Buddhagosha, who was famous for spreading Buddhism, had united the Buddhism of Burma and Cambodia. He often stayed in Cambodia; thus he disseminated Buddhism into the territory that was to become Thailand. He was revered by the royal family and the common people, and thus Buddhism became the national religion. Subsequently, the year of Shakyamuni Buddha's death was made the starting point of the Thai Buddhist calendar. Thai Buddhism takes Hinayana Buddhist thought as its standard.

Young men in Thailand must enter Buddhist temples and become monks for a time. There they receive a Buddhist education. All the Thai people take Buddhist principles as their standard of self-cultivation. Whatever form of schooling they receive, when they begin school and when they graduate they must formally recite Buddhist scriptures. When they reach the legally prescribed age, young Thai men must leave home and live as monks for a period of three months or one year. During this period, they curb their desires and devote themselves to learning Buddhist forms of conduct and studying Buddhist thought. This training provides them with moral standards for dealing with the world in later life. When a new king comes to the throne in Thailand, his installation must be carried out and proclaimed according to Buddhist ritual forms.

Thus, from top to bottom, throughout the whole country, all Thais are Buddhists. The Buddhist monks all wear yellow robes and the whole nation could be said to be a purely Buddhist country robed in yellow. Many Buddhist monks participate directly in politics. Deeply qualified monks are given titles as monk-princes. Buddhist images and temples are everywhere throughout the country. Temple buildings occupy 40 percent of the total area of the capital, Bangkok. The famous Wat Po temple is the most splendid structure in Bangkok. Wat Mahathat is a major Buddhist center to which monks from all directions come to study. Wat Bonchamabopit is the one of the oldest Buddhist temples. It contains many statues of Buddha in various postures, ranging in size from many tens of feet to a few inches, all rich in artistic value.

Thailand is an ancient Buddhist land and it preserves many of the customs of early Indian Buddhism. The Southeast Asian Buddhist countries of Thailand and Burma are both strongholds for the preservation and dissemination of Buddhism. As the great wheel of time advances on these tranquil Buddhist lands, they still remain serenely in the Buddhist realm of blue skies and lush forests. Will the changing situation of the 20th century keep Thailand as a Buddhist land, or lead the country into demonic delusion? It all depends on the leadership of an enlightened royal family and the wise choices of the Buddhist sangha.

Vietnam

Vietnamese Buddhism was originally brought in from China, but later also received the influences of the Hinayana Buddhism of Burma and Thailand. Mahayana thought was unable to plant deep roots in Vietnam. As in the other Southeast Asian countries, in Vietnam, the understanding of the concepts of Mahayana Buddhism was always somewhat unclear. Buddhist temples and Buddhist monks in Vietnam did not follow the Chinese monastic system.

During the second half of the 19th century, Vietnam was invaded and occupied by the French. From this point on, the religious situation no longer remained simple. Before Vietnam regained its independence, the ancient Buddhist faith, which had relied on the protection of the royal family, had fallen into the gap between the new and the old eras and had run its natural course. At present, Vietnamese Buddhists have declared their struggle for independence. There have been several waves of this struggle that have risen up and overthrown governments. Monks and nuns have even immolated themselves in this struggle to demonstrate their adamant resistance to anti-Buddhist measures, and this has already attracted the attention of the whole world. At present, it is very difficult to judge whether this movement will succeed or not, and we must leave this for future historical judgment.

Tibet

From the seventh century A.D., the region of Tibet formally accepted Buddhist civilization. Within one or two centuries, the whole area of Tibetan culture, extending from the Lhasa area to Xikang in the east and to Qinghai in the north, had become an area of Buddhist civilization. For a thousand years after this, there took place internal sectarian divisions within Tibetan Buddhism, but there was no outside interference.

All political, economic, and military power was concentrated under the control of the Buddhist lamas. Every place where the lamas had a temple was equivalent to a center of local political power. This could be compared with the situation of the Papal States in Italy, but the wealth, resources, and political authority of the lamas may have even surpassed that of the popes in the Papal States. With its mineral resources, Tibet is one of the world's famous centers of mineral wealth. At the same time, the Tibetan people voluntarily gave about two-thirds of their income to support the lamas and their temples as a way of acquiring the merit to be reborn in heaven and to attain enlightenment.

Through this period, the social structure and customs of the Tibetans remained at a fairly primitive level as one of China's border peoples. For example, their marriage practices were relatively free and allowed for polygamy and polyandry, as well as monogamy. If a family had more than two male children, one son was sure to become a lama, either for life or for a limited period, as he wished.

In the vastness of their snowy mountains and high plateaus, the Tibetans lived an idyllic life. Consequently, in the view of the Tibetans of olden times, only a Buddhist-influenced society could achieve a utopia. Down through the ages, during periods of political upheaval and change in China, the Tibetans watched which way the wind was blowing and adjusted their course accordingly. They would profess allegiance to the new dynasty, and so the Chinese emperors generally looked upon them with favor. The Chinese government would invest the lamas with official titles and employ them as its local administrators. Thus the lamas could enjoy an untroubled existence and pay no attention to Chinese affairs. During the reign of the Qianlong Emperor (1736–1795), the Manchu Qing dynasty sent troops to Tibet, and from then on there were usually Qing troops posted in Tibet. Even then, these garrison troops were soon converted to the Buddhism of the lamas.

During the later part of the 19th century and into the 20th century, due to the decline of the Qing dynasty and the warlordism that followed, China was afflicted by internal strife and its external problems multiplied. The British occupied India and had designs on Tibet. Many times, the British tried to provoke ethnic animosity between the Han Chinese and the Tibetans; they wanted to incite conflict between the two sides, from which they could profit. Thus there commenced in Tibet a conflict, sometimes open and sometimes hidden, between the faction that wanted to be allied to the British and the faction that wanted to be allied with China. Broadly speaking, the previous Panchen Lama was in the party that favored the Chinese and the previous Dalai Lama was in the party that favored the British.

Starting in the 19th century, a considerable number of Europeans and Americans came to Tibet in order to study Buddhism, or else used this as a pretext to further their other schemes. More Tibetans came to be able to read English than were able to read Chinese. British and French missionaries, or men posing as missionaries for their own protection, entered Tibet. They penetrated as far as the upper reaches of the Yangzi River in southwest China. Their intention was to take advantage of the ignorance of the backward peoples along China's borders and roll up China's southwest frontiers. Later, the Japanese also noticed this Chinese weak point, and, under the pretext of studying Buddhism, many of their agents penetrated deeply into Tibet and the southwest border region to carry out their aggressive ambitions.

After 1949, when the Communists came to power, the Tibetan lamas, due to their lack of political sophistication, thought that this was no more than another Chinese drama of a change of dynasties. None of them realized that, before long, there would be no room for them to preserve their traditional religious preeminence in the Tibet which they had thought of as a Buddhist pure land, and that they could scarcely dream of seeking to preserve their tradition of religious political rule.

Fundamentally, culture, history, and politics are three aspects of a single whole. In the spirit of reflecting on modern times in light of times past and restudying ancient times in order to gain new insight about the present, with the utmost respect I present this simple account of the experience of Tibet and offer it for the consideration of the Buddhist nations of Southeast Asia. It is up to them to ponder for themselves the sequence of cause and effect in this, and to discover the important theoretical principles.

To summarize briefly, in the 20th century, in the final analysis, it is not possible to amalgamate religion and politics into one whole.

Other Regions of Southeast Asia

Among the other regions of Southeast Asia in the early period, Buddhism flourished the most in Sri Lanka, Java, and Sumatra. About A.D. 450, the eminent Buddhist monk Gongdekai came to Java to propagate Buddhism. From the king and queen down, all the people in the country put their faith in him and Mahayana Buddhism became very popular. Late in the seventh century, the eminent Chinese monk Yijing passed through various regions of Southeast Asia as he made his way by sea to study in India; he spread the Buddha Dharma as he went. Buddhism in Sumatra was brought there from Java during the seventh through ninth centuries, but nowadays it has already withered away.

Throughout Southeast Asia, in Laos, Indonesia, Malaya, and the Philippines, wherever there are overseas Chinese, no matter how many or how few, Buddhism exists on a small but concrete scale. Some of these countries have been influenced by the Hinayana Buddhism of Burma and Thailand. Some have been influenced by the Pure Land school of Chinese Mahayana Buddhism. The sound of the Pure Land invocation "Hail to Amitabha Buddha" (*Namo Amitajo*) is present everywhere, and there are Buddhist temples being built all over the area.

BUDDHISM IN EUROPE AND AMERICA

Now that the conditions of Buddhism in Korea, Japan, Burma, Thailand, Vietnam, Tibet, and other Asian areas have been examined, it's time to examine the conditions of Buddhism in the West.

Britain

After the British had taken control of all of India by 1796, they began to pay attention to Indian civilization and to study Buddhist texts. Many talented people emerged among the British researchers on Buddhism. There were two among them who were particularly outstanding: Max Muller (1823–1900) and T. W. Rhys Davids (1843–1922). Muller was a specialist in Sanskrit. Starting in 1879, he began to publish the *Sacred Books of the East* series in forty-nine volumes. For this, he received the respect of the learned world of his time. In this collection, there were several Buddhist scriptures, such as the Hinayana code of monastic discipline, the *Larger Agama Sutra*, the *Sutra in Praise of the Deeds of Buddha*, the *Contemplation of Amitabha Sutra*, the *Greater Amitabha Sutra*, and the *Lotus Sutra*, along with English translations of various Sanskrit texts that had been discovered. This collection aroused British interest in investigating Buddhism. In 1881, Rhys Davids founded the Pali Text Society. The Society put out translations of various Buddhist texts that were in circulation in Sri Lanka, including sutras, shastras, vinaya texts, commentaries, histories, and biographies. Having received the support of the king of Thailand, the Society published the Pali canon. This did even more to encourage the interest of Europeans in studying Buddhism.

As related above, Muller and Rhys Davids performed a major service in transmitting Buddhism to the West. Many scholars from Britain, France, and Germany took part in this process, which injected a new current into the learned world of Europe in the 18th and 19th centuries. Lecturing on Buddhism at the major universities of Oxford and London, Max Muller and Rhys Davids had a great influence. The London Buddhist Association made Rhys Davids its president, and Mrs. Rhys Davids also translated many Buddhist texts.

The British Mahabodhi Society was founded in 1927 by the Sri Lankan Angarika Buddhapala. A considerable number of British Buddhists joined it, along with Buddhists from India and Sri Lanka. Attached to it were a research society and a lecture society. Every month it published a journal called *The British Buddhist*, which achieved a wide circulation. In addition to this, there was the London Students' Buddhist Association, founded by Dr. A. P. DeZoysa, and the Buddhist Layman's Association, founded by

Christmas Humphreys. Both were organizations devoted to promoting Buddhist learning.

Germany

After the British, among German scholars a new movement began to study Indian Buddhism. In 1881, Hermann Oldenberg published *The Life and Teachings of the Buddha*, based on Pali textual sources, in which he related the immortal deeds of Shakyamuni Buddha. This book circulated very widely.

A famous contemporary of the British scholar Max Muller was the German specialist on Indian studies, Richard Karl von Garbe. He was the most eminent figure in research on the Agama Sutras. His student Hermann Weller taught in Berlin, and was renowned for his expertise in Sanskrit and Tibetan. Among the students who studied with him for many years were the Japanese Buddhist scholars Watanabe Kaikyoku and Ogihara Unrai.

In addition, there was Max Walleser, who had mastered Sanskrit and Tibetan, and who was an authority in the German scholarly world. He wrote a book called *The Question of the Self*. His works include, among others, *The Philosophical Foundations of Ancient Buddhism*, published in 1904, and *The Sects of Ancient Buddhism*, published in 1927. He also established a Buddhist Studies Association to encourage the study of Buddhism by European scholars and to draw together the scholars of various countries, especially those of eastern Asia, to do joint research on Buddhism. The activities of Dr. Walleser included work on translating Buddhist texts, publishing articles and a newsletter, establishing a Buddhist library, publishing study materials for university courses on Buddhism, and organizing Buddhist lectures outside the universities. The center of the Buddhist movement in Germany was the Buddhist retreat established in the suburbs of Berlin by Paul Dahlke. At present, this is one of the famous sites near Berlin, housing many original texts, Buddhist books and journals in Eastern languages, and Buddhist works of art. It is unmatched in Europe for the richness and breadth of its collection. This center also published many accounts of Buddhism. At the same time, it functioned as a retreat and as a meditation center for the real cultivation of Buddhist practice. Not only did it engage in theoretical discussion, but it put a major emphasis on practice and realization. It was truly a pioneering effort in Europe for emphasizing the cultivation of practice.

There were many other famous German Buddhist scholars besides these, such as Wilhelm Geiger, Moritz Winternitz, Ernst Windisch, Richard Pischel, Erich Frauwallner, Heinrich Zimmer, Hermann Beckh, Wilhelm Stede, and Kurt Schmidt.

France

French research in Buddhism and Eastern civilization was inaugurated by Eugene Burnouf, who opened up a new era in Western culture. Burnouf was born in Paris in 1801. He was an expert in the languages of the East, such as Pali, Sanskrit, Persian, ancient Babylonian cuneiform, and others. His representative work is *A Treatise on the History of Buddhism in India,* based on over a hundred and seventy Buddhist texts in Sanskrit which had been discovered in Nepal, and which he used to write a biography of Shakyamuni Buddha and to research the principles of the Buddhist teaching. This set of texts included the flower of the Mahayana Scriptures, such as the *Prajnaparamita Sutra,* the *Lankavatara Sutra,* the *Avatamsaka Sutra,* the *Suvarnaprabhasa Sutra,* and the *Lotus Sutra.* Burnouf also translated the *Lotus Sutra* in its entirety, making the first translation of a Buddhist Sanskrit text into a European language.

Among Burnouf's students, the most famous as Buddhist scholars were such men as Miyouluo and Emile Senart. Senart edited the texts of various scriptures and, based on Mahayana scriptural sources, wrote an essay on the biography of Buddha and other works. Fuxini, a professor at the University of Paris, wrote several works on Mahayana Buddhist art. There was also Fu-ai-ye, who edited and published the *Samyutta-nikaya* from the four Agamas.

Apart from these men, the most authoritative figure in the study of Eastern learning, and especially in Buddhist studies and Indian culture, was Dr. Sylvain Levi. His books on Buddhism include a Sanskrit text and French translation of the bodhisattva Asanga's treatise on the *Mahayanasutralamkara* published in 1911, a French translation of the first chapter of Cheng-you's explanation of the *Abhidharmakosha,* and Sanskrit texts and French translations of Vasubandhu's *Vimshakakarika-shastra* and

Tridashakarika-shastra, and Sthiramati's explanatory treatise on the *Tridashakarika-shastra,* all published in 1926. He also compiled a French Buddhist dictionary and he was planning to compile a great collection of Buddhist music from the Asian Buddhist lands.

There is also a joint project of French and Japanese Buddhist scholars, who have formed a large-scale Japanese-French Buddhist Association, which is now flourishing and making great progress.

United States of America

American Buddhist studies have really contributed greatly to Buddhist studies in Europe. In the early period of Buddhist studies in America, a significant contribution was made by Henry Warren, who put out the book *Buddhism in Translation* in 1896. In 1902, A. S. Edwards wrote *A Buddhist Bibliography* and translated the *Dhammapada* under the title *Hymns of the Faith.* Professor Lamman of Harvard was the editor of the Harvard Oriental Series, which included the Agama Sutras and various other Buddhist scriptures. In addition, there were also such works as *The Gospel of Buddha,* by Anderson.

The leader of the Buddhist revival movement, the Sri Lankan Angarika Buddhapala, founded the American Mahabodhi Society and established a meeting place for it in New York City. Every year, on the fourth day of the fifth lunar month, he would gather together people from the various countries of the world and hold a large commemorative ceremony.

There are two or three hundred thousand Japanese immigrants in the United States. They are engaged in various areas with their religious and community activities involving the various sects of Japanese Buddhism. Gradually, this has attracted some Americans who have come to believe in Buddhism. In recent years, some Americans have even become Buddhist monks and nuns. In Hawaii, where Japanese Americans are very numerous, there are scores of centers for the propagation of Japanese Buddhism and Buddhist temples. Among these, the most fruitful has been the outreach work of the Honganji Shingon sect.

The number of Americans who are becoming Buddhists is continually increasing, and there are also Buddhist study associations. In recent years, more and more Buddhist groups and temples have been established. Americans go to Japan to study, and more and more Americans are investigating Buddhist learning and thought. They are particularly interested in investigating Zen.

In Brazil, because of the colonies of Japanese immigrants, Buddhism is also developing more and more.

The Japanese must bear the boundless shame and inner pain of unleashing the disasters of the Second World War. But their work since the war in bringing the culture of eastern Asia to the West, and providing extra spiritual nourishment for the people of the West, mired, whether intentionally or not, in the depressing life of their materialistic culture, seems almost to have made up for this mistake and is very much to be commended. When we reflect on our own relatively meager contributions in spreading Buddhism to the West, we Chinese must indeed regret our shortcomings.

Russia

In 1887, the Russian Buddhist scholar Minayeff published his famous treatise on Buddhism. In 1889, he also published the original text of the *Bodhi Practice Sutra*. Such was the early development of Buddhist studies in Russia. Comparable to Rhys Davids' Pali Text Society in Britain, the Mahayana Buddhist Publishing Society was attached to the Russian National Academy. In 1895, the society edited and published many Sanskrit Buddhist texts that had never before been published. Among the principal Buddhist scriptures they published were *Mahayana Treatise on the Learning of the Bodhisattvas*, edited by Xibiante-er and published from 1897–1902, the *Sutra of the Questions of the Protector of the Nation*, published from 1901 to 1909 by Fuyinlao, the *Selection and Assembly of the Hundred Phenomena Scripture*, published by Stcherbatsky in 1902 (Stcherbatsky was an expert in Buddhist logic), La Vallee Poussin's translations of Nagarjuna's *Madhyamika-karikas* and the appended commentaries, published in 1903, and the joint studies by Kern and Nanjo on the *Lotus Sutra*, published from 1908 to 1916.

With the outbreak of the Russian Revolution in 1917, Buddhist studies in Russia were throttled.

CHAPTER SUMMARY

In the various countries of Asia, Buddhism still retains its traditional prestige. But the times are changing, and Buddhism is also in the midst of changes. It is difficult to anticipate what kind of religion Buddhism will become in the future. Nevertheless, from a religious standpoint, there are still many countries in Asia that are Buddhist lands. This is especially true in Southeast Asia.

Nevertheless, Buddhist learning in Southeast Asia is still confined within the limits of Hinayana thought. There are also religious phenomena in the Southeast Asian lands that show a mixing together of Buddhist elements with the worship of spirits. But the banner of Buddhism is still bright in these countries. There are precedents, however, that give us cause for concern: "Where we have gone, the enemy can also go." When we investigate the overall trend of Buddhism in Southeast Asia, it cannot help but make us feel a secret worry.

In recent times, most of the Westerners who believe in or study Buddhism have taken the Southeast Asian version of Buddhist thought as the original form, or else they have been deeply influenced by the later manifestations of Japanese Buddhism. The Buddhism of China, the second great homeland of the religion, continues to be overlooked or deliberately slighted. I think that this is something that all intelligent Chinese Buddhists and their sympathizers must guard against!

The circumstances of the transmission of Buddhism to Europe and America have been described above. In the past half century, many Chinese have heard that Europeans and Americans are also studying Buddhism, and they have become enthusiastic about this. Thinking that Chinese Buddhism has already been propagated in the West, they take this as an honor. Some Chinese think that Westerners have brought the scientific spirit to the study of Buddhism, and that their Buddhism must be even better than Chinese Buddhism itself. They are ready to follow the Westerners gladly, and are going to Western countries to study Buddhism there. This blind mentality is really quite ridiculous.

Frankly speaking, the study of Buddhism by Westerners may possibly cause Buddhist studies to become more meticulous about textual criticism, but this is a far cry from being an impetus to a revival of the Correct Dharma. Moreover, at present, Buddhism is just beginning to be disseminated in the West, and how long it may take for it to be able to flower and bear fruit there, we will have to wait until the 21st century to see.

For now, I will mention five basic causal factors which will enable us to understand the trends in world Buddhism.

1. The translation of the Buddhist scriptures: When Buddhism was transmitted to China from India, it took four or five centuries, from the late Han period through the Sui and Tang periods, before there were genuine results. It is also necessary to be aware that Chinese civilization at that time already had its own brilliant accomplishments and was not some newly arisen upstart with shallow foundations.

Therefore, for Buddhist concepts to undergo translation into Chinese and become commonly understood in China was no easy matter. This was even more true because translating Buddhist scriptures is not comparable to translating ordinary books. The first requirement is to have a high level of literary cultivation in two dissimilar languages. The second requirement is that the translator must have already had personal experience of the realms reached by cultivating the practice of the Buddha Dharma. Just to reach a high level of literary cultivation in two languages is already far from easy, and the work of genuinely cultivating true practice is even more difficult.

The famous adepts in China's past who translated the Buddhist scriptures, like the Central Asian Kumarajiva and the Chinese Dharma master Xuanzang, were at the same time both talented literary scholars and men with a high level of attainment in cultivating realization of the Buddha Dharma.

Even so, they still had to rely on the support of the state, which established translation institutes staffed by several thousand people who devoted themselves to the work of translating the scriptures. Often the way a term was translated would be discussed over and over again for several months before they could decide on a translation.

Moreover, after a certain period of time, if there were people who thought that the translation was not exactly right, the text would be retranslated. Thus, there are usually several different translations of each Buddhist scripture. Only after several centuries did one of these translations get to be generally acknowledged as a reliable version.

Westerners use various different languages. After a few years of studying Buddhist texts, they make haste to translate and comment on Buddhist scriptures. They of course employ the customary ways of thinking of their own countries, claiming that they are being objective, but actually this amounts to subjective study. How reliable their translations ultimately are is really hard to say.

Even if Chinese try to translate Buddhist texts into foreign languages, they still must meet the conditions mentioned above before they can succeed. Thus, when it comes to the popular scriptures and examples of Buddhist thought translated by modern-day Westerners, we must be very cautious and seek confirmation of their accuracy.

2. The basis in the Buddhist scriptures: The Hinayana Buddhist thought that Europeans have taken up, and the Indian-language texts that they have discovered, usually represent texts from the late period of Indian Buddhism. There are great divergences between such texts and the texts of a thousand years earlier, from the time of Shakyamuni Buddha and King Ashoka. These texts must be compared with the various Chinese translations of the Buddhist scriptures and corrected in light of them before they can be considered comparatively reliable. But the modern-day Western translations of Buddhist scriptures have been undertaken without doing this work, and there is still a tendency not to take the Chinese versions of the Buddhist scriptures seriously. Moreover, the modern Western culture that has been formed on the basis of the Hellenic heritage has its own independent cultural tradition of several thousand years, and this must be comprehended.

3. Cultivating realization of the Buddha Dharma: Buddhist learning is not only a system of thought. Buddhist philosophy does indeed have a resemblance to Western philosophical thought. But Buddhist methods of cultivating realization must be pursued within the person himself. They are not like the methods of physics for studying the natural world. When Buddhism first entered China, men like Fotudeng and others could make the Chinese believe in them and accept the Buddhist teaching only because they themselves could show as proof spiritual powers based on their own attainments in cultivating realization.

In modern times, if people trying to promote Buddhism in the West do not seek the proof within themselves, but instead just try to spread Buddhism based on its texts and its philosophical thought, it will naturally appear as merely a system of Eastern thought, and it will detract greatly from the Buddhist spirit of bringing salvation to the world.

4. The dissemination of Zen: The message of the Zen school is a special transmission beyond the scriptural teachings, an approach that does not establish verbal formulations as sacred, but puts its real substantive emphasis on cultivating realization. The Dharma words, meditation cases, and pointed sayings of the Zen school that became popular in China from the Tang and Song periods on have already become indivisible from Chinese literature and Chinese common colloquial language. But when they came to Japan from the 13th century onward, they changed in character. These days, no matter whether in China or Japan, those who talk of Zen are many, but those who cultivate and realize it are few.

There are already many barriers for Chinese people to study Zen, and many points that are hard to comprehend if they are not deeply versed in the classical literary language and the various regional dialects of the Song period. Zen studies in modern-day Europe and America are in a state of flux: from a quick superficial impression, Westerners get some idea of the Zen realm of informality and humor, and then assume that Zen is just like this. If we Chinese are not able to give the countervailing evidence, and we just go along with these Western misconceptions and do nothing to correct them, then the misunderstandings will be endless.

5. The transmission of Buddhist concentration and wisdom: Indian yogic techniques and Tibetan Tantric methods of self-cultivation are currently becoming popular in Europe and America. The average Westerner who practices these methods takes them as a kind of Eastern mystical exercise for strengthening the body, and may even confuse them with hypnotic techniques. It goes without saying that, fundamentally, the meditative techniques of the true Buddha Dharma have not been transmitted to the West. Most of the people who try to spread so-called Eastern mystical exercises in the West do not even understand them themselves. They travel to the West and teach others only as a way of seeking empty fame. Are they misleading others or misleading themselves? Are they acting on behalf of Buddhism, or are they acting for themselves? We must reflect deeply on this and offer frank criticism.

For all these reasons, I would say that, in all the countries of the West in the late 20th century, Buddhism is in the beginning stages of being disseminated and there are bound to be mistakes made.

The introductory explanations of the *Ming Yi* ("Injury to Illumination") and *Jia Ren* ("People in the Home") hexagrams 36 and 37 of the *Book of Changes* say: "When it enters, there must be injury, so it is received with injury to illumination. Injury means damage. Damage to the outside must return to the family, so it is received by people in the home." All of us Chinese must alert ourselves to this, for the sake of Buddhist civilization and for the sake of Chinese civilization!

THE DECLINE OF CHINESE BUDDHISM SINCE THE QING PERIOD

Though the Chinese people still believed in and respected Buddhism during the period after the establishment of the Manchu Qing dynasty as rulers of China in the middle of the 17th century, all was not well.

In order to keep the peoples of the Mongolian and Tibetan border regions of their empire under control, the Qing rulers paid particular reverence to Tantric Buddhism. Imperial patronage of Tantric lamas for political purposes had been the pattern ever since the Yuan dynasty and had become a traditional policy of the government.

As for Buddhism within China proper, from the Yongzheng reign (1723–1735) onward, the Zen school maintained in form its traditional transmission under the protection of the Zen monastic system, but, in reality, Zen had already collapsed. Only the Pure Land school was still able to preserve the stature it had enjoyed in times gone by and was diffused universally throughout popular society. Apart from these two, the Tiantai school barely made its presence felt and was hanging by a thread. Schools of Buddhist philosophy like the Huayan school and the Yogacara school in the main no longer had any real substance and had become attached to Zen, Tiantai, or Pure Land. This was the general situation of Buddhism in China at that time.

Sectarian Decline

In the history of Chinese learning and thought, strictly speaking, the relative level of Buddhist learning and the position of Buddhist learning in China had already reached its zenith and begun to decline by the period of the late Ming and early Qing in the 17th century. Because of the widespread popularity among the 16th and

17th-century intelligentsia of the Neo-Confucian teachings of Wang Yangming, among the relatively small number of genuine Zen masters and Dharma teachers in the late Ming period, there were those who, although they were Buddhist monks, understood the Buddhist teachings on mind from the perspective of Wang Yangming's theories.

Thus we can observe two general trends over the three centuries of the Qing dynasty (1644–1911). In the main, the Chinese social elite, the educated gentry, devoted their energies to the great task of rebuilding the social order and mostly focused on branches of learning connected to political administration and managing practical affairs. Moreover, the Buddhist monks who had left secular life were without any special achievements in terms of the Buddhist perceptions of truth. Thus, Buddhist learning could no longer regain the prestige among the intelligentsia it had enjoyed since the Tang and Song periods.

In addition, Buddhism itself saw a decline in the talent of its adherents and there were extremely few Buddhists in this period who could match the eloquence or the virtuous conduct of the eminent monks of the Tang and Song periods and be models for the times. From the middle years of the Qing period onward, there were many so-called Zen masters who acted for the sake of empty reputation and to secure meaningless lineage credentials. Some even became involved with opium and alcohol. To win over educated types who had failed on the official examinations, they plagiarized from the collected sayings of the previous generations of Zen masters and, behind closed doors, concocted what they called precious Zen sayings to be transmitted to their followers. They urged their disciples to struggle to have these included in Buddhist canonical collections for their own glory.

As for the relatively more learned and prominent monks, they vied with each other for positions at the capital and flocked to the gates of the powerful, congregating around the officials' offices. They were intent on currying favor with high-ranking men and hoped to obtain titles from the emperors. If they managed to obtain any sort of imperial commendation or title, then they could pass themselves off as National Teachers and boast of their glory among the credulous common followers of Buddhism. Thus the lament of the popular saying: "In the capital a monk, outside the capital putting on the lofty airs of an official."

These tendencies began in the late Ming and, by the Yongzheng era early in the 18th century, they had already become rather serious. Thus the Yongzheng Emperor repeatedly issued edicts forcefully declaring that monks should not study poetry and literary composition and warning them against being intent on relying on their literary efforts to form relationships with rich gentlemen. The Yongzheng Emperor said to them, in effect: "Even if you write good poetry, you will never be able to match the scholars of our Hanlin Academy. Since you have left home to become monks, you must devote all your efforts to cultivating practice and realizing the fruits of enlightenment. How can you work so hard contending with literati for literary fame!" These are indeed very true words, spoken earnestly and sincerely. We should not neglect them because of the dubious quality of the man who said them.

During the Qing period, there were only two well-known Buddhist centers that placed their emphasis on true study and genuine realization and took as their standard studying Zen through sitting meditation: the Jinshan Temple and the Gaomin Temple in southern China. Ranking below these were temples like Tiantong and Yuwang.

The Change in the Character of Monks and Temples

Due to the legacy of the official temple system that had come down from the Tang and Song periods, all over China there were Buddhist hermitages, halls, temples, and monasteries with varying amounts of private property, like forest lands and cultivated fields. Altogether, there was a considerable amount of such property. In the early years of the Chinese Republic, proclaimed in 1911, someone did some preliminary studies and found that the aggregate wealth of all the Buddhist temples in China was probably equal to the wealth of the Roman Catholic Church. Though this study may not have been accurate, still, it allowed us a glimpse of the incontestable fact that the Buddhist temples in China, taken altogether, possessed great wealth.

But from the late Ming through the Qing period, this originally admirable system had already developed major abuses. Throughout China, only a small number of famous large temples still retained the system of common ownership and common use of their assets and wealth and functioned as public temples. Most local temples had already been transformed into hereditary temples that were private domains. In the so-called hereditary temples, when the Dharma succession was handed down through the generations from teacher to disciple, at the same time the successor also received the authority to control the property of that temple. If a teacher had several disciples, they divided the temple property into shares, just as a family in lay life would do. Struggles over power and profit in such situations showed up everywhere. In this connection, there were many cases where monks formed ties with the local officials and set themselves up as petty tyrants in their areas.

Apart from the hereditary temples, the Buddhist terminology of the time also spoke of "little temples" which in the south were further divided into "Zen gates" and "ministering gates." In the so-called "Zen gates," the monks paid attention to practice. In the so-called "ministering gates," the monks specialized in performing rituals. They chanted sutras, held rites of repentance, and even officiated at funerals: for this they earned payment and thus eked out a living. It was easy for them to attract disciples and form groups of loyal followers.

If we trace back history, we see that, in the old days, Shakyamuni Buddha, with his great vows so full of compassion, founded Buddhism to save the world. By this time, Buddhism in China had no time even to save itself, and had reached the lowest point in its decline. All religions prohibit us from going against our consciences and telling lies, so when I write of this, all I can do is tell the truth and make the general situation clear. I do this so that far-sighted Buddhists will undertake an urgent examination of the cycles of flourishing and decline and success and failure of Buddhism and carefully reflect on it.

THE BUDDHIST REVIVAL OF THE
LATE QING AND EARLY REPUBLICAN PERIODS

From the Sui and Tang periods onward, Chinese Buddhism became one of the three great streams of Chinese civilization. Confucianism, Buddhism, and Taoism were like the three legs of a tripod. Over the course of China's historical development, through the succession of dynasties and the cycles of prosperity and decline, up until the last century, behind the succession of dynasties there was still a continuity of tradition which seemed to be unchanging. But in recent history, beginning with the Opium Wars between China and Britain and extending through the war between China and Japan, China was subjected to a continuous series of painful lessons: disasters and humiliations, losses of territory, and the payment of indemnities. Under the deep impact of these outside stimuli, the Chinese people, who had been content to follow in their traditional ways, woke up as if from a dream and began to pay attention to Western culture. Gradually, the Chinese transformed their ideas of Western culture and began to study it deeply.

Along with this, Western culture was continuously entering China. Christian missionaries from various countries came to China, spreading the Christian gospel on the one hand and disseminating Western learning on the other. If we investigate the background of the missionary movement, it was not without a certain coloration of so-called cultural aggression. The missionaries came to China, bringing with them the concealed power of the imperial nations. In the conditions of the time, this was an inevitable tendency. The decline of the power of the Qing dynasty was already completely exposed. At the same time, the Westerners basically did not understand what the legacy of thousands of years of Chinese civilization was, and so they looked down upon the Chinese in general as a barbarous people in a backward region.

Even up to the present day, the Chinese and the Westerners have still not fully understood and totally dissolved these discriminatory, conflicting views. This has been a great barrier in the history of the interchange between Eastern and Western civilization. It is because of this barrier that Westerners have suffered many incalculable losses in their appreciation of the position of the Chinese in history. Even though at present they are researching Chinese civilization and are gradually acquiring a comparatively better understanding of it, and there are signs of a change for the better, the future success of this increased understanding still must await the test of history.

When we have a full knowledge of cultural history as a whole, and when we give a simple treatment of 20th-century Buddhism, we will be able to give a logical account, enabling us to reflect on the past in order to better know the future. This tentative essay on Buddhism in the 20th century will be divided into three sections:

the revival of Chinese Buddhism, the development of Chinese Buddhism, and trends in world Buddhism.

The Revival of Chinese Buddhism

When we discuss the revival of Chinese Buddhism, first we must give credit to virtuous and scholarly Buddhist laymen. At the end of the last century and the beginning of this century, the Buddhist monks whose traditional task was to uphold Buddhism, like the Qing government, did not understand the great trends in the world. In general, they were people who had shut themselves into a self-contained world and were following the old ways. The impetus for the renewal of Buddhism could only be given by the scholarly Buddhist laymen among the intelligentsia who had changed along with the trend of the times, and who were restudying the old traditions to gain better insight into the new world.

As is common knowledge, the most credit for initiating this movement of renewal must undoubtedly be given to Yang Renshan of Shidai. Master Renshan's personal name was Yang Wenhui, and he was a native of Shidai, in Anhui Province. Modern-day scholars honor him as the great teacher, Yang Renshan. His grandfather was a contemporary of the famous Qing dynasty statesman, Zeng Guofan, a leader in the victory over the Taiping rebellion in the 1850s and 1860s. When Master Renshan was in his teens, he accompanied his grandfather and met Zeng Guofan. When Zeng Guofan met him, he immediately appreciated his talents and told him to work hard to become successful. Master Renshan replied: "I do not want to seek success under an alien dynasty." Zeng Guofan just laughed and let it go at that. But from then on, he bore the young man in mind and later, he instructed his son, Zeng Jize, to be sure to nurture this talented young man.

When Zeng Jize went as an ambassador to Europe, he invited Master Renshan to assist him. Master Renshan bore the title of counselor, but he actually held major power in his own hands. During his travels in Europe, Master Renshan became very interested in science. Later, Master Renshan also went to Japan. With the help of the Japanese Buddhist scholar Nanjo Bun'o, he discovered many Buddhist texts from the Tang and Song periods that were still extant in Japan, but not in China.

When Master Renshan returned to China, he gave up his intention of having a career as an official and resolved to devote his life to spreading Buddhist learning. Later, he donated one of the family houses to become a center for the printing of the Buddhist scriptures. With his disciple Master Ouyang Jingwu, he established in Nanking the famous Jingling Sutra Printing Agency and undertook the work of promoting Buddhist learning. The editions of the Buddhist scriptures and other essential Buddhist works that they printed were always carefully prepared and edited. These editions of the Buddhist classics became very well known at the time and influenced such men as Tan Sitong, who was one of the leading figures in the Republican revolution of 1911, and Liang Qichao, one of the pioneers of modern Chinese culture, and even Zhang Taiyan, the dean of the National Academy, to turn their efforts to Buddhist studies.

In sum, in the last years of the Qing dynasty and the early years of the Republic, Master Renshan was influential among important men in the capital and throughout the country. Throughout his life, he worked hard to promote Buddhist learning and, in his role as a Buddhist layman, he responded with appropriate teachings for sentient beings. Such men are indeed hard to find.

The man who later took up Master Renshan's mission of promoting Buddhist learning was Master Ouyang Jingwu. Master Jingwu's personal name was Ouyang Jian, and he was a native of Yihuang, in Jiangxi Province. Along with Master Li Zhenggang and others who had studied with Master Renshan, Master Jingwu could be called a giant of Buddhist studies, one of the outstanding figures of Buddhism. Scholars also honor him with the title "great teacher." Carrying out the intention of Master Renshan, he founded the Chinese Institute of Inner Studies, which specialized in propagating the Buddhist *prajna* philosophy and the philosophy of Yogacara Buddhism. Among his students were both Dharma teachers who were monks and scholars who were laymen. Lu Qiuyi, Xiong Shili, Wang Enyang, Liang Shuming, and Huang Chanhua were all his disciples. Many of the current Chinese Buddhist scholars are second-generation descendants of his school or have received his influence indirectly. During the war against Japan, the Institute of Inner Studies was relocated to Jiangjin in Sichuan Province, and Master Jingwu himself died in Sichuan. The Buddhist scriptures and the prefaces to them published by the

Institute are all outstanding works in beautiful language based on careful research. Most of these were edited by Lu Qiuyi after he had studied all the Sanskrit and Japanese editions. We can imagine how serious Master Lu's attitude was. At this time in northern China, there was also the famous Buddhist teacher Master Han Qingjing, so most scholars speak of this as the period of Ouyang Jingwu in the south and Han Qingjing in the north.

The era of Yang Renshan and Ouyang Jingwu was the beginning of the Republican period in the early part of the 20th century. Various people in the area of Nanking worked to propagate Buddhist learning under the influence of Master Renshan's school. Among them were Master Ding Fubao, who edited the *Buddhist Studies Dictionary;* Master Mei Guangxi, who lectured on Yogacara philosophy; Master Nie Yuntai, whose generous patronage helped protect the Dharma; and Master Ma Yifu, who founded the Fuxing Shuyuan publishing house and harmonized the theories of Confucianism, Buddhism, and Taoism, founding a school of thought that advocated combined study of Zen principles and the Confucian classics. We can be sure that all these developments were due to the direct or indirect impetus of Master Yang Renshan.

In summary, in the first years of the Republic in the early part of the 20th century in Chinese learned circles, the tendency to undertake the study of Buddhism made an obvious break with the previous pattern of neglect and began to advance briskly. There was vigorous growth and development on all sides, and various manifestations of the new interest in Buddhist studies appeared like sprouts after a spring rain, like flowers turning toward the Sun. This tendency developed continuously for several decades, until the Communists came to power on the mainland and throttled it, anticipating that Buddhism would be totally wiped out.

Whenever a trend forms in learning, it is sure to have its background in the sense of the times, its progression of cause and effect. As the saying goes, phenomena do not arise in isolation and towers cannot appear out of thin air for no reason. This will be the basis for our discussion of the 20th-century revival of Buddhist learning and the trends within 20th-century Buddhist thought. Both of these must adhere to this general principle and have their own necessary sequences of cause and effect.

What is the explanation for the revival of Buddhist learning in China? Frankly speaking, it was a response to the stimulus of Western culture and thought. In the last years of the 19th century, the Chinese were directing their attention to Western culture and thought by studying natural science and discovering the Western social sciences and political thought. Thus, the Chinese were continuously importing various Western political theories, and new currents of thought arose in China with great vigor. To investigate Western political thought, the Chinese naturally had to trace it back to the philosophies that were guiding it and so, all kinds of Western philosophies, from the ancient Greek philosophy onward, were also imported into China. Particularly prominent in this was the newly arisen materialist philosophy, which swept in like a tidal wave, inundating everything.

The entry of this new current of thought into China forced a revolutionary change in Chinese history. Up until then, in the realm of learning and thought, the Chinese intelligentsia had been generally following along in the pattern of Song and Ming Neo-Confucianism, while others had gone along in isolation, laboring to construct philosophies from various combinations of Confucianism, Buddhism, and Taoism. Unexpectedly, the Chinese intelligentsia were directly confronted with various imported Western philosophical theories. Suddenly, they had the erroneous feeling of being left behind, unable to catch up. Because of this, a force resisting the intrusion of Western ideas began to form imperceptibly in the latent consciousness of the young intelligentsia, who were rich in nationalist consciousness, comparatively conservative, and rather well trained in Chinese learning. Reflecting back on themselves, they began to think that traditional Confucian philosophy had locked China up for more than two thousand years in a cage of moralistic social ideals. They wanted a pure system of thought in order to go beyond the materialistic philosophy of the West. They felt that Confucianism had no arguments to offer against materialism, and that they must leave it behind in order to develop further and shed new light on the situation. Thus, when intellectuals of great purpose like Master Yang Renshan went to Japan and came into contact with Yogacara philosophy, they discovered that it contained within it an unsurpassed metaphysical-philosophical theory that could encompass both idealist and materialist philosophy. They saw that Yogacara, with its clear logic and its closely worked-out moral theories and principles of cultivating the body and mind, was all-inclusive. Thus they felt that this is where the true Path must lie and so, unexpectedly, they ended up dedicating themselves to the Dharma Ocean of Buddhist studies and took great compassionate vows to enlighten the world and save its people. From this point on, where the winds of their influence blew, the grasses all bent down. All Chinese of deep learning, whether they were scholars of ancient or modern things, gave them their unending respect and immediately flocked to them. Thus did Buddhist studies become popular again in China's learned circles.

On the other hand, there were many scholars who tended more toward Western culture. There were also many who advocated harmonizing Chinese and Western thought. But these developments are outside our subject here, and we need not discuss them in detail.

What was the tendency of this revived Buddhist thought? Frankly speaking, the initial motive of the early 20th-century revivers of Buddhist studies was to use Buddhist principles to comprehend both Eastern and Western thought. But later, as they delved into Buddhism more and more deeply, without being fully aware of what was happening, they turned into sincere Buddhists. Almost imperceptibly, they entered into the religion's Dharma Gate of nonduality and naturally vowed to try to straighten out the decadent Buddhism that had come down to them from the Ming and Qing dynasties. But, since they thought that decadent Buddhism was unable to save the world or save itself, the result was that, unintentionally, they came to be at odds with the Buddhist monks, and the antagonism went so far that some monks argued that for laymen to spread the Dharma was against the Dharma. Thus, the learned laymen who acted as revivers of Buddhist studies were unable to rescue the decadent Buddhist religion. This was truly lamentable.

Master Yang Renshan and his disciple, Ouyang Jingwu, were discriminated against by many within the Buddhist religion. This caused so much trouble for them that it almost reached the state of inflicting upon them irreparable wrongs and intolerable mistreatment. Thus, in the sixth article of his discussion on refuting errors and promoting the correct Path, Master Jingwu directly dealt with whether or not monks and laymen were entitled to spread the

Dharma. From this, we can see that the debate provoked by Yang Renshan and Ouyang Jingwu over whether laymen as well as monks could propagate the Dharma was very serious indeed. This issue between Buddhist monks and laymen has extended up through today and really is a major wound within Buddhism.

After this, the style of learning of the Chinese Institute of Inner Studies started to move in a new direction. Because disciples of Master Jingwu, like Xiong Shili, did not get results in their studies of Buddhism, they began to feel again that to rely on Buddhist studies was not fully adequate for the path of enlightening the world and opening the way for its people. Thus they turned their attention back to their former learning and created a style of learning that combined and synthesized Confucian and Buddhist thought. Xiong Shili aligned the principles of the *Book of Changes* with Yogacara concepts. He authored books like *A New Treatise on Yogacara,* broke with his teacher, Master Jingwu, and started his own school. Actually, the level of Xiong Shili's attainment in studies of the *Book of Changes* and in Yogacara theory is open to debate.

All the writings that came out of the Institute of Inner Studies after Master Jingwu were modeled in their style on Dharma master Xuanzang's translations of Yogacara texts. Because of this, they were very obscure and hard to understand. After the May 4th movement and the move toward writing in the vernacular language, when the younger intellectuals accustomed to modern writing read these works, they felt them too lofty and enigmatic to fathom.

Thus, after the transmission of this revival of Buddhist studies from Master Yang Renshan to Ouyang Jingwu and then to Xiong Shili, the so-called "New Confucianism" and "New-Style Neo-Confucianism" took shape and came to life. When the mainland fell to the Communists, the efforts of these gentlemen over many decades were scattered like smoke and ashes.

The Development of Chinese Buddhism

From the foregoing account of the renewal of Chinese Buddhism, we can understand the movement of Buddhism in the early part of the 20th century, at the end of the Qing dynasty and the beginning of the Republic. Although in this period the Buddhists who were monks were feeling the pressure of the times, they continued to live their lives in their monasteries and temples, aloof from worldly events, in the spirit of the saying: "When the Sun rises I work, and when the Sun sets I rest: What does the Emperor's power have to do with me?" Among the monks there was no one qualified, as the Zen masters and Dharma teachers of the Tang and Song periods had been, to act as leaders of learned thought, and so the Chinese monks in this period were not only confused about the trends of the times and the transformations in world affairs, they were fundamentally uninformed or even incurious about them.

In 1911, the Qing emperor abdicated and the Chinese Republic was founded. Yuan Shikai, the general who became the first president of the Republic, harbored evil intentions to make himself emperor. The Buddhist community was reflecting on the organization of the religions being brought into China from overseas and their planned movement to spread their teachings, and at the same time the community was also feeling the influence of the new developments in political thought. At last, on the initiative of a poet-monk who was famous at the time (the "Eight-Fingered Ascetic"), a meeting was called of representatives of the Buddhist monastic communities from all over China. They convened in Liuyun Temple in Shanghai and founded the "General Association of Chinese Buddhism." They settled on a charter for the organization and requested government sanction.

But before this approval was granted, the Yuan Shikai government had cast its eyes on the property possessed by Buddhist temples throughout the country as a means of providing funds for its plans to restore the imperial system. So in 1912, the second year of the Republic, the issue of turning over public and private temple property to the government arose and the Eight-Fingered Ascetic went to the capital to struggle against this. But his demands were not met and he died of indignation. Since such a famous poet-monk had given his life struggling against the expropriation of temple property, the level of public indignation was such that eight of his former associates, like Xiong Xiling, Yang Du, and others, got to hold closed-door talks with Yuan Shikai. Because of this, the charter of the General Association of Chinese Buddhism was approved and promulgated by the government, and thus the property of Buddhist temples became a little more secure.

The Eight-Fingered Ascetic was a native of Xiangtan, in Hunan Province. His family name was Huang, his Dharma name was Fajing, and his literary sobriquet was Jichan. As a boy, he was a poor orphan and worked for other people tending oxen. He did not get a chance to go to school and was illiterate. When he grew up, he was a friend outside official circles to many famous literati of the time, like Master Wang Xiangqi. On the basis of his austerities and his cultivation of practice, he was suddenly enlightened. When he was first enlightened, he came out with the famous line, "The waves of Lake Dongting see the monk on his way." The line was so elegant, it was as if he had previously composed it. Master Xiangqi and the others greatly appreciated his poems and, from this point on, the Eight-Fingered Ascetic became known as a famous poet. Later, he served as abbot in various of the famous temples and he was held in high esteem throughout the country.

The Nationalist Revolution had still not achieved complete success. After the death of Yuan Shikai in 1916, China entered a period of fragmentation into territories of rival warlords. During the fighting, there was much devastation and the well-known Buddhist temples were invaded and plundered more and more, becoming garrison points for the warlord armies. It was a severe form of the situation described in the famous verse: "All the famous temples under Heaven were occupied by troops."

During this period, among the disciples of the Eight-Fingered Ascetic, it was Dharma teacher Taixu who was best equipped with modern knowledge and was able to continue his legacy. Over the succeeding decades, Taixu worked resolutely to protect Buddhism, not caring when he was mocked by people as a political monk. Several times he carried out reforms of the Chinese Buddhist Association. He founded schools for the education of monks and published journals like *Haichaoyin,* "The Sound of the Tide." Indeed, Master Taixu accomplished many things for Buddhism in the new China that were worthy of respect.

Dharma teacher Taixu was a native of Haining, in Zhejiang Province. His family name was Zhang. He was orphaned as a boy and, when he was 14, he became a monk. He devoted himself to cultivating practice. He was skilled in poetry and literary composition, and thus he formed friendships with various famous literati of the time.

When he was 30, under the influence of the revolutionary monks Huashan and Qiyun, he began to take part in the work of the Nationalist Revolution in the Canton area. With the Wuchang rebellion in 1911 that sparked the downfall of the Qing dynasty, China began to recover its former glory. Dharma teacher Taixu had a personal interview with Dr. Sun Yatsen, the Father of the Republic. At Jinshan Temple, Taixu organized the Buddhist Cooperative Progress Society with the intention of creating through reforms a new Buddhism for the new China. In the Chinese Buddhist world of the time, he became famous for what he was doing at Jinshan Temple and was known as the revolutionary new monk Taixu.

During the first year of the Republic, Taixu again immersed himself in the cultivation of practice and went into seclusion at Putuo Xilin Zen Temple. For the next thirty years, Taixu worked wholeheartedly for the movement to renew Buddhism in China. He traveled all over giving lectures and spreading the Dharma, and took charge of many projects for the education of Buddhist monks. He also initiated the World Buddhist Federation movement. In 1922 and 1923 at Lushan, he raised the standard of the World Buddhist Federation. Many eminent Buddhist monks and Buddhist scholars from Japan met with him, and Buddhists from Britain, Germany, France, Finland, and other countries also participated. Later, Taixu traveled to Japan and lectured on Buddhism at various places there. Subsequently, Taixu intended to establish a Chinese Buddhist University and a World Buddhist Institute, but, due to lack of funds, his intentions were not realized.

Around the time of the Second World War, Taixu established the South Fukien Buddhist Institute in Amoy, the Wuchang Buddhist Institute, and the Hanzang Buddhist Institute to train talented monks for the new Buddhism. This did in fact result in the nurturing of many outstanding scholar-monks, like the famous monk Fafang, who spread the Dharma in China and studied in Sri Lanka, and who was one of Taixu's favorite disciples. After World War II, Taixu organized groups of Chinese Buddhists and led them on tours of the various Buddhist countries of Southeast Asia.

Though Taixu's lifelong hopes of reforming and reinvigorating Buddhism were not always fulfilled everywhere, the strength of his vows and his resolve for the mission are indeed worthy of respect. In his writings and his life, both pure Buddhist conduct and errors appear together, and his thinking was very novel. He advocated "the Pure Land of the human world" and always used the slogan: "Look up to Buddha, but perfect your human character. If you achieve true humanity, you achieve buddhahood: this is called true immediate reality." This is the spirit of renewal for the new China and the new Buddhism, replete with boldness of vision and with understanding. We must admit that this, his most famous saying, can provide a stimulus for Buddhists now and in the future. Taixu also advocated developing a movement of friendly associations among all the world's religions and personally took part in the work of making this happen. He truly had a far-seeing vision.

Many people in the present-day Chinese Buddhist world and many religious personages from abroad have made oblique criticisms of Taixu, and have even claimed that he was enamored of politics or too fond of fame. But, in reality, these criticisms are ill-founded. In reality, Taixu could be called a monk who practiced austerities. What I mean by austerities is that Taixu's aspirations brought much pain. He wanted to reinvigorate Buddhism and he was an ardent Chinese patriot: both of these came forth from his true sincerity. He was born in a period where new ways of thought were replacing the old and in a new period of democratic politics. He was perhaps overzealous, and he was unable to complete all his projects. He lacked a correct political understanding of world trends. Toward Chinese Buddhism, with its deep accumulation of traditional practices, he did not follow the path of gradual change, but wanted to use revolutionary methods and force an abrupt transformation, and so his hopes went unfulfilled.

The new way of educating monks which Taixu initiated had a wide influence and, after the success of the Nationalist armies' Northern Expedition in 1928, not only were branches of the Chinese Buddhist Association established in all the provinces and county seats that came under the Nationalist regime, but Buddhist studies academies were also set up in most of the county seats. All of these, directly or indirectly, were subject to the influences of the new way of educating monks associated with Taixu's new Buddhist movement. The result of this new way of educating monks was that the Buddhist monks became relatively more aware of the common knowledge of the new era. But, with regard to the principles of Buddhism and the methods of cultivating realization of the Buddha Dharma, on the other hand, they became more and more misinformed, and they were not as knowledgeable about these things as monks had been originally, before the new way of education. This was really one of the most regrettable effects of the new system of educating monks.

Both the Eight-Fingered Ascetic and Dharma teacher Taixu adapted to the needs of the times: they were our wise predecessors who extended Buddhism's life of wisdom. In the modern history of Chinese Buddhism, they must be counted as disciples of Buddha who should be respected. In the end, their accomplishments outweighed their errors, and they were men who merit full-scale biographies.

Apart from these two, there were several outstanding Buddhists in those years who stuck to established practices and who were models for the period in adhering to the Buddha Dharma and cultivating its practices. Among these were Dharma teacher Yinguang of the Pure Land school, Dharma teacher Dixian of the Tiantai school, and the great teacher Hongyi of the Vinaya school. In the Zen school, there was Master Xuyun, whose prestige was enormous. There were also several others who were acclaimed at the time as preeminent figures in the Zen school: Master Chuanben of Golden Peak Temple on Mount Emei, Master Nengyuan of Bell Drum Tower in Wanxian, Master Daojian of Qionglong Mountain in Suzhou, and Master Laiguo of Gaomin Temple in Yangzhou. All these men were able to maintain the customary style of the Zen school and stand out as distinguished, independent figures, acting as mainstays of the Buddha Dharma.

Among the Buddhist teachers of the time, these adepts were representatives of virtuous qualities and profound learning. For almost half a century, from the end of the Qing dynasty in 1911 to the Communist victory in 1948–1949, they shone brilliantly, exerting a big influence on trends within Chinese Buddhism, on the intelligentsia, and on all those who studied Buddhism. To a greater or lesser degree, directly or indirectly, their call was felt by men and women, by young and old, by everyone from eminent statesmen to humble peddlers. They held together the worldly path, maintained popular support for Buddhism, and silently did their part to remedy the shortcomings of the nation's political and educational situations. It can be said that their efforts were not made in vain, and that their accomplishments cannot be effaced.

Apart from the eminent monks mentioned above, in every province and every region of China, there were some Buddhist teachers who set an example with their virtuous conduct. In a brief account like this, it is hard to tell of them all.

Among the eminent monks previously discussed, the most famous were Yinguang, Xuyun, and Hongyi, who were the most noted monks of the time.

The great teacher Yinguang was originally a Confucian gentleman at the end of the Qing dynasty. Before he left home to become a Buddhist monk, he venerated Neo-Confucian philosophy and repudiated Buddhism. After he became a Buddhist monk, he taught people in a plain and genuine way on the basis of his life-experience. He often used the moral principles for human life taught by Confucius and Mencius as a bridge to the study of Buddhism. He considered sincere invocation of the buddha-name as the ultimate Dharma Gate. His writings, his speech, and his conduct were permeated with compassion, and various of his writings, such as *Dharma Master Yinguang's Essays* were in wide circulation.

Master Xuyun was a man of great virtue who was even more universally venerated throughout China. Collections recording his words and deeds are in wide circulation within China and abroad, so there is no need to give another introduction to his teachings.

Before Dharma teacher Hongyi left home to become a Buddhist monk, he was already a noted scholar recognized for his special talents, and an artist as well. He was a master of calligraphy, painting, music, and all forms of poetry, and a man of superlative talents. Before he became a monk, his elegant verses were already quite popular in the Shanghai-Hangzhou area and in Japan. After he became a Buddhist monk, he practiced austerities and diligently cultivated the Dharma: he had only a single robe and a begging bowl, and he was very strict in maintaining the precepts of discipline. This made people admire and respect him. He spent relatively long periods in places like Fuzhou, Quanzhou, Amoy, and Wenzhou. Among his lay disciples were men like the famous painter Feng Zikai, who responded to his call and spent his whole life painting works that promoted the Buddhist ideas of compassion and nonviolence.

In addition to these men, among the noted Dharma teachers of the time in southern China, in the Yangzi Valley and the Zhejiang regions, were such figures as Yuanying, Cizhou, and Yingci.

In northern China, there was Dharma teacher Tanxu. In southwest China, in the region of Sichuan and Guizhou, there were Changyuan and Jiechen. All these were eminent monks who advocated the Pure Land practice of invoking the buddha-name. Appearing somewhat later were Dharma teachers like Chisong and Chaoyi, who propagated Japanese-style Esoteric Buddhism. Dharma teachers like Nenghai and Fazun promoted Tibetan-style Esoteric Buddhism.

Apart from these was the figure of Su Manshu, who was given prominence by Zhang Taiyan and the poets of the Southern Society. He took the lead in the literary style of the so-called "Lovers and Butterflies" school, and became famous for writing such emotionally expressive novels as *Duan Hong Ling Hui Ji* ["Broken Geese and Scattered Sparrows"]. In his conduct, he abandoned himself to sensuality and his mind was sunk in emotional desires, so Su Manshu was definitely not a genuine monk. By temperament, he refused to be bound by formalities. In a temple in Guangzhou, he happened to obtain the ordination certificate of a deceased monk, so he changed his name and became a monk. From this point on, he moved freely in and out of literary circles and became a much talked-about figure of the time: he was really an unusual character. His followers gave him the Buddhist title of "great teacher" and this caused confusion about whether he was really a monk or a layman. Many people at the time mistook him for a Buddhist monk and mentioned his name alongside Dharma teachers like Taixu and Hongyi. In fact, he was an anomaly in the annals of the Buddhist monks of the Republican period. Nevertheless, Su Manshu was a man of unique temperament.

This, then, was the overall outline of Buddhist activity in the Republican period. In terms of the distinction between esoteric and exoteric Buddhism, these are all events in the exoteric Buddhism of the recent period. Esoteric Buddhism in this period had a different style and appearance, which we will now proceed to consider.

During the founding of the Republic, people throughout the country followed the nationalistic call of Dr. Sun Yatsen, the Father of the Republic. Everyone understood that the the five major ethnic groups, the Han, the Manchus, the Mongols, the Hui (Chinese Muslims), and the Tibetans, were all one nation, were all the descendants of Yandi and Huangdi, the legendary culture heroes of Chinese civilization. From this, in response to the movement of the times, arose the fashion for opening channels between the Han and Tibetan cultures.

During the Yuan, Ming, and Qing periods, the ruling dynasties paid their respects to the Buddhism and the great Buddhist ceremonies of the Mongol and Tibetan regions and honored its leaders with the titles of Dalai Lama, Panchen Lama, and Jangjia, following precedent in officially recognizing them as Khutughtu. For example, the President of the Republic, Jiang Kaishek, sent special emissaries to take part in the great ceremonies for the installation of the two living buddhas, the tenth Panchen Lama and the fourteenth Dalai Lama (now in India). The Republic recognized their positions, as previous Chinese governments had, and treated them with full honors. The nineteenth Jangjia, a leading incarnate lama in Mongolian Buddhism, came to Sichuan with the Nationalist government during the period of the war against Japan, and, after the Communist victory, moved again with the Nationalists to Taiwan. He adhered to the Nationalist government all along and held a succession of high positions in its administration.

The organization known as the Western Borderlands Cultural Institute was active in Beiping, the modern Beijing, in the early years of the Republic and, during the war of resistance against Japan, relocated along with the Nationalist government to Sichuan.

Thus, from the early years of the Republic to the fall of the mainland to the Communists in 1949, over three or four decades, eminent monks from the various schools of Tibetan esoteric Buddhism came to China proper to propagate the methods of esoteric Buddhism. During the same period, Dharma teachers and Buddhist laymen from China proper were going to Tibet to seek the Dharma there. Tibetan teachers on their way to China and Chinese Buddhists on their way to Tibet were going back and forth frequently through Xikang and Tibet, and parties of these travelers were always on the road.

Among the Tibetan Lamas who came to China proper to spread the Dharma in this period were the representatives of all four sects of Tibetan Buddhism: Nyingmapa, Sakyapa, Kargyudpa, and Gelugpa. Among them were the lamas known to the Chinese as Baipuren, Nuona, Gonghe, Gensang, Dongben Gexi, and Awang Kanbu. None of them had previously set foot outside Tibet and Xikang, but, after the founding of the Republic, they all came in person to China proper to transmit the Dharma.

From the Song and Yuan periods on, Chinese Buddhism had held to the idea that Tibetan esoteric Buddhism was something mysterious. Those who studied the teachings of esoteric Buddhism were mostly confined to the imperial palace, and esoteric Buddhism had very little currency among the Chinese people in general. In the Republican period, once the aura of mystery around esoteric Buddhism was lifted, the average Chinese studying Buddhism suddenly came into contact with methods of cultivating practices which they had hitherto viewed as mysterious, and there was a tendency to turn toward it in dizzy enthusiasm. Many people who were devotees of the mysterious thought that only Tibetan esoteric Buddhism was the correct way to become enlightened in this lifetime and, even though they did not dare to look down on all the other forms of Buddhism, at least they had a sense that they were not worth trying.

In fact, those who study Buddhism correctly and are the least bit concerned with later Indian Buddhist thought, and those who have had any contact with such aspects of Indian religious philosophy as Brahmanism and the techniques of yoga, can then understand the source of the so-called mysterious side of esoteric Buddhism and its philosophical foundations. But the fashion for the study of esoteric Buddhism, from the first years of the Republic up through the conclusion of World War II, grew stronger and stronger in Chinese Buddhist circles. With the Communist victory of 1949, however, all forms of Buddhism, no matter whether exoteric or esoteric, met with unprecedented ruinous misfortune, and even Tibet, which had previously been called a mystic Buddhist country, suffered the same fate. The future revival and vitality of Buddhism will depend on the spirit and the continuous hard work of the worthy people of the time and their successors.

CONCLUSION

In more than two thousand years of continuous transmission of its teachings, Buddhism has made glorious contributions to learned thought, political life, and education in both India and China. After Buddhism came to China, over the period from the third to the ninth century, it became one of the major streams of Chinese

learned thought. Buddhism led and guided learning and contributed to philosophical thought. It upheld the moral orientation
of the secular world and knit together the hearts of the people,
helping to make up for the shortcomings of the political order. Its
achievements can never be obliterated. If we pass over without
comment the errors and abuses committed by the followers of
Buddhism in later generations and just take the overall view, we
can without error praise Buddhism as *the* philosophy among
philosophies and *the* religion among religions. As for the range of
its abuses, in many instances they can be blamed on society. These
abuses were the peripheral streams of Buddhism that resulted from
an accumulation of wrongs coming to be considered as right, and
they had nothing at all to do with true Buddhist principles or with
the great spirit of Buddhism.

Nevertheless, if we observe the style of present-day Chinese
Buddhism and the Buddhism of the various countries in Southeast
Asia, we cannot be optimistic about the future. Rather, there is
cause for worry and concern. Although all worthy people in the
Buddhist world feel apprehensive about its future adaptations, it is
still the case that accumulated momentum is hard to reverse, and
there is no way to make a clean break with the past and start fresh.
Thus I will try to make six concluding points about the present situation of Buddhism, and offer them for the consideration of present-day Buddhists. I am just jotting down this conclusion and
cannot say I have anything to propose. Even less am I offering a
critique: I am merely writing to ease my feelings, and no more.

Concerning the fate of Buddhism: From the time of Shakyamuni
Buddha, the founder of the religion, there has been the system of
four groups of Buddhists: the male home-leavers, the monks; the
female home-leavers, the nuns; and the male and female householders, the Buddhist laity, sometimes distinguished as laymen
and laywomen. Shakyamuni Buddha gave to the monks the responsibility for taking charge of the forms of Buddhism and for
propagating the Buddhist teaching. The responsibility for protecting the Dharma Shakyamuni Buddha placed on the rulers, on their
great ministers, on the community elders, and on the Buddhist laiety, who were to uphold and protect Buddhism. Based on this,
over the generations in China, India, Japan, and other Buddhist

countries, the fate of Buddhism always depended on the protection of the political authorities and the social elite.

Since the end of the 19th century, the democratic political system has toppled the evil practices of several thousand years of monarchical rule and its monopoly on political power. Chinese Buddhists do not have a thorough enough knowledge of democracy and freedom and do not understand the rule of law sufficiently. They still try in unwholesome ways to make connections among prominent people and climb the social ladder. They rely on the remnants of the old-style political powers. From the present day onward, in the new period from the 20th century into the 21st century, if Buddhists go on as they have before without changing, trying to curry favor with those in high position in order to prolong their moribund existence, and do not seek for themselves a means by which to stand on their own in the new century, I'm afraid that the fate of Buddhism will be hanging from a thread, and that the position of Buddhism will be as precarious as a pile of eggs.

Concerning the economic position of Buddhism: For over two thousand years, no matter whether in China, India, or Japan, Buddhism has always lived on the surplus of an agricultural society by begging. It has never given careful consideration from the economic point of view to the economics of its religious communities. Moreover, because the codes of monastic discipline directly forbid concerns with economic matters, knowledgeable people within Buddhism have never dared to make proposals about this issue. Only in the case of Chinese Buddhism, after the establishment of the Zen monastic system in the Tang period, was there a somewhat systematic economic basis for Buddhist religious communities, resembling a system of collective agricultural production. Later, along with the forms and religious principles of Buddhism, this system was transmitted to Japan.

But at the present time, this kind of system, which relied totally on the form of production of the old agricultural society, is no longer viable. On one hand, in mainland China, it has met with destruction at the hands of the Chinese Communists' Cultural Revolution. On the other hand, in the capitalist parts of eastern Asia, it has been subjected to the influences of the development of capitalism, of the intense competition within industry and commerce, and the total economic and social transformation which has come about. Buddhist monastic communities can no longer survive by their own strength, and so rely on begging and collecting funds in return for ritual services. For the future, we must reflect on the fact that, if we use this type of dependent existence to maintain Buddhism, it will not take any outside forces to destroy it: fundamentally, Buddhism will have no way to keep its foothold.

Concerning the unity of Buddhists: The teachings of all the world's religions basically advocate individual freedom and true liberty. The Western religions also have an understanding of religious administration of politics and have concrete organizational guidelines. We can say that, in Buddhism, the principle of the liberty of the individual reaches its ultimate point. This can easily be transformed into absolute egotism, at least in form. If you say that the Chinese people are all lacking in the propensity to unite, I think that the disunity of Chinese Buddhists is a prime example of this. All through the history of Chinese Buddhism, and up through the present day, we see disputes over whether monks or laymen should teach, disputes for power and profit between the followers of various teachers, sectarian disputes, disputes over prestige and status within groups of lay Buddhists, disputes over whose lineage is better or worse, and disputes over such trivial matters as how to dress and so on, to mention just a few.

When Shakyamuni Buddha was in the world, he always taught that the Buddhist community should be united in harmony and mutual respect. With these disputes, the Chinese Buddhist community has destroyed and defeated itself, to the point where there is nothing left. If Chinese Buddhists do not reflect seriously on this and take action to remedy the situation, if we just want to walk on high beyond the world, I'm afraid that we may no longer exist after the 20th century.

The conditions of Buddhist education and learning: In the past, when Buddhism was flourishing in China, this was entirely due to the deep learning and knowledge of the Buddhist teachers and the standards they set of moral quality and cultivation of practice. They became figures who were universally revered at all levels of society. Buddhism achieved its honored place and its greatness only because of this. But in most cases, these great teachers already had reached a high level of cultivation in general knowledge before they had left home to become monks, or in the early phase of their lives as monks. To this, they added the essential principles of Buddhist learning. Only then were they able to become teachers for their time. Moreover, they themselves were true educators.

What is the situation today? The level of ordinary education that Buddhist monks have received is not adequate. All they have to do is put on a monk's robe and be able to explain a few lines of Buddhist theory or interpret some Buddhist terms and they immediately view themselves as teachers of devas and humans. In reality, they should hasten to reflect back on themselves, acquire some learning, and strive hard to improve and strengthen themselves. Only then will they be able to avoid being ashamed in front of the deeply learned founder of their religion.

In the past, in the later period of Indian Buddhism, it was proposed that a Great Vehicle bodhisattva must be equipped with five kinds of understanding: inner understanding (this comes from cultivating the Path and awakening to the Path); understanding causation (this means mastering logic and, in the present day, this must include mastery of the various religious philosophies and the human and natural sciences); understanding sound (this means linguistics and literature); understanding medicine (this means being an expert on medicines and healing); and understanding practical techniques (in the present day, this must include the skills associated with science and technology).

Now in the later part of the 20th century, education and knowledge are becoming more and more widespread. If we Buddhists do not immediately reflect back on ourselves and rapidly make plans to solidify our own educational base, then I'm afraid that Buddhism, which has always been a model teacher of humankind, will be hard put to justify itself. Though at present there are several areas where the education of Buddhist monks is being undertaken, we must humbly recognize that education is a great long-term undertaking. If Buddhist education is managed by nonspecialists who have no basic understanding of education, or who only know about religious education, I'm afraid that mistakes will be made repeatedly and may become irreparable. "The stone of another mountain can be used to polish the jade"—we can learn by the example of others. We must accept in all humility the sincere advice of those both inside and outside of Buddhism. This is surely a course that will bring many benefits and little harm.

Concerning the lack of cultivating realization: Apart from the surpassing excellence of its philosophical thought, the most important thing about the principles of the Buddhist teaching is that they are not empty theoretical talk. They require each and every person really to put them into practice and test them with body and mind and to work to carry them out. Only by this kind of personal practice can one experience realization of the complete answer. Because of this, from a modern point of view, Buddhist learning itself has a very scientific spirit. It has been able to stand the test of time. Moreover, besides its philosophical thought, it also is very rich in scientific principles. Indeed, Buddhism is a rich treasury that has still not been opened up on any large scale by the world's people.

In present-day Buddhism, there are many who talk theory, but few who cultivate realization. In the 20th century, the scientific era, what proof can they show that will make people respect Buddhism? Moreover, due to the shortcomings of Buddhists in cultivating realization, even when they talk theory, they come out with many distorted theories. This is an extremely frightening, dangerous situation, which threatens Buddhism with self-destruction. We must adjust our ideas realistically and work hard on our realization and insight.

Concerning the tendency to mix in politics: In keeping with the prevailing democratic current in the thought of the 20th century, in all the enlightened nations of the world, the freedom of religious belief and the freedom of religious groups to participate in politics legally must be beyond question. But how should the Buddhist message of great compassion be applied to the various kinds of political ideologies and political systems in the world?

If there is no concrete way to settle on a Buddhist theory of political advocacy, then I'm afraid that Buddhist leaders will almost always go wrong when they try to mount the political stage by simply relying on their zeal and their ardent desires. They attempt to show the fearless bravery of the founder of religion when they, themselves, have always been lacking the practiced habits of political cultivation. This point is worth careful consideration. We must first seek an excellent level of knowledge and also take our stand on invincible ground before we can participate in politics.

Let us try to analyze the future of Buddhism. From the point of view of religious belief, it seems that the farther we follow the old road, the narrower it gets. From the point of view of learned thought, the new realm of Buddhism is getting broader and broader. This is because Buddhism has an expansive message, profound principles, a well worked-out thought system of surpassing wisdom, and a theory that is great, far-reaching, and perfectly synthesized. What's more, Buddhism has a long history and a multitude of faithful believers. There is no lack of committed, outstanding people of vision and insight within the Buddhist communities who are ready to express their views and do all they can for Buddhism to protect the Dharma. They will base themselves on the will to act with true humanity, the stamina to endure, and the spirit to see their duty and boldly carry it out. They will take up the responsibility of the Tathagata's enterprise and reinvigorate the bold style of Buddhism in order to adapt to future currents and win glory in the future era. Indeed, the process of reinvigorating and reviving an enfeebled Buddhism begins with an act of will. This is the author's sincere hope and prayer.

The Zen Monastic System and Chinese Society

A The term "society" refers to the situation in which there are established relations and a sharing of benefits among several groups; on this basis they work together to attain a set goal and organize into an integral collectivity. In common parlance, the Chinese word *she-hui,* "society," is used as a term designating a group of people who share certain kinds of common enterprise or a certain type of similar status, like the "Upstream Society" or the "Labor Society." It is also used for groups with a certain regional character, like the "Shanghai Society" or the "Hankou Society."

In 1838, the French scholar Auguste Comte created the term "sociology" (Chinese: *she-hui-xue*). He used it to mean the branch of science that studies society. In the past, we also used the term *qun-xue* for this. Ever since the British scholar Herbert Spencer followed this usage of the term "sociology," it has become a term for a specialized branch of science. The specialized study of social organization is called social statics; the specialized study of the growth and development of social organizations is called social dynamics. In general, there are three objects of sociological study: the nature of society, the process of social progress and transformations, and the basic principles of social progress and transformation. Some sociologists bring in evidence from biology and some from psychology.

THE DIFFERENT SOCIETIES OF EASTERN AND WESTERN CIVILIZATION

If we delve back into the history of our Chinese culture, one hundred years ago there was basically no such term as "sociology." This branch of learning had not been established. We cannot say that this was because, in the past, we were unscientific. All we can say is that, in the past history of our culture, we did not have need of this concept. This was a matter of the difference in spirit at a time when the material basis of culture was different.

From the viewpoint of economics, China in the past was always an agrarian country. Its territory was large and materially rich and the land was not densely populated. There were ample natural resources that could be used to support a prosperous life and it was not necessary for the

Chinese to go abroad and struggle for profit in order to survive. In addition to this, the traditional culture always taught the Chinese to live in peace, be happy with their occupations, and be content with their destined lot. Thus, in traditional China, people only had to give the prescribed social forms their due, obey the law, and pay their taxes to the government. In the society of the farming villages, it was very common for people of neighboring hamlets to live out their lives without ever seeing each other. The poem by Fan Chengda of the Song dynasty says:

> Green fills the mountain meadow, white foamy rivers
> In the cuckoo's cry, the rain is like mist
> In the village in June few are idle
> They're tending the silkworms and planting the fields.

Such a beautiful picture of a natural way of life! Who would prefer life in a society obsessed with industry and commerce, with its hustle and bustle and its frantic pace that makes people forget themselves? In the main, our ancestors in old China lived peaceful, harmonious, healthy, and happy lives. The exceptions were the nomadic herding peoples of the northwest and northern borderlands, who lived a harsh existence described in the verse, "in felt tents under the moonlight, the sad sound of the flute," and so had to launch raids to rob and plunder.

In old Europe, things were not as in China, because it history was different from ours. They did not experience an early unification like that carried out in China by the Qin and Han dynasties. The Europeans lived in small domains under local feudal chieftains. Since they lacked broad territories, they could not base their nations on agriculture alone. Hence, in many regions, the premodern Europeans could not depend on the products of the soil for their entire livelihood. Thus, the characteristic pattern of European politics developed from a state of raiding and plundering to aggressive wars among nations. By undertaking long distance trading ventures, the Europeans in the medieval period developed organized handicraft and commercial groups, and all the societies of Europe came to need these organizations. By this means, Western society grew and developed and, in this context, such organizations very naturally became a central need of human group life. Economic needs dictated the main primary purpose of society.

Sociological concepts such as "the social system" and "divisions within society" all developed gradually during the 19th century as more and more problems developed within European society: other examples are "social movement," "social revolution," "social policy," "social psychology," and so on. When problems arose for 19th-century European society, their sociological theorists took this problem as their focus, analyzed it and studied it, and made it into a special branch of learning.

Under such conditions, the socialism of Marx and Engels thus could arise very naturally. If Marx and Engels had been born in China's agrarian society, it is very possible that they might have turned out like the eminent poet Du Fu, lamenting and composing verses full of pity for the human condition like this:

> How heartbreaking! Spring along the river is about to end.
> Leaning on my staff I make my way slowly along the
>   sandy islands overgrown with fragrant plants.
> Crazy willow fronds dance in the wind.
> Delicate peach blossoms float with the current.
> The falling flowers make the stream flow red.
> Without saying anything I blame the east wind.

As Western society and the Western economy advanced into modern times, Europe and America developed into societies based on scientific industry and commerce. Thus, all kinds of corporate organizations, interest groups, and trade associations developed. From economies based on exploitation and aggression, the Western countries have developed into economies oriented toward social welfare. National laws set the guidelines for organizations and the organization of society influences national legislation.

In one main variant of the Western tradition, the political ideology of liberal democracy developed as a reflection of commercial competition in the marketplace. In the other main variant, from the Western emphasis on political economics, the ideology of socialism and of communist dictatorship developed.

When our historical Chinese culture came into the modern period, it was just at the time when these Western developments were taking place. China was thrust into these vast contradictory world currents and it was up to the Chinese, through their own efforts, to unify and synthesize them and stand up firmly in their midst.

The Differentiation of Patriarchal Clan Society

To explain the social history of our historical Chinese culture from a sociological point of view, some call it a patriarchal clan society, since, in the past, the social structure was based on clans. Strictly speaking, this is problematic, because a society is an organization put together on the basis of common interest or a common purpose. The patriarchal society of our ancestors was just a representation and symbol tied together by the spirit of the Chinese people as an ethnic group. It did not forget the basic origin of the people, and so it transmitted and perpetuated the virtues of the ancestors and demanded that their descendants in later generations carry forward their greatness and glory.

Thus, traditional Chinese society was not an organization founded on collective laws, as Western society was. Nor was it an organization dedicated to some common interest, or to reaching some political or economic goals. All we can say is that the patriarchal system was the expression of the *li*, the ritual and social norms, that were the heart of the traditional culture. This term, *li*, has both a seemingly religious character and also a sense of human relatedness. It is a refined expression of the spirit of human civilization that gives equal weight to human nature and to ideal standards. *Li* emphasizes human nature, and so it honors the natural and slights artificial organizations. *Li* emphasizes ideal standards, and so it speaks of proper forms of behavior and standards of duty and justice by which to rule human nature and make it conform to the necessary norms of group life. The concept of *li* is very different from Western society's emphasis on organization.

I think that the highest form of organization in the human world is put together on the basis of the true feelings between people. This is what is called the ultimate expression of both human ideals and human sentiments. Only after this comes faith, or religious belief as an organizing principle. This produces what is called obedience based on reverence. After this come laws and regulations as the basis for organization. At an even lower level than this are groups based on considerations of gain and loss, which use power and coercion to create limits. This is like commerce in the marketplace.

Any form of organization that is not closely based on natural patterns and that goes against human nature and human sentiments is bound to come to ruin. As social history shows, organization based on considerations of gain and loss may be able to endure for a time, but they can never last for an extended period. As an example of a tightly-knit organization based on considerations of gain and loss, nothing surpasses the modern-day Communist Party. But if we judge them on the basis of historical patterns, we can be absolutely certain that very soon we will see the time when the Communist Party is on the verge of ruin.

The basic unit of our historical patriarchal clan society was the family lineage. The clan was made up of linked lineages. The state, with its altars and ancestral shrines, was based on the clans joined together to form the Chinese people as an ethnic group. The imperial altars and ancestral shrines were emblems of the linkage between the human realm and the heavenly spirit. The emperor, who was honored as the Son of Heaven, had to stand in awe of the Will of Heaven, and so he had to respect the altars of soil and grain, the ancestral shrines, and the spirits of the mountains and rivers. For the common people, to not pay respect to the clan and to the clan shrine would be to commit a very serious offense of disrespect, from the point of view that ritual norms were the heart of the law. From the point of view of the traditional culture's thought system, this would be an offense against heaven and an offense against the clan spirits. If this offense could not be expiated, then the offender would have nowhere to pray.

Although this was the established rule in terms of the traditional culture's customs, governing rites, and duties, and in the eyes of the national law, this was not the same as the social organization to be found in Western culture and in modern social groups. The ancestral shrines of the period from the Han through the Tang dynasties were later called the shrine halls of the various clans. But this, too, was not a form of social organization: all we can say is that it was connected to the heart of the popular spirit. These clan shrines were close to religious in character and most of the time had no functions in social life. At harvest time, the clan elders would lead the clan members to sacrifice to the ancestor of their own clan.

Though the clan elders had the highest status in the clan, this was not a product of any legal organization: this was just the natural respect rendered to him by people acting from the viewpoint of the ritual norms of the traditional culture. If it happened that any members of the clan did anything that violated the traditional ritual norms and obligations, then the clan elders would call together all the members of the clan, open the doors of the shrine hall, and pay obeisance to the clan ancestors, entreating them to pass judgment according to the clan laws and decide the innocence or guilt of the parties involved in the particular case. The judgment also had to accord with the heavenly pattern, with the national laws, and with human sentiments. This was an arrangement based on accepting and upholding the ritual norms and standards of duty: it did not have the same character as a legal code or an organized system.

The Qing dynasty followed the practice of the Tang and Song dynasties and established a local government and mutual security system by appointing village chiefs responsible to the higher authorities for the maintenance of order called *li-zheng*, *bao-zheng*, or *she-dong;* these were like the modern-day village chiefs. From Song times on, there were village granaries which were local welfare projects to store up supplies and provide famine relief; later, they were also called "righteous granaries." From Ming times on, there were local schools which carried out popular education in the villages.

If we trace things back before the unification of China by the Qin and Han dynasties, the relationship between society and politics was even simpler. In the culture and thought of that period, political rule and education were basically not that sharply divided. The idea was that the rulers should be at the same time lords, teachers, and parents to the common people. In spirit, they were still almost preserving the simple concepts of ancient times. These functions were three aspects of a single whole. In the tradition of ritual and social norms and standards of duty and obligation, what was influential in local society was the spontaneous respect for elders and the veneration of the worthy. The term *lao-he-gong,* used in Qin and Han times, was an appellation indicating reverence and respect, not a title representing an official leadership post in society. The term *san-lao,* "three elders," found in the ancient classic, *Zuo Zhuan,* according to the Fu Qian commentary meant "the craftsmen's elder, the merchants' elder, and the farmers' elder." The ancient emperors treated these three elders with the etiquette due to fathers and elder brothers. In the biography of the emperor Han Gaozu, it is recorded: "Anyone over fifty who is cultivated and who can lead the masses to do good deeds is to be appointed *san-lao.* From among the *san-lao* of all the villages, one man is to be appointed chief *san-lao.*" The Song dynasty scholar Song Qi said: "The Qin system was to have a *san-lao* in each village to take charge of the education of the people." The Han dynasty followed this system.

Thus in our historical civilization, it is really hard to find the kind of society that resembles the social organization of the West. The first example of a thought system in China that proposed something like a model social system was the philosophy of Mo Di in the pre-Qin period. After this, the next deliberate construction of a social system was the Zen monastic system that began in the Tang dynasty. The Zen system influenced Chinese history and society during the Yuan, Ming, and Qing dynasties, and it also influenced the secret mutual-aid societies which advocated popular revolution against the imperial order. But the Zen monastic system was not the same as the religious societies of the West, nor was it the same as the theological academies in the West that had religious education as their main purpose.

What about the organization of the Chinese secret societies? They merged the traditional spirit of righteous resistance against injustice with political activity. It would be correct to say that they were the contemporary revolutionary groups dedicated to restoring justice. If we compare them to social groups in the West, or to vagabond groups, and we trace back their original intent, naturally the Chinese secret societies were very different.

If we concentrate on sociology and study the issues of social history, there are different standpoints and different concepts. We should adopt a different kind of explanation. We can say that over the past sixty years, we have been subjected to the influence of Western culture and thought, and that this produced the concern with social issues. So the theoretical basis and the tendency in culture and thought of China and the West are quite distinct and different.

By reflecting on what is proper for the present and considering the lessons of the past, I only want to give an account of the Zen monastic system of the Tang and Song periods and how it influenced the organization of the secret societies in later generations. By doing this, I want to offer to those concerned with social issues some study materials that will let us absorb and synthesize both Eastern and Western culture and advance into the new era.

THE EARLY BUDDHIST MONASTIC SYSTEM

Zen is one of the schools of Buddhism: its teaching is a special transmission outside the scriptures that does not establish any verbal formulations, but rather points directly to the human mind to enable people to see their true nature and become buddhas. Because Zen did not necessarily require written texts, after it was transmitted to China, it became a form of Buddhism with a Chinese cultural style. If some say Zen was a revolutionary school of Buddhism, this is definitely not accurate because Zen did not change anything about Buddhism or introduce any innovations into it. The Zen teachings and the Zen road of cultivating practice did not alter the original face of the Buddha Dharma and were not created in China. The Zen school only took the original Buddhist monastic system transmitted from India and precisely altered it to suit the popular sentiments and customs of Chinese civilization. This initiated a new look in Chinese Buddhism and also influenced the contours of the various strata of the society in the subsequent generations. But, in keeping with the quiet approach taught by Buddha, the Zen system accomplished a great mission within Chinese society, although this took place quietly without anyone realizing it. The system created by the Chinese Zen school indeed accomplished something extraordinary with regard to Buddhism and, at the same time, established the organizational guidelines for later generations of Chinese society and its various layers.

Before Shakyamuni left home and began his quest for enlightenment, there were many religious faiths in India already. People who left the conventional world to devote themselves to religious cultivation were all called *shramanas*. They were like the lofty people in ancient China who shunned the world, the people we Chinese generally call "recluses," or *yin-shi*. The Chinese recluses were not necessarily free of family ties, but in India, the *shramanas* were all people who had left their family and fled the world.

After Shakyamuni founded Buddhism, all those who formally left home and became disciples of the Buddha Dharma had to shave off their beards and hair and wear monastic robes; they had left conventional life behind and had no family ties. The men were called *bhikshus* and the women were called *bhikshunis*. The term "bhikshu" has several connotations: for example, "one who begs," "one who strikes fear into the demons of delusion," or "one who has slain the robbers of affliction." They were called "beggars" in that they begged for the Dharma from Buddha and begged for food from other people. "Bhikshu" also contains the meaning of one able to slay the robbers of affliction or one with the awe-inspiring virtue to make the legions of demons tremble in fear. Thus, the bhikshus who strictly observed the Buddhist regulations generally practiced austerities and resolved upon a regime of purification and diligent effort. Those among them who placed special emphasis on austerities were called *dhuta*, which means "ascetics."

The early Buddhist bhikshus followed the Buddhist codes of discipline and also had to cultivate the austere practices of ascetics. Not only did they have to follow a system of cultivating the true nature of mind and, in their conduct, observe all kinds of precepts of discipline, they also settled upon systems regulating various aspects of their individual lives, such as what they should wear, what they should eat, where they should stay, and how they should walk.

As for clothing, monks and nuns could not own more than three garments. If they had more, then they had to give them away. They were required to collect old scraps of cloth discarded by other people and patch them together into clothes to wear. These were called "rag garments." After Buddhism was transmitted to China, this practice was changed and monks and nuns wore a Chinese-style long robe, patched together from scraps of cloth which the monks obtained by begging. These were called "patchwork robes."

As for food, monks and nuns could only eat one meal a day or, at the most, one meal in the morning and one at noon. They could not eat after noon. This was because monks and nuns looked upon food and drink only as a way to maintain their lives, as medicine to cure the disease of starvation.

As for where they should stay, monks and nuns had to be content wherever they were. Whether under the eaves of houses, in the corridors of temples, under the trees, in the fields, or in deserted graveyards, they would spread out the mats they carried with them or a woven straw cushion, sit cross-legged, and pass the day or night there with their minds at ease.

As for how they should walk, monks and nuns had to go barefoot or wear straw sandals, and walk bareheaded in a dignified manner. In old India, they could carry an umbrella to shield them from the Sun and the rain. When Buddhism came to China, the umbrella was replaced by a straw rainhat. Thus we find the expression in Chinese literature: "the ascetic in his straw sandals and conical hat." Besides this, monks and nuns carried at most a water jug to provide for drinking and washing, a begging bowl to eat from, and also possibly some sutra texts.

With this kind of austere life, dedicated to purity and diligent effort, Buddhist monks and nuns did all they could to abandon the entanglements of material desires and lived a continuation of the life of primitive mankind. They did this in order to concentrate on seeking enlightenment and to show that they were finished with this physical life and had said goodbye to worldly affairs. Although they still had the intention to benefit the world and help sentient beings, in their daily activities they kept apart from the worldly crowd. It was said that a Buddhist ascetic never spent three nights in the same place in order to avoid growing fond of any material things. In Buddhist terms, this could be called renunciation, and it also could be called inner giving. Buddhist ascetics appeared superficially to be totally selfish, in accord with the doctrine of the classical Chinese philosopher of egoism, Yang Zhu, but at the same time they had the intention of benefiting the whole world in every way they could, in keeping with the philosophy of the classical Chinese philosopher of universal love, Mo Zi.

There were also some bhikshus who lived together in groups to cultivate the work of the Path. This was called the sangha, which means a group of monks. The one in the group who was qualified to act as the teacher of the whole congregation and lead the sangha was called *he-shang,* which means "master" or "teacher." In China, the general term for the bhikshus was *seng,* "monk," and, by a confusion of terms, the term *he-shang* came to be applied to monks in general. Thus *seng* and *he-shang* came to have the same meaning.

When the Buddha Dharma was first transmitted to China in the reign of Emperor Mingdi of the Han dynasty (A.D. 58–75), it was brought in by two eminent monks from India, who are known in Chinese as Shemoteng and Zhu Falan. The Han court installed them in the imperial capital, Luoyang, at a place called Baima Si, "the White Horse Office." So in China thereafter, Buddhist temples and monasteries were called by the Chinese terms *si* and *yuan.* In fact, *si* was originally the term for government offices attached to the court, the central government. A notation to the record of Emperor Yuandi in the official History of the Han dynasty says: "Any place where there was a government office was called a *si.*" Examples are such institutions of the central government as the Honglu Si and the Taichang Si.

The eminent monks from the "western regions," meaning Central Asia and, by extension, India, who came to China during the Han, Wei, Western and Eastern Jin, and Northern and Southern dynasties from the first to the sixth centuries A.D. were not necessarily all ascetics who practiced austerities, but in general they were all bhikshus who adhered strictly to the precepts of monastic discipline. Because they kept the precepts rigorously and followed the Buddhist monastic system, they lived by begging for food. They depended on the offerings of those who believed in them and accepted them as teachers. But, as the number of Buddhist monks and nuns in China kept increasing, this finally came to be a problem.

In Indian culture, people had always believed in and respected the *shramanas*. In central and southern India, the climate was mild and there were many edible wild plants which the *shramanas* could gather to satisfy their hunger if their begging did not bring enough food. But in China, it was not that easy to obtain subsistence from nature.

Popular sentiment and customs were far different in China than in India. Except for those who were destitute and had no recourse, and who had sunk to the level of beggars, in China even the recluses obtained their food and clothing by tilling the soil themselves. People who relied on begging to live would be considered lazy or worthless.

The view of the traditional Chinese culture was that a person's body, including the skin and hair, had been received from his or her parents, and should not be injured. When the bhikshus shaved off their hair and beards, they were committing a major sin of disrespect and a breach of filial piety. The average Chinese would look askance at Buddhist monks for this, and even more so because they begged for food. So such practices were not easy to follow in the Chinese cultural context.

Because of the reasons cited above, most of the Buddhist monks in China before the Sui-Tang period could only manage to live on the offerings they received from the social elite. At the same time, some of them also had to rely on payments they received for ritual services or other means to support themselves. There were many incidents where such behavior provoked major revulsion against the Buddhist clergy in China. Still, at that time, due to local conditions, it was already the case that Chinese Buddhist monks and nuns could not fully adhere to the original Buddhist monastic rules. Some had already built temples and gathered together to live in groups. There were only a few who concentrated on cultivating practice and wholeheartedly sought enlightenment, dwelling in solitude in wilderness retreats, and living the life of *aranyakas,* the Indian term for those who dwelt in pure religious retreat. The rest had to change the forms of Buddhist monastic life in order to be able to adapt to Chinese conditions.

THE ORIGIN OF THE ZEN MONASTIC SYSTEM

Traditionally, the Zen school began in China when the great teacher Bodhidharma came here in the early sixth century, during the reign of Emperor Wu of the Liang dynasty, and transmitted the Zen Dharma Gate of the Buddha Mind-Seal.

At that time, there were not many monks who accepted Zen. According to the classic Zen biographical collection, *Jingde Chuan Deng Lu,* there were only three of four people who formally took Bodhidharma as their teacher and got the Dharma from him. Of them, it was Shenguang who received Bodhidharma's robe and bowl, accepted the mind-seal, and so became the Second Patriarch of Zen in China. Although the number of people who studied Zen gradually increased over the generations, there was a single line of transmission of the position of Zen patriarch. This position was eventually passed to the Sixth Patriarch, Huineng, who spread the Zen path widely from Caoqi in Guangdong Province. Students gathered there from all over.

With the Sixth Patriarch, we can say that the Zen school was like the Sun rising in the east, shining forth into the distance. The transmission of the robe and bowl stopped with the Sixth Patriarch. Many disciples received the Dharma from the Sixth Patriarch, and they spread it far and wide. Two branches of Zen developed from two of the Sixth Patriarch's leading disciples: Zen master Nanyue Huairang in Hunan Province and Zen master Qingyuan Xingsi in Jiangxi Province. The Qingyuan branch began to show signs of decline after a few generations, and the Xingsi branch carried on the lineage of the Path alone.

Later, there appeared Zen master Mazu Daoyi, who propagated the Zen message on a wide scale. He was called Mazu, "Ancestor Ma," because his lay surname was Ma. Mazu produced some seventy-two enlightened teachers from among his disciples who could function as Zen adepts. A few of them were truly outstanding, especially Zen master Baizhang Huaihai of Hongzhou in Jiangxi Province. It was Mazu and Baizhang, teacher and pupil, who changed the Chinese Buddhist monastic system and inaugurated the new Zen monastic system. It was particularly through the efforts of Baizhang that the guidelines for the new monastic system were formalized and passed down, so traditionally Baizhang has been called the founder of the Zen monastic system. According to what is recorded in the *Chanmen Zhengtong:* "In the ninth year of the Yuanhe period [A.D. 814], Zen master Baizhang Huaihai first established rules for the Zen communities throughout China. These were called the Pure Rules."

In fact, Baizhang lived in the middle years of the Tang dynasty, in the eighth and ninth centuries, whereas Buddhism had formally entered China in the Han, Wei, and Jin dynasty periods, the first through the early fifth centuries, and already by Baizhang's time it had undergone four or five centuries of evolution. Buddhism had been assimilated with Chinese culture and had been influenced by Chinese popular sentiments and the customs of Chinese society. Its monastic system had gradually changed during this period, as was logical and inevitable under the circumstances. Before Baizhang, the monk Fayun, who lived in the Liang dynasty period in first half of the sixth century and dwelt at Guangxiao Temple, had already received an imperial order to establish a system of pure rules. But Fayun did not have the clear vision and daring of Baizhang to boldly and decisively change the monastic regulations and establish a new set of guidelines. And even after Baizhang, the system of monastic regulations was still not fully perfected. It was possible to overstep the limits of the Zen monastic regulations, and so, to add to the authority of the system, it was declared that it was Zen master Baizhang himself who had constructed the Zen monastic system.

Before Baizhang, the influence of the Zen school was widespread mostly in the region south of the Yangzi River. The regions where it flourished most were the provinces of Guangdong, Hunan, Hubei, Jiangxi, Fujian, Jiangsu, and Sichuan. It had not yet been able to make its influence felt to any great extent in the Central Plain of northern China, which was at that time still the cultural and economic heart of the Chinese Empire. In the region north and south of the Yellow River, the style of Buddhism that had been transmitted to China in the early period still remained. There were still great numbers of devotees of schools of Buddhism other than Zen, as well as Dharma teachers who devoted themselves to mastering Buddhist theory and to lecturing on the sutras and shastras, who were called "monks learned in Buddhist theory." Generally, the people who zealously studied the theories of the sutras and shastras were either too accommodating or too pedantic. Even if they themselves were not tumbling in the currents of the times, if anyone had publicly proposed changing the old rules, they naturally would have gotten very angry. So when Baizhang first established the new rules for the Zen communities, he was reviled as a monk who was breaking the precepts. This, too, was inevitable.

Zen masters like Mazu and Baizhang were all men of bold spirit and penetrating wisdom, with the outstanding brilliance necessary to take charge of the contemporary world. They took up the responsibilities of the mind-seal of instant enlightenment. When Baizhang courageously reformed the monastic regulations, this was certainly due to his surpassing perception of truth and *samadhi* power. It was also a proper adaptive response to the contemporary situation.

After Baizhang, in the late Tang and Five Dynasties periods of the ninth and tenth centuries, the Five Houses of Zen were established. The system of guidelines for Zen monks in the main still followed Baizhang's *Pure Rules* for the Zen communities. There were some minor differences among the various Zen communities, however, in their methods of teaching and their prescribed forms of behavior due to differences in the people, the places, and the times. These cannot be counted as substantive differences: they were just different forms of behavior and teaching methods, which can be termed the family styles of the various Zen schools. Thus, in the Zen communities of later generations, each Zen temple had its own particular family style.

This was the pattern up through the late Qing and early Republican periods. Strictly speaking, the guidelines handed down in the various Zen temples had already undergone centuries of changes and, naturally, they were not totally in accord with the old views from the time of Zen master Baizhang. Throughout the various regions of China, every temple had its own different family style and set of rules and guidelines. But if we trace back to the source of these developments, no matter how much these rules and guidelines had changed in form, when we get back to the basic source, we can reach the following conclusion:

The characteristic style of the Zen communities has its source in the development of the Zen monastic system. The Zen monastic system and its regulations are a development that sprang from the Buddhist Vinaya, the precepts of discipline. The Buddhist precepts of discipline were devised by Shakyamuni Buddha. They were established in order to regulate the collective life of Buddhist monks and nuns and enable them to cultivate and realize the essence of body and mind. The Buddhist precepts have the spirit and function of the behavioral norms found in Chinese culture in the *Book of Rites*, of law, and of societal guidelines.

THE ZEN MONASTIC SYSTEM
ITS REGULATIONS AND GUIDELINES

In Chinese Buddhism, the term *cong-lin* was originally a special term for the communities of Zen monks, equivalent to what the Buddhist sutras call "the congregation of those cultivating practice" or "the pure ocean assembly." *Cong-lin* cannot mean one particular temple or the guidelines of one particular temple. *Cong-lin* refers to Zen temples, not Buddhist temples in general. However, in the Ming and Qing periods in some areas, temples that were not necessarily Zen temples also adopted this appellation, and called themselves *cong-lin* temples; there was no strict distinction made.

The Abbot

The abbot was in charge of all temple activities: teaching, administration, rules and discipline, and preaching to the laiety. In his power over the temple economy and the administration of its wealth, he was the equivalent to the head of state in a government, or to the leader of a society.

The abbot's dwelling place in the temple was called the *fang-zhang,* which means "ten foot square room." This is derived from the

Vimalakirti Sutra, which says that though Vimalakirti's room was only ten feet square, it could hold a vast assembly of enlightened beings. Because of this, it was also common to call the abbot of the temple himself the *fang-zhang*. The abbot was also called the *zhu-chi*, which literally means "dwelling in and upholding." This was based on the sutras' sense of dwelling in and upholding the true Dharma.

The *Chanyuan Qinggui Pure Rules of the Zen Gardens* calls the abbot "the venerable adept who upholds [the True Dharma]," saying: "He takes the place of Buddha in spreading the teaching, and takes charge of making the teaching known, so this is called transmitting the Dharma. In the area where he is, he continues the Buddha's life of wisdom, and so he is called 'the one who dwells in and upholds [the True Dharma].' When [the abbot] first turns the Wheel of the Dharma [by teaching publicly], it is called 'appearing in the world.' This has a basis in what he received from his teacher, so it is called 'transmitting the lamp.'"

The Selection of the Abbot

The abbot was nominated by the congregation of monks and had to meet several conditions. First, he had to be a disciple of the Zen school who had received the Dharma from his teacher. He had to have genuine cultivation of practice and perception of truth and be qualified to be the teacher and guide of the congregation. His demeanor had be upright, correct, and without defects. Second, his virtue and his genuineness had to be recognized by the community and he had to be endorsed by the elders and abbots of other Zen communities. Third, his selection as abbot required the consent of the central or local government authorities.

If the prospective abbot met the condition of enjoying the general confidence of the community, he underwent a solemn ceremony and, only then, was elevated to the position of abbot. If his own teacher was still alive at his installation ceremony, there were various other procedures known as "handing on the Dharma," "succeeding to the Dharma," "entering the temple," "viewing the credentials," and so on, which were considered to complete the installation process. This corresponded to the modern-day transfer of the teaching, or transfer of office.

The Retiring Former Abbot

When the former abbot retired, he was known as the "retired old master." He lived at leisure and was no longer consulted about affairs. Sometimes he went into seclusion to devote himself to cultivating practice. Most retired abbots were already greatly respected for their lofty accomplishments and had attained perfection in their cultivation of practice and their virtuous conduct. The retired abbot and the new abbot who was taking over the position and the teaching duties viewed each other as father and son. The new abbot was required to treat the retired abbot with the utmost respect and care for him and serve him to the best of his abilities until he died, and do all he could to support him, as would a filial son. Otherwise, the new abbot could be reproached by the elders of the other Zen communities and by his own congregation and, in extreme cases, punished for violating the *Pure Rules*. In Tang and Song times, most retired abbots were detached and aloof from worldly concerns and would never do anything that smacked of being eager to hold on to their previous position.

The Relationship Between the Abbot and the Government

In the past in Chinese politics, although there were always controversies down through the ages about the system by which to regulate Buddhist and Taoist institutions, due to the great tolerance of Chinese culture, the ultimate decision was always to treat Buddhist and Taoist monks and nuns with the courtesy due to religious teachers. When Buddhist and Taoist monks had audiences with the emperor, they did not have to kneel, but only to join their hands and salute.

During the Eastern Han dynasty (A.D. 25–219), Buddhist monks and nuns were under the jurisdiction of the government bureau known as the Honglu Si. Between the Han and Tang periods, such short-lived regimes as the Later Qin, Qi, and Liang dynasties in the fifth and sixth centuries appointed officials known as the *da-seng-zheng* and *da-seng-tong* (roughly: "general supervisor of monks") to control the Buddhist clergy.

The Tang dynasty changed this and established the Bureau of Sacrifice to take charge of such matters as issuing credentials to all the Buddhist and Taoist monks and nuns in the empire. Government departments like the Bureau of Sacrifice and the Supervisor of Monks were equivalent to the modern Nationalist Chinese government's Office of Religion. In the Tang dynasty, the Bureau of Sacrifice was under the Bureau of Rites. The *Tang Huiyao [Collection of Essential Documents of the Tang Dynasty]* says: "On the fifteenth day of the fifth month of the first year of the Yanzai era (A.D. 694), an imperial edict put all the Buddhist monks and nuns in the empire under the control of the Bureau of Sacrifice." By this, the registration of all the Buddhist monks and nuns in China was put under the control of the Bureau of Sacrifice, and special registers were established for registering monks and nuns.

In the second year of the Yuanhe period, 807, in the reign of Emperor Xianzong, the office of *seng-lu*, "registrar of monks," was established for the left and right divisions of the imperial capital of Chang-an. This corresponded to earlier official positions established to take charge of the Buddhist clergy, such as the Later Qin dynasty's *seng-zheng*, "corrector of monks," the Later Wei dynasty's *shamen-tong*, "general controller of monks," and the Southern Qi dynasty's *jingyi seng-guan*, "capital monk-officer." The Tang court filled this position by selecting an eminent monk of great virtue, learning, and cultivation, and summoning him to the capital to serve as a monk-official to take charge of supervising all the Buddhist and Taoist monks and nuns in the empire.

When the Mongols ruled China during the Yuan dynasty (1279–1366), they established regional governments. These took charge of Chinese Buddhist clergy and laiety and also the Tibetan lamas, whom the Mongol rulers brought to China and patronized, as well as border affairs and so on.

During the Hongwu era (1366–1398), the reign of the founder of the Ming dynasty, the government established an Office for Monks, *seng-lu-si*, in the capital and, subordinate to it, *seng-gang-si*, Offices for the Control of Monks in each province, as well as Offices for the Correction of Monks, *seng-zheng-si*, in each prefecture. These titles were continued during the Qing period.

Ordination certificates, *du-die*, were the credentials issued by the government to Buddhist monks and nuns which officially recognized their status. They were similar to the modern-day identity documents. In the Tang dynasty, these were also called *ci-bu-die*, "certificates of the Bureau of Sacrifice," and they were issued by that bureau. The ordination certificates for the Taoist clergy were also called *lu*.

Although the abbots of Zen temples were chosen by the congregation of monks, it was also necessary for the imperial court or the local government officials to concur in the appointment. If an abbot was guilty of any lapse, the government could dismiss him from office. In extreme cases, it could even revoke his ordination certificate and order that he be returned to layman's status, to be subject to the control of the government's law like any ordinary commoner.

This sort of system continued from the Tang dynasty up through the Qing dynasty, when it gradually changed its character and was no longer very strict. In spirit, the Qing dynasty, with its Manchu ruling elite, represented the rule of an alien people over China, and this slackening of regulations over Buddhism had its own political function.

Though political authority in China through the ages did not have constitutional guarantees of the freedom of religious belief as in modern states, it did always tolerate freedom of religious belief. The measures the government adopted in the past toward Buddhism and Taoism certainly did not embody a policy of strict control, but only a supervision of the orderliness of Buddhist and Taoist institutions.

The Duties Carried Out by the Abbot

While the abbot occupied his position, he was the chief of the entire temple. He chose monks from among the congregation to take charge of various duties, but this was called "inviting them to take up the post," not assigning them. This was as if to say the abbot was politely extending an invitation, not that he was commanding particular monks to undertake the duties of the post. Though each responsible duty-holder was appointed by the abbot, once his appointment was decided, it was up to him to carry out his responsibilities himself and manage things according to the common interest. He could not show favoritism, even to the abbot. Because these monks enjoyed the highest trust and respect of the congregation, they had to exert themselves to the limit of their abilities and do everything for the sake of the permanent endowment of the temple: only this would be meritorious conduct on their part.

Chang-zhu, "permanent abode," which in a narrow sense referred to the temple property, was a term that referred to the temple as a whole, derived from the phrase in the sutra, "a permanent abode for the Buddha Dharma." In reaching a decision on any matter that pertained to the temple as a whole and its congregation, the abbot had to convene all the monks in managerial posts to pass judgment on it. The abbot could not act alone according to his own opinion. At the very least, the responsible elders of the two echelons of monks or a small number of the monks with important managerial posts had to participate in the decision for it to be valid. Thus, while in his post, the abbot was not like the chief in an autocratic government. Rather, he was like the honored teacher of the whole body of disciples in China's old-style educational institutions. Because his most important duty was to guide the cultivation of practice by the congregation of the whole temple and to supervise their character and conduct, in this area, he had supreme authority and a feeling of unlimited responsibility.

Thus, in the Zen monasteries of the past, there were some abbots who never asked about the mundane affairs of the institution and considered that there were already people in charge of all such supervisory responsibilities and it was not necessary to oversee them further. These abbots thought that their principal duties were to work hard at cultivating practice, to expound the Dharma as the occasion arose, to teach by personal example, and to make sure that their students did not stray from the path.

The Abbot's Appointment of Leaders for the Two Echelons of Monks

Once the abbot assumed his post, he had to select overseer monks for the entire temple. In Baizhang's classic guidelines, these overseer monks were called *zhi-shi*, "those in charge of affairs." The classic guidelines called the leaders of the echelons of monks *tou-shou*, "head monks." To fill these supervisory posts, the abbot had to select from the congregation those monks whose abilities were up to the task and who were sufficiently respected and trusted by the whole congregation. When abbot was about to publish the roster of the various monks to whom responsible positions were being assigned, first he had to obtain their consent to the appointments. Then he would write their names and positions on a signboard (like a modern-day signboard for public announcements) and hang it up. Then everyone in the congregation had to follow his decisions. These signboards had to be posted every year on the fifteenth day of the first or seventh lunar month. A few days before the abbot invited monks to take up these posts, he would prepare refreshments in his quarters and order his attendant to invite the monks in question to have tea with him. After the abbot had extended the invitations to take up certain posts to them face to face and obtained their consent, he would inscribe their names and posts on the signboard and post it for the whole congregation to see.

Later, on the day they were to take up their posts, the abbot's appointees were escorted first to the eating hall for the noon meal, where they took their seats and were served in their order of rank. After the meal, they circumambulated the buddha-image and were escorted to the great shrine where, arrayed according to rank, they paid homage to the Buddha and were installed in their posts. After the evening recitation, each of the newly appointed supervisory monks went to the abbot's quarters to pay homage and report for duty. The abbot gave them instructions and admonished them to devote themselves to their duties and to obey the *Pure Rules*. After withdrawing from the abbot's quarters, they went back to the rooms of the senior holders of the supervisory posts and bowed to them: this was called "making the rounds of the rooms." (This term will be discussed further in the section on the code of discipline.)

This, then, was the simple procedure for inviting monks to take up supervisory posts. When the abbot invited monks to take up these posts, he would sometimes invite two monks to fill the same post so they could assist each other. Sometimes he even invited several monks to a single post. There were also cases of choosing supervisory monks by lot. Even though monks were appointed to supervisory posts by the abbot, this was not like a hierarchic bureaucratic organization. All the supervisory monks were equal in rank. We can say that there was a circular relationship among them, not relationships of superiors and inferiors, or vertical and horizontal ties of subordination. Toward the abbot they had the respect of disciples for their teacher, but not the rank-consciousness of subordinates for their superior.

The Abbot's Post According to the Old Pure Rules *Fell Subject to Six Events*

1) The Abbot's Daily Duties (which the old version of the *Pure Rules* called the abbot's daily functions)

[Teaching and Expounding the Dharma]:
Shang-tang, "going up to the hall" to preach to the assembled monks.
Ye-can, "evening meetings" with select groups of students.
Xiao-can, "small gatherings" with select groups of students.
Gao-xiang, "announcing offerings of incense."
Pu-shuo, "general talks" on the Dharma, given to audiences of all comers.
Ru-shi, "entering the room," private lessons given to advanced students in the abbot's quarters.

[Overseeing Temple Personnel]:
Nian-jing, "reciting the scriptures."
Xun-liao, "visiting the rooms" of the elderly monks.
Su-zhong, "calling the congregation to order." Instructing the novices. Giving general talks to the temple workmen.

[Other Duties of Ordinary Administration]:
Accepting the Dharma Robe.
Attending on the venerable ones, the elderly monks.
Responding to the invitations of donors to appear at the vegetarian feasts they sponsored for the monks, and preaching the Dharma.
Accepting offerings from Dharma successors.
Adhering to the testament of the Dharma teacher.

2) The Procedure for Inviting a New Abbot
A special emissary was dispatched and the new abbot accepted the invitation. Having accepted the invitation, the new abbot went up to the teacher's seat at his former temple to announce he was leaving. The emissary presented offerings of food for him. At the temple gate, there was a reception for the new abbot and the special emissary.

3) Entering the Temple and Viewing the Credentials
At the temple gate, there was a vegetarian feast for the new abbot, who formally opened the teaching hall and offered salutation to the Emperor. Tea and broth were served to the new abbot at the temple gate. The evening that he entered the temple, the new abbot held a small gathering for the leading monks. He preached to the patrons of the temple, and he also extended invitations to the two echelons of monks and gave them thanks. Items of daily use were distributed. The new abbot received meritorious offerings from the two echelons of monks.

4) The Abbot's Retirement

5) The Abbot's Death

The abbot's corpse was placed in a funerary urn. An overseer of the funeral and monks to take charge of the funeral arrangements were appointed. The monks put on mourning clothes. There were ceremonies to Buddha. The funerary urn was moved. The portrait of the deceased abbot was displayed and there was a wake. There was a small gathering to mourn the abbot, to chant the scriptures, and to make ritual offerings of tea and broth. The corpse was taken out, the portrait displayed, and offerings were made. The corpse was cremated and the remains were interred in a stupa.

The last testament of the deceased was read. There was a reception for the overseer of the funeral and those who had taken charge of the funeral arrangements. (Either the whole body or the relics remaining after the cremation could be interred in the stupa, according to conditions.)

6) Proposals for the Selection of a New Abbot

The Two Echelons of Monks

The heads of the two echelons of monks were appointed by the abbot. The two echelons of monks were somewhat comparable to the system in the ancient imperial courts, where the officials were divided into a civil echelon and a military echelon. Thus the two groups of monks were called the two echelons.

According to the old *Pure Rules*, these were the various posts that went with the two echelons of monks:

The heads of the western echelon:
The head monk, *shou-cuo;*
The head of the western hall, *xi-tang;*
The chief of the hall, *tang-zhu;*
The secretary, *shu-ji;*
The overseer of the scriptures, *zhi-zang;*
The study leader, *can-tou;*
The attendant of the images of the Zen patriarchs, *zu-shi;*
The monk in charge of burning incense, *shao-xiang;*
The recorder, *ji-lu;*
The attendant of the image of Manjushri, *sheng-seng-shi.*

The duty posts of the western echelon:
The monk in charge of the buddha-shrine, *dian-zhu;*
Head of the residential quarters, *liao-yuan;*

Monk in charge of ringing the bell, *zhong-tou;*
Monk in charge of beating the drum, *gu-tou;*
Monk in charge of the seal room, *yin-fang;*
Night watchman, *ye-xun;*
Monk in charge of communal discipline, *qing-yuan;*
Monk in charge of incense and lamps, *xiang-deng;*
Monk in charge of water, *si-shui;*
Monks in charge of the elderly monks, *qi-su;*
Monk in charge of the retired monks' quarters, *xian-zhu;*
Monk to care for the sick, *hu-bing;*
Sweepers, *da-sao;*
Workmen, *hang-zhe;*
Latrine orderlies, *jing-tou.*

The heads of the eastern echelon:

General supervisor of the temple, *du-jian-si;*
Supervisor of the halls, *jian-yuan;*
Duty distributor, *wei-na;*
Assistant supervisor of the temple, *fu-si;*
Head of the storehouses, *ku-tou;*
Supervisor of the congregation, *zhi-zhong;*
Monk in charge of visitors, *zhi-ke;*
Visitors' attendants, *zhao-ke;*
The supervisor of the congregation, *yue-zhong;*.
Quartermaster, *dian-cuo;*
The harvest evaluator, *zhi-sui;*
The overseer of the baths, *zhi-yu;*
The supervisor of the harvest, *jian-shou;*
The monk in charge of robes and bowls, *yi-ben;*
The monk in charge of medicine, *yao-zhu;*
The abbot's personal attendants, *shi-zhe;*
The overseer of the temple's fields, *zhuang-zhu.*

The duty posts of the eastern echelon:

Chief of teaching the laity, *hua-zhu;*
Senior supervisor of the monks' quarters, *liao-yuan;*
Chief supervisor of the monks' quarters, *liao-zhu,* and his assis-
    tant, *fu-liao;*
The chief of the life-prolonging hall (equivalent to the modern-
    day nirvana hall for mortally ill monks), *yuan-shou-
    tang-zhu;*
The monk in charge of the latrines, *jing-tou;*
The monk in charge of rice, *mi-tou;*

The monk in charge of cooked food, *fan-tou;*
The monk in charge of tea, *cha-tou;*
The monk in charge of the garden, *yuan-tou;*
The monk in charge of the grinding mill, *mo-tou;*
The monk in charge of water, *shui-tou;*
The monk in charge of ashes, *hui-tou;*
The monk in charge of vegetables, *cai-tou;*
The monk in charge of firewood, *chai-tou.*

The Responsible Posts in a Zen Temple

There were ten categories of responsible posts in a Zen temple: administration, economy and finances, supervisory functions, ministering and external functions, teaching functions, organizational and disciplinary functions, attendance on the abbot, general affairs, "pure and essential" posts, and general labor. Each had its own characteristic duties.

Temple administration: There might be one temple supervisor, *jian-yuan,* or several. They were in charge of administering all the internal and external affairs of the whole temple. In the old system, this post was called the temple chief, *si-zhu.* Along with the duty distributor, *wei-na,* and the head monk, *shou-cuo,* the temple chief held one of the three chief posts in a Zen temple, termed the *san-gang.*

The colloquial term for the temple supervisor was *dangjia-shi,* "the teacher in charge," "the managing teacher," "the boss." If there were two of them, they were called the inner and the outer teachers in charge. If there were three or more, they were ranked by number. They divided up the duties of managing internal and external affairs, revenues, accounting, and so on. Most of the smaller Zen temples had only one monk in this post.

There were one or more assistant temple supervisors, or *fu-si.* They were like the assistant managers of the temple, who took part in the oversight of the temple affairs and took charge of the finances and the revenues of the temple properties. In the old system, the assistant temple supervisor had to make an account of expenditures every ten days, and record it in a ledger. This was called the *xun-dan,* the ten day account.

Economy and finances: There might be one or more heads of the storehouses, *ku-tou.* In the old system, this was one of the assistant administrator's titles. Another name for this post was *du-cang,* supervisor of the storehouses. He was in charge of expenditures and revenues, and in charge of storing up all the necessary supplies and food, like a modern-day warehouse manager. Colloquially, this monk was called the "storehouse master." He was responsible for maintaining everything in the temple storehouses, like food and clothing and so on, in good condition and keeping them clean and dry.

The *Pure Rules* say: "[The abbot] must select someone with intelligence who can read and write and do arithmetic, and who is very frugal and diligent to take charge of the temple storehouses." It also says: "In the old rules the assistant temple supervisor was called the storehouse head. These days the temples refer to him as the keeper of the treasure chest, and in the north this post is called [the keeper of the temple] wealth. All these are [different names for] the same post."

Supervisory functions: In each temple there was a single general supervisor, *du-jian*. In the old system, this was called the *du-si*, the general overseer of the temple, and also the *du-guan*, the general manager. His responsibility was to oversee the temple's administration, its economic affairs, and its personnel matters. Generally, the monk who filled this post was appointed by the previous temple supervisor. In later generations, this became a kind of sinecure post that was similar to a nominal promotion but also like a demotion in the government. In the old system, this post was above the temple supervisor, and it was called general supervisor because it called for the overall supervision of the temple. Other names for this post were *du-zong* and *du-shou*.

Ministering and external functions: Each temple had one or possibly two or three monks in charge of visitors, *zhi-ke*. In the old system, these were called by such general terms as registrar of visitors, *dian-ke*, monk in charge of the baths, *zhi-yu*, monk in charge of the storehouses, *zhi-ku*, or monk in charge of the shrine, *zhi-dian*. They were in charge of receiving and entertaining outside visitors, and the duties involved in maintaining relationships with other institutions. They also undertook the functions of chanting the scriptures and performing rituals for people. If there were two monks in this position, they were called the chief *zhi-ke* and the subordinate *zhi-ke*. Thus the monks in charge of visitors also could be the equivalent of the outside manager, or the assistant temple supervisor. Every evening, they made a general account of the day's receipts received from outside donors and turned this over to the temple storehouse. If there was an excess of funds in the temple storehouse, it was handed over to the abbot for him to take care of. These days, it would be deposited in a bank.

For these posts, it was necessary for the abbot to choose monks who were possessed of both virtue and authority. Often monks who concentrated on cultivation of practice and regulating their conduct declined these posts with their heavy involvement in financial affairs. But if it happened that there were no other suitable people from which the abbot could choose, these reluctant candidates had to resolve to take on these responsibilities, for the sake of the permanent endowment. This was like leaping into a fiery pit for the sake of the community.

Under the monk in charge of visitors, there were two or more monks to attend to visitors, *zhao-ke*. In the old system, these were called visitors' attendants. Their duty was to assist the monk in charge of visitors and obey his commands. They were chosen from among the young novices for their intelligence and quick wits.

Teaching functions: The head monk, *shou-cuo*, also called the *yuan-cuo*, "first seat," in the old system, was the chief of the monks. He was one of the three top monks, along with the temple supervisor and the duty distributor. He assisted the abbot in preaching the Dharma. Generally this post was assigned to a monk recognized as a man of knowledge throughout the Zen communities or to a monk chosen from among the abbot's disciples for his deep learning. At the same time, he could be the abbot's designated successor. He was permitted to hold the teacher's whisk, take the abbot's place on the teacher's seat, and give instructions to the whole congregation. In the old system, five of the leading monks were considered qualified to hold the teacher's whisk, symbolic of the authority to teach: the head monk, the head monk of the front hall, the head monk of the rear hall, the keeper of the canon, and the secretary.

For the posts of chief of the hall, *tang-zhu*, chief of the rear hall, *hou-tang*, and chief of the west hall, *xi-tang*, the abbot could appoint one or more monks.

In the old system, chief of the hall was a general term, and there were various monks in charge of the various halls, with corresponding titles. Though they were called *tang-zhu*, this was not the same as the later use of the term to designate only the chief of the meditation hall. Here I am using the term only to refer to the *tang-zhu* who was in charge of the meditation hall and the cultivation of practice that went on there. In the old system, the abbot was also sometimes called the "master of the hall." The chief of the hall was the leader of the meditation hall, and took charge of the congregation's cultivation of practice. At the same time, he could also take the abbot's place in preaching the Dharma. Thus, in later generations the term "small gathering" was also given to occasions when the chief of the hall explained the Dharma. The monk chosen to be chief of the hall had to be someone whose cultivation of practice was genuine and who had real knowledge.

In the system in recent times, the chief of the hall would be promoted to chief of the rear hall, and the chief of the rear hall would be promoted to chief of the west hall, and the chief of the west hall would be promoted to head monk. The head monk could substitute for the abbot in such duties as presiding at the Buddha-shrine, eating in the monks' hall, and preaching the Dharma. When the chiefs of the halls got old and retired from their posts, they were no longer consulted on temple affairs.

Within the meditation hall there were several posts, like monk in charge of incense, *jian-xiang*, the supervisor of the congregation, *yue-zhong*, and the monk in charge of the sitting mats, known variously as *dan-tou*, *liao-zhang*, or *xi-tou*.

Each temple had one or more secretaries, *shu-ji*. They maintained the written records of the temple and were like the secretaries in government offices. They were in charge of all the written documents related to temple affairs. In the old system, the secretaries wrote on Buddhist matters and often used the parallel line literary style. In later generations, the post of secretary became the term for the monks who wrote out the abbot's letters and made records of his Dharma talks. They were like the chroniclers in the entourage of the old Chinese emperors who recorded the words and deeds of the rulers. The temple secretary recorded the abbot's Dharma talks and wrote accounts of his sayings and doings. Thus for this post, it was necessary to choose monks who were proficient in the written word.

Sometimes too, the secretary's post was made an honorary one and was awarded to monks in the congregation who had practiced hard for many years so they could be given private quarters. From the post of secretary, a monk could be promoted to chief of the hall. In the old system, another term for the secretary was *ji-shi*.

Organizational and disciplinary functions: The duty distributor, *wei-na*, was one of the three major officers of the whole temple. He was ranked as one of the top leaders, along with the temple supervisor and the head monk. These three were called the *san-gang*, i.e. the three *gang*: *gang* has the meaning of guide and upholder. The three *gang* were the ones who acted as guiding leaders and upholders of discipline in the temple.

In Zen temples and Vinaya temples, the duty distributor was called *wei-na*; in temples devoted to scriptural studies, the term used was *du-wei-na*. In the old system, other terms for the same function were *ci-di*, "ordinator," *zhi-shi*, "supervisor," *yue-zhong*, "supervisor of the congregation," *shi-hu*, "temple protector," and so on. In fact, the term *wei-na* comes from a term in the vinaya section of the Buddhist canon. In *The Brief History of the Sangha*, it says: "In the eastern and western regions, the supervisory monk is called the *karmadana*. This is translated [into Chinese] as *zhi-shi* and also as *yue-zhong*, meaning the one who is in charge of the affairs of the monks and keeps the congregation happy."

In general, whenever the monks chanted sutras or recited the vinaya or performed any rituals, they were led by the duty distributor. If the monks broke the precepts of discipline, or offended against the Zen *Pure Rules*, these were enforced by the duty distributor by such measures as expulsion from the community. (The precepts of discipline call this being expelled; the Zen technical term is being made to move. These are both expressions for being driven out of the temple.)

Another term for duty distributor, *wei-na*, was *tang-si*, "controller of hall." Sometimes this term, *tang-si*, was used directly to mean the duty distributor's quarters, or his position. There was also another term for both of these meanings: *ji-wang-liao*, "the controller's room."

The abbot's attendants: The abbot could have several attendants who stayed near him and carried out errands on which he sent them. In the old system, there were sometimes five and sometimes six attendants. When there were five attendants, there was an attendant in charge of incense, one in charge of written documents, one in charge of receiving guests, one in charge of medicines, and one in charge of robes. When there were six, there was one in charge of the towels and washbasin, one in charge of receiving guests, one in charge of written documents, one in charge of the robe and bowl, one in charge of tea and rice, and one for carrying out other specific tasks. In later generations, the attendant in charge of the abbot's robe and bowl was the general overseer of the abbot's quarters. The attendant in charge of written documents was later termed the attendant for writing down the abbot's teachings, and he was responsible for recording and collecting the abbot's words of instruction and posting them on signboards for the congregation to see.

The monks who were the abbot's attendants were like a retinue, and were usually selected from among the abbot's closest disciples. It was a very honorable post.

The Buddhist sutras say that attendants should have eight qualities: their roots of faith must be solid and strong; they must be intent on advancing in the Path; they must be free of physical illness; they must make energetic progress; they must be mindful; they must not be arrogant; they must be able to concentrate; and they must be sufficiently learned. In sum, to be worthy of the post, the abbot's attendants had to be ready to forget their bodies for the sake of the Dharma, be rigorous in both knowledge and practice, and not spurn the milk of the Dharma bestowed on them by the abbot.

General affairs: The quartermaster, *dian-cuo*, was in charge of daily affairs: his function was like that of a modern-day general affairs department. A note to the *Record of Zen Master Linji* says: "According to Baizhang's *Pure Rules*, [a Zen temple] has a *dian-cuo* 'quartermaster' but no *fan-tou* 'monk in charge of food.' The *dian-cuo* is in charge of food for the whole congregation and all offerings for their support." The book, *Pure Rules for the Monks' Hall*, says: "This office takes charge of the food for the whole congregation. Thus, if he makes sure there are frequent changes in the food, the congregation will be wonderfully content and happy." In later generations, in some cases, the *dian-cuo* became the officer in charge of all internal affairs of the temple.

The "monks serving in turn," *seng-zhi*, were monks in charge of some particular duty for the term of a year. Such a post was rotated and was filled in turn by each of the monks in administrative positions.

The monk in charge of food, *fan-tou*, was responsible for preparing meals. The *Pure Rules for the Monks' Hall* says: "The monk in charge of food *fan-tou* and the quartermaster *dian-cuo* divide the work of overseeing the food. They often work together with various others like the monk in charge of medicines and the monk in charge of grain supplies to protect and husband the temple's permanent endowment. The monk in charge of food has the same concern as the quartermaster: to see to it that there is neither too much nor too little food. The monk in charge of food should be well-versed in the book called *Precious Lessons for Quartermaster Monks*."

Zen temples often assigned certain monks to certain jobs. The monk in charge of the fire, *huo-tou*, supervised the stoves. The monk in charge of the garden, *yuan-tou*, supervised the planting of vegetables. The monk in charge of vegetables, *cai-tou*, supervised the cooking of vegetables. Several chief workers, *hang-tou*, were in charge of the workers in the vegetarian meal hall. Other monks were assigned to taking charge of firewood, *chai-tou*, of removing ashes, *hui-tou*, of buckets, *tong-tou*, of milling grain, *mo-tou*, and of cleaning pots, *huo-tou*. There were differences here over time and due to local conditions. Some temples made these job assignments and some did not: there was no uniform rule.

There was a latrine orderly, *jing-tou*, who was responsible for the cleanliness and hygiene of the latrines. Oftentimes, the head monk and the heads of the two echelons of monks or other monks from the congregation volunteered to take on this job, considering it to be a good way to repent of their sins and accumulate merit. Another name for this job was toilet orderly, *qing-tou*; in the old system, it was also called *dong-si*, "eastern orderly."

There might be one or more monks in charge of the temple's fields, *zhuang-zhu*. Large Zen temples with a lot of agricultural land outside established this post to take charge of the tenant farmers and collecting rents. The colloquial term for this was "the outside manager." He controlled other temple officers, like the harvest supervisor.

There might be one or more monks serving as wardens, *xun-shan-liao-zhu*. They were in charge of protecting the forests owned by the temples and guarding against robbers and poachers. Major temples in the mountains always established this position, but ordinary temples might not have it. Generally, monks who were strong and skilled in the martial arts were chosen to fill this post. If there were special quarters for the holder of this post, then the monks in charge of gardens and in charge of firewood would also be assigned there.

If there were small retreats attached to a temple, then there would be monks living there in charge of them. If the temple had stupas, then there would be monks in charge of them.

The monks in charge of ringing the temple bells were called the bell-monks, *zhong-tou*, and the monk in charge of beating the temple drum was called the drum-monk, *gu-tou*.

The "pure and essential" posts: A temple might have one monk in charge of the canon, called the *cang-zhu*. In the old system, the term used was *zhi-cang*. His job was to take charge of the canonical texts and the religious pictures owned by the temple library. He was like a modern-day library chief or library manager. Usually, a very learned monk was chosen to fill this post, and he might also be the temple secretary. In many large temples, there was a special building in which to store the scriptures, and so this post was very important.

A temple might have a monk in charge of the buddha-shrine, *dian-zhu,* and monks in charge of the incense and lamps. The *dian-zhu* took charge of all the duties connected with the shrine where the image of the Buddha was housed, and he would have a monk in charge of incense and lamps to assist him in this. The other shrines that were part of the temple would have their own monks in charge of incense and lamps, but these were not called *dian-zhu.* In the old system, all this was included in the job of the chief of the hall, the *tang-zhu.*

There was also the chief of the nirvana hall (called the life-prolonging hall in the old system), which was the infirmary for mortally ill monks, and the chief of the arhats' hall. The Vinaya school temples called the nirvana hall "the hall of impermanence." The Zen temples called it the nirvana hall or the life-prolonging hall. This was the place where sick monks on the brink of death were placed so they could contemplate impermanence.

Temples had one or more monks in charge of teaching the laity, *hua-zhu.* Their special task was to travel outside the temple to spread the Buddhist teaching. By the donations they received from lay Buddhists who engaged them to perform rituals, they contributed to the support of the congregation of the whole temple and provided resources for the temple's permanent endowment. They turned in an account of the funds they had received by their teaching work to the monks in charge of visitors, *zhi-ke,* or to the chief of the storehouse, *ku-tou,* who recorded it in the temple account books and turned it over to the abbot's control. The monks in charge of teaching the laity were often traveling outside the temple all year round, and led a comparatively leisurely life.

Working monks: Many monks took upon themselves the laborious work and the various jobs that needed to be done around the temple. Often they volunteered to do this, seeking to perform the difficult jobs in order to spur themselves on to virtuous conduct. There were many worthy monks who took on these tasks, and most of them were not seeking people's recognition.

There are many examples of famous Zen masters serving in menial posts. The *Transmission of the Lamp* says: "When Guishan was in Baizhang's congregation, he acted as the quartermaster, and he ordered that the work of straining and ladling water be assigned to the quartermaster." The *Five Lamps Meeting at the Source* says: "When Xuefeng was at Dongshan he was the monk in charge of food. Qingzhu was the monk in charge of rice at Guishan. Daokuang was the monk in charge of the buckets at Zhaoqing. Guanqi was the monk in charge of the gardens at Moshan. Shaoyuan was the monk in charge of the fields at Shimen. Zhitong was the harvest evaluator at Guishan. Xiaocong was the monk in charge of the lamps at Yunju. Jishan was the monk in charge of firewood at Touzi. Yihuai was the monk in charge of water at Cuifeng. Foxin was in charge of cleaning the privies at Haiyin."

All these are examples of eminent Zen masters taking on jobs that involved hard labor. It was even more common for monks of high attainments to serve as temple quartermasters.

In years past, when I was traveling around studying at various Buddhist centers, I wrote this poem:

The wind from Spirit Peak is high, climbing in the ancient footprints
Studying Zen with the ancestral teachers of the north and south
Traveling on foot in those days across rivers and lakes
Visiting all the famous mountain temples, those hard-practicing monks.

I wrote this to express my feelings of admiration for the virtuous conduct among the Zen monks over the generations who practiced austerities.

The Chief Administrators, Visiting Monks, and the Pure Congregation

The monks in administrative positions under the abbot generally had private quarters. If the temple did not have enough rooms to assign to them, private quarters were assigned according to the importance of the positions, and sometimes two monks would share a room. The rest of the congregation, no matter whether they lived in the Zen hall or were travelers passing through, were called the "pure congregation," *qing-zhong*.

Later on, since Buddhism had become widespread in China, there was a need to influence the beliefs of the common people, and monks were invited to go outside the temples to chant the sutras and perform Buddhist ceremonies. At the same time, this was the way the temple as a whole and the congregation of monks earned their collective and individual incomes. Thus, there came to be a group of monks within each temple who specialized in ministering to the people by chanting sutras and conducting ceremonies. Generally, they were distinguished from the "pure congregation," who devoted themselves to pure cultivation, and they were called the ministering monks, the monks who responded to the people's needs. In the late Qing and early Republican periods, in the region of Fujian and Zhejiang, the general custom was to call them "ministering teachers." This may have been a corruption of the term "ministering teaching monks."

The quarters of the monks who were passing through the temple on their travels were called the "clouds and rivers rooms," *yun-shui-liao*; in the old system these were called the "river and lake rooms," *jiang-hu-liao*, and they were also called the "group rooms," *zhong-liao*. This referred to the rooms set aside for monks who were staying at the temple temporarily during the course of their travels to study Zen.

What is the derivation of the term *jiang-hu-liao*? In Zen tradition, *jiang-hu*, "river and lake," meant Jiangxi and Hunan provinces. In the Tang period, monks studying Zen either went to Mazu's place in Jiangxi or to Shitou's place in Hunan; many monks traveled back and forth between these two and congregated at the teaching centers of these two great teachers, and so they were called *jiang-hu* monks. But a note to the famous literary collection, *Wen Xuan*, also says that *jiang-hu* means beyond the rivers and by the side of lakes, which were locations where recluses went to dwell. The *Biographies of the Eminent Worthies of the Lotus Society*, in its section on Zhou Xuzhi, says: "His mind was running off to the palace of Wei, but the rivers and lakes locked him in." A preface by Luo Binwang says: "The temple with its verandas is aligned with the rivers and lakes." Fan Xi, Master Wenyan, says in his note on the sacrifice hall: "Once the constellations had shifted, he returned to the rivers and lakes." All these testify to this derivation. In fact, the original meaning of *jiang-hu* comes from *Zhuang Zi*, where it refers to the air of a recluse. "When the spring dries up, the fish in it are stranded on dry land, gasping for moisture, sputtering out bubbles: it's better to forget the rivers and lakes."

Variations in the Zen *Pure Rules* Over Time

More than a thousand years have passed since Baizhang instituted his *Pure Rules*. The original regulations were lost long ago, and in the various versions of *Pure Rules for Zen Monastic Communities* that have been passed down from later generations to us today, there are many passages that do not resemble the practices of olden times. But this is nothing to be surprised at.

In 1338, under orders from Emperor Shundi of the Yuan dynasty, Zen master Dehui of Baizhang Mountain, the abode of Baizhang Huaihai, the originator of the *Pure Rules*, prepared an edition of the *Pure Rules* of Baizhang in eight fascicles which circulated through the empire. The emperor commanded that all Buddhist monks in his realm practice according to this version of the *Pure Rules*.

During the Ming dynasty (1368–1644) the imperial authorities repeatedly decreed that those monks who did not abide by these *Pure Rules* were to be dealt with as lawbreakers and, in later generations, this was taken as the standard.

In 1823, under the Qing dynasty, Zen master Yuanhong wrote *Qinggui Zhengyi*, a ten fascicle textual criticism of the *Pure Rules* of Baizhang that circulated widely and established the accepted text.

Because of differences in time and place, there are various differences in other versions of the *Pure Rules* in use at various temples. In recent generations, there are versions in use that are even more different from the old system. In reality, this has been brought about by the trend of the times. There have been the difficulties of unavoidable changes. There have also been many cases where people did not know what they should base themselves on and have falsely introduced changes prompted by their own pretensions to be teachers.

As Zen master Yuanhong said: "There are many differences in the *Pure Rules* between older and more recent versions. For example, the older versions call the head monk *tou-shou*, while the more recent ones use the terms *shou-cuo* or *cuo-yuan*. The older versions call the temple supervisor *jian-si*, while the more recent ones use the term *jian-yuan*. The term for the temple secretary, *shu-zhuang* has been changed to *shu-ji*, and the term monks' hall *seng-tang* has been changed to Zen hall *chan-tang*. In all these cases there has been a change of term but no change in meaning. There are also instances where a particular regulation is present in the older versions but absent in the more recent ones, and vice versa."

Generally, in the case of any kind of social organization, the earliest form is always very simple. The more time goes by, the more complicated the situation becomes, and so more and more regulations are added. Although Baizhang's original *Pure Rules* have been lost, the preface to them by the Song dynasty writer Yang Yi is still extant. The situation he describes is naturally much simpler than that of later generations. For example, he writes: "The assembled students, no matter how many or few, should all enter the monks' hall, with no distinctions of rank. They should be seated according to how many summers they have spent as Zen monks. They are provided with meditation benches, a rack to hang their robes, a place to hang up their bags, and sitting mats. When they recline, they must use a slanted pillow and a bed and lie on their right sides for an auspicious sleep. After they have been doing sitting meditation for a long time, they will only rest briefly." Yang Yi also explains the purpose of Baizhang's *Pure Rules* as follows: "To keep the pure congregation from defilement, and to engender respect and trust. To avoid violating the proper form for monks, and to follow the Buddha's rules. To avoid trouble with the authorities, and eliminate lawsuits. To avoid gossip outside the temple, and to preserve the guiding principles of the Zen school."

Judging from Yang Yi's preface, and from the text of the great teacher Cijue's *Mirror and Guide*, the focus of attention in the *Pure Rules* was actually on what has come down to the present as the meditation hall. But in later generations, except at a small number of major Zen temples, most of the Zen temples that still use these standards to regulate the congregation instead relegate the meditation hall to a subordinate position. What a grave mistake! By doing this, they have made the decline of the Zen school inevitable. The purpose behind leaving home is to wholeheartedly seek the mind of enlightenment. How is it that the meditation hall should therefore occupy anything but the most prominent position? Those of us today who are responsible for such matters should think deeply on this.

THE INFLUENCE OF THE ZEN COMMUNITIES

In the Tang and Song periods, during the heyday of the Zen school, in general there were four types of situations in which people left home and became monks and nuns.

1. Those who studied the Buddhist sutras and shastras were called *yi-xue* monks, monks devoted to doctrinal learning. Some of these became monks when they were granted official ordination certificates, *du-die,* after passing the examinations conducted by the government in Buddhist scriptures.

2. Some developed the aspiration for enlightenment on their own. They left behind conventional society to seek the Path, and requested ordination from eminent monks of great virtue.

3. Sometimes the imperial court issued edicts allowing commoners throughout the empire to become monks and nuns freely as they wished. During the Tang period, the imperial government on several occasions resorted to the sale of ordination certificates to raise revenue and allowed anyone who purchased one to freely become a monk or nun.

4. Sometimes the old and weak, or widows and widowers with no recourse and no one to support them, became monks and nuns.

In any of these circumstances, those who wanted to leave home but had not reached adulthood, according to the Buddhist rules, had to obtain the consent of their parents and their clan before they were permitted to leave home.

Equality of Status and Collective Living

After having left home, received the precepts, and obtained an ordination certificate, a monk could go to a Zen temple and seek admission to become a long-term resident. In general, there were two forms of seeking admission to a temple, each with a different procedure.

Generally, staying at a temple for a few days or for a short period of time was called *gua-da*, "hanging up one's bag." (Colloquially, this was also called *gua-dan*, "hanging up one's mat.") The monks who were staying at a temple for a short time were those who had come from afar to study there on account of their respect for the reputation of that temple's abbot, or else those who were passing through the place on their travels. In either event, the newcomer had to go first to the guest hall and follow a prescribed form to offer salutations, announce himself, and set down his traveling gear. After doing so, he was received with due courtesy by the monk in charge of guests. The monk in charge of guests would ask him, according to the Zen school's prescribed formula, about his journey. When the monk in charge of guests had found out the newcomer's intention to stay at the temple, he would escort him to the guest rooms and call for water to wash with, and food and drink.

Generally, the room where visiting monks stayed was called the *liao-fang*. Another term was *yun-shui-liao*. In the Tang and Song periods, it was called by the older term, *jiang-hu-liao*.

Generally, traveling monks who stayed for a time at a temple were entertained with three meals a day, and were made to feel at home. They were not discriminated against at all. With a monk who was traveling for his studies, some of the bigger Zen temples would give him some money for his travel expenses when he was about to depart. This was called "money for straw sandals." Those visiting monks who stayed for some time at the temple would go along with the congregation to the buddha-shrine to chant sutras and would take part in the work of the temple. Even though they were staying in the guest quarters, they followed the same routine of work and rest as the other monks.

If visiting monks wanted to stay at the temple for a long time, this was called *tao-da*, "seeking [a place to put] the bag." If they wanted to live in the Zen hall and cultivate their studies there, this was called *tao-hai-da*. If they sought to live in the Zen hall, they would be counted as regular members of the temple's congregation of monks. For this, it was necessary first to follow the procedures of "hanging up the bag" for a short sojourn, and stay at the temple for some time and be checked out by the monk in charge of guests and the other leading monks of the temple. If they gave permission, then the newcomer could become a long-term resident. In the old system, this was called *an-da*, "settling the bag."

Every year, in the Spring and in the Fall, the congregation of monks who were long-term residents at a temple were issued a set of robes, or else money for robes so they could have robes made. In addition to donations made by the temple's patrons, every three months the permanent endowment of the temple gave out a small sum of pocket money to each monk. This was called *chen-qian*, "lining money."

Among the permanent residents of a Zen temple, everyone who had already accepted the precepts and who had an ordination certificate was completely equal in status and way of life. Status and way of life were the same for everyone, from the abbot to the monks doing manual labor. In matters of clothing, food, dwelling places, and conduct, they all had to adhere strictly to the Buddhist code of discipline and the *Pure Rules* of the Zen monastic community. When there were violations of the code of discipline or the *Pure Rules*, if they were minor, the punishment might be to kneel holding incense or to do hard labor. If the violations were serious, they would be punished according to the code of discipline, which might result in expulsion from the community. Colloquially, this was called "being driven out of the temple gate."

The Monks' Clothing

Monks generally all wore the long robes that were the legacy of the Tang and Song periods. They also dressed like this when they practiced Zen and did sitting meditation. When the monks did manual labor, they wore short tunics. These are the monastic garments that have been passed down to the present. When formal courtesy requires it, monks wear long robes. Modern-day monks call this long robe *hai-qing*, "ocean blue." When they go up to the buddha-shrine to chant the sutras or pay homage to Buddha, or listen to the sutras being chanted or to a teacher expounding the Dharma, monks put on a *kashaya*, a Buddhist monk's formal robe. The *kashaya* worn by Chinese monks underwent changes in the Tang and Song periods and is not the same style as the original Indian version. At the present time, we can see a bit of Chinese traditional culture in the Buddhist monks' long robes and, in their air of elegance and dignity, we can catch a glimpse of the style of the elite dress of old China. There are set regulations for the way monks put on and fold their robes: they have been carefully trained in this and have had long practice at it, so that even if a thousand monks are walking along, it is hard to hear any sound of garments rustling.

The Monks' Food

According to the Buddhist code of discipline, monks can only have two meals a day, in the morning and at noon. For all sorts of good reasons, monks do not eat after noon. When they eat, they use a bowl and a spoon for their food. Buddhist monks did not eat like other Indians, scooping up the food with their hands. But this practice has already been changed since Buddhism came to China, and Chinese Buddhist monks eat with bowls and chopsticks, like ordinary Chinese. But if Chinese monks fully carry out the teachings of Mahayana Buddhism, they follow a vegetarian diet consistently throughout their lives and they never eat after noon. The only ones who may dare to eat a meal in the evening are those monks who do heavy manual labor: this is done for fear their physical strength may not be adequate, with the thought that this is like taking medicine to cure starvation.

When the monks ate, it was always in the *zhai-tang*, the vegetarian hall, also called the *shi-tang*, the eating hall. This was also called the *guan-tang*, the contemplation hall, taking from the Buddhist scriptures the idea that eating food is to be seen as a cure for a sickness, and is not to be done for the sake of indulging the desires of the mouth or the belly. The rules regarding eating had to be followed uniformly by all the monks, and no exceptions could be made, even for the abbot. If there were guests from outside, they were accompanied by the monk in charge of guests and given a meal in the guest hall. Sometimes there was no choice but for the abbot to eat along with the guests.

There were set regulations for mealtimes for the congregation. Even if there were a thousand monks or more at a temple, as soon as they heard the sound of the wooden sounding board being struck, they knew it was time to eat. All the monks would put on their long robes, arrange themselves in order, and noiselessly file into the eating hall, seating themselves in the proper sequence. There was a set procedure for the placement of the bowls and chopsticks and platters of vegetables. Everyone sat upright: no one was permitted to lean on the table. Each monk held his bowl in his left hand and his chopsticks in his right. They were not supposed to make any sounds while sipping their drinks or chewing their food. There was a set rule for putting rice and vegetables in the monks' individual bowls. The monks at work serving the meal were not allowed to talk or call to each other. At the head of the vegetarian hall was the abbot's seat. When the abbot took up his bowl and lifted his chopsticks, then the whole congregation could start to eat. When the entire group had finished the meal, they would file out together in silence to return to their quarters. If the abbot had something to say to the congregation, he would stop eating during the meal and tell them about it. This was called *biao-tang,* "making an announcement in the hall." On the first and fifteenth of every month, extra dishes would be added to the meal of the laboring monks. When the patrons of the temple made donations to give a vegetarian feast for the monks, extra dishes would also be added to the meal.

The Monks' Dwelling Places

The monks who devoted themselves to practicing Zen meditation in the Zen hall were called the "pure congregation." They lived there in the Zen hall day and night. The other monks had their own rooms: sometimes a monk had his own room and sometimes several monks shared one room. In keeping with the Buddhist precepts and the Zen *Pure Rules,* if these monks were not otherwise occupied, they sat quietly in their rooms, except in the morning and evenings when they were in the buddha-shrine chanting sutras, doing exercises, listening to the sutras, or listening to explanations of the Dharma. They were not allowed to go from room to room to engage in idle chatter, or to wander around to various places. They were not allowed without reason to gather together to talk or to make a lot of noise. If the abbot, one of the monks holding responsible positions, or one of the senior monks happened to pass by, the monks had to get up and stand in a dignified fashion with the palms joined in salute to show their respect.

The Monks' Way of Walking

When the monks were walking, or when they lined up with the rest of the congregation, they had to adhere to the regulations in the code of discipline. They had to walk at a slow even pace in silence, with faces cast down and hands placed evenly over their breasts. They were not allowed to look to the left or to the right, or to keep their gaze high, or to take large steps. If there was some matter that required them to go outside the temple, they had to go to the guest hall and report their absence to the monk in charge of guests. When they returned to the temple, they had to go again to the guest hall and report. They were not permitted to come and go in and out of the temple as they pleased. Even the abbot and the monks with responsible positions had to inform the monk in charge of guests when they left or reentered the temple, and when they spent a few days away from the temple, they also had to announce their departure and their return in front of the image of Buddha.

There were regulations for the other activities of daily life, such as bathing and washing clothes. When monks were sick, the larger temples had their own pharmacies to prepare medicines. The sick monk would ask for leave, spend time in his room recuperating, and be excused from going along with the rest of the congregation to the buddha-shrine and the meditation hall. If a monk was gravely ill, he would stay in the *ru-yi-tang*, the "wish-granting hall," where he was cared for by monks who gladly ministered to the sick. The *ru-yi-tang* was called the *an-le-tang*, "peace and happiness hall," under the old system. When a monk died, he was moved into the nirvana hall and subsequently cremated. Afterward, the bones and ashes were collected, and placed in the *ling-gu-ta*, the "spirit bone stupa" (colloquially called the *gu-hui-ta*, the "bones and ashes stupa").

In summary, the collective life of genuine Zen communities had achieved equality in all respects, and was guided by regulations in every particular. Starting with the management of the individual's body and mind, and extending to the life of the whole community, every aspect of life was carried out according to rules and regulations. There were detailed rules for everything. Thus, when the great Song dynasty Confucian Cheng Yi observed the life of the monks in the Zen communities, he exclaimed: "The rites and music of the Three Dynasties are all here in this." Confucians revered the ancient Three Dynasties as the fount of correct social and ethical norms.

Equality of Labor and a Prosperous Economy

When Baizhang established rules for the Zen monastic communities, his most crucial innovation was to change the system whereby the monks were not productive and depended on begging for their food. According to the monastic code of primitive Buddhism, the monks could not till the soil and plant crops for fear of injuring living things in the soil. This may have worked in certain regions of India, but in China, where agriculture had always been esteemed, this could not prevail. Such a system could not endure forever in China. So Baizhang boldly established a new set of monastic regulations, paying no attention to other people's rebukes. In this system, the Zen monks cleared fields in the mountain forests around their retreats and supported themselves mainly by their own farming, with the donations they got from the laiety as a subsidiary source of income. Tilling and planting and gathering the harvest, the Zen monks were like the ordinary people, and according to the government's laws and regulations, they too had to pay taxes. Thus the Zen monks in China were not a special class of people and were not outside the social order.

In their daily activities, the Zen monks were devoted to cultivating practice and seeking realization of the Buddha Dharma. But in addition to this, whenever there was agricultural work or other tasks to do, they all had to participate in manual labor according to the directives of the *seng-zhi-shi* (the monk who issued the orders and acted as the leader), no matter whether they were of high or low standing in the community. In the technical language of the Zen communities, this sort of thing was called *chu-po*, "going out to the slopes." In the old system it was called *pu-qing*, "the general call to labor." When the monks went out to work in the fields, the abbot had to lead them in person and act as a model for the other monks.

When Zen master Baizhang reached old age, he still did not stop working. His disciples could not bear to see this, so they surreptitiously took his farming tools and hid them. Unable to find his tools, he could not go do his work that day, so he went without food for the day. Thus the Zen school traditionally extols Baizhang's lofty style with the saying: "A day without work means a day without food." This saying has been used to spur on the Zen monks of later generations. From this, we can see the inspirational qualities of Baizhang's great personality. In modern times, Master Xuyun reached the age of 120, but he still personally took part in manual labor. Master Xuyun upheld this practice consistently throughout his life.

In the economic system of the Zen communities, all receipts and expenditures were made public. The technical term for this was *gong-zhong*, "public community." All the income of the temple went for the well-being of the entire congregation. If there was a surplus, it was invested in landed property in the hope that this would support a greater number of the nation's monks. Most of the monks holding administrative posts clearly distinguished between community affairs and their own private interests, and absolutely would not dare to appropriate for their own use any of the temple funds and property. This was not only because the monastic regulations prohibited this, but because the monks firmly believed in the principle of cause and effect and karmic retribution.

There was a common constantly repeated maxim: "A single grain of rice belonging to the Buddhist community is as big as Mount Sumeru. If I do not complete the Path in this lifetime, I will come back [as an animal] wearing fur and horns." Thus everyone did his utmost to protect and care for the monks who were really engaged in cultivating practice in the Zen hall. They did not want to cause them any trouble or alarm. They hoped that those monks would consummate the Path, and thus repay the benevolence of the nation and society at large, and of the temple's patrons and donors.

In the past, there was a Zen master named Baoshou, who was in charge of the storehouse at Wuzu Temple. Master Jie, who was the abbot of the temple at the time, happened to take some medicine because he was sick. He needed fresh ginger, so his attendant went to the storehouse to get some. Baoshou rebuked him and sent him away. When Master Jie was informed of this, he had his attendant take some money to pay for the ginger: only then did Baoshou give it to him. Later, Dongshan Temple needed someone to serve as abbot, and the prefectural governor sent a letter asking Master Jie to find someone to be its abbot. Master Jie said, "That guy who sold me the fresh ginger can go." So Baoshou went to be the abbot at Dongshan Temple. Because of this, a saying was passed down in the Zen school: "Baoshou's fresh ginger will be pungent for ten thousand years."

In the 1940s, when I was in Chengdu, I met the retired abbot of Baoguang Temple in Xindu. He was as upright as an ancient pine and his visage was imbued with the Tao: he was indeed a venerable figure. He had been the abbot of a major temple for several decades. When he came there, he had only the clothes he was wearing, and when he retired, he still had the same set of worn-out robes. He had never taken a penny of the temple funds for his personal use. He said of this that if his virtuous conduct had not been worthy of inspiring the congregation, he would have been unable to bear the karmic retribution. Having a few words with him made me feel the serenity that comes from contemplating the ancient Zen masters. His was the style of a great abbot of a Zen temple.

Equality of Faith and Discipline in Speech and Action

The Chinese term for the Zen communities was *cong-lin,* which literally means "dense forests." The meaning is obvious from the term: many of the early Zen centers were located in mountain forests. In fact, the term also implies that those who understood the Path and were cultivating practice in these Zen communities were as numerous as the trees growing thick in the forests.

Those who lived in the Zen communities were all people with a firm belief in the Buddha Dharma, and especially in the Zen school's method of attaining buddhahood in the mind-ground. They wanted to live in Zen communities in order to devote themselves wholeheartedly to the method of attaining enlightenment by cultivating realization of the mind-ground. Thus, besides adhering to the *Pure Rules* of the Zen monastic communities, in the Zen temples they also held faithfully to the Buddhist code of monastic discipline, the vinaya.

The story goes that, in the past at Guoqing Temple on Mount Tiantai, there was an eminent monk who had attained the Path and who already possessed spiritual powers. One evening he was sitting in meditation in the Zen hall. He left his seat and whispered to the monks in the other seats: "Are you hungry?" The other monks did not dare answer. But one monk said: "If we are hungry, what can we do about it? The rule is that we cannot eat after noon, and who would dare break this precept? Even if we wanted to eat, there is nothing in the kitchen, so how could there be anything to eat?" The adept said: "Don't worry. If you want to eat, I will make something for you. There are some rice cakes in the kitchen." As he finished talking, he reached into his left sleeve with his right hand and brought out a big rice cake and invited the monk to eat it.

The abbot of the temple also had spiritual powers. He observed the precepts strictly and would never casually display his spiritual powers. The next morning, the abbot made an announcement to the congregation: "Last night in the Zen hall, there were two monks who broke the precepts. According to the code of discipline, they will be expelled from the temple." The monk with spiritual powers then took his robe in one hand, prostrated himself in front of the abbot, and admitted that he had violated the precepts. So (regardless of possessing super powers or not), because he had violated the precepts, he was driven out of the temple.

In the Southern Song period, before he attained the Dharma, Zen master Dahui stayed with Zen master Zhantang. One day, Zhantang looked at his fingernails and said to him: "Didn't you recently wash the latrine cleaners' stick?" Dahui knew that his teacher was rebuking him for being fond of leisure and averse to hard work, so he immediately cut off his long fingernails and went to take the place of Huanglong Zhong as the latrine cleaner for nine months.

From examples like these of the conduct of the Zen masters of old, we can see how natural and yet strictly disciplined they were in regard to observing the rules and precepts, in their speech and their actions, and in the example they set.

Equality of all Sentient Beings

The Buddhist teaching does not only regard all people as equal, it actually wants to achieve solidarity between humans and all beings. It regards all sentient beings as equal in inherent nature.

The regulations for the Zen monastic system were created in response to the times and to social conditions in China. On the surface, there seem to be differences between the Zen *Pure Rules* and the Buddhist Vinaya. In reality, the *Pure Rules* took the Buddhist code of monastic discipline as their basic framework. Thus, within the Zen *Pure Rules*, strict adherence to the Vinaya was still very important. For example, when a Zen monk was walking, he would not dare to trample upon worms or ants: how could he dare to harm living creatures?

Because Buddhist belief and teaching calls for treating all things equally in the universal exercise of compassion, Zen communities adopted a style of doing things that recognized all the people in the world as members of a single family. When Zen monks were traveling on foot all over the country, no matter where they were, in major towns or country villages, as long as there was a Zen temple, and they understood the regulations, they were permitted to "hang up their bags" and stay there temporarily. This practice was observed throughout China, and traveling monks were permitted to stay for a time even in small temples in little towns and in hereditary private temples. In the past, monks could travel on foot all over China without having to carry any money with them. Even if there was no temple for them to stay in, it did not matter because they could pass a day in peaceful meditation under the trees.

From the Yuan and Ming periods on, though there seemed to be differences in religious faith between Buddhism and Taoism in certain aspects Buddhists and Taoists acted like one family. For example, if a Taoist monk arrived in a locality where there was no Taoist temple, he could go to a Buddhist temple and stay there. It was the same way for Buddhist monks: when they needed to, they could stay at Taoist temples. When the time came for the congregation to go to the shrine hall and chant the scriptures, the visitor had to accompany them there, but he was free to chant the scriptures of his own faith. As long as the visitor abided by the rules, the resident monks could not discriminate against him.

Indeed, it was even possible for monks to stay at temples inhabited by nuns and vice versa. But in such cases, the rules of discipline and decorum between monks and nuns had to be observed very strictly. For example, if a monk stayed temporarily at a temple inhabited by nuns, in temples that abided strictly by the *Pure Rules*, he could only stay there for one night, sitting in meditation in the great hall. At temples that were a bit more accommodating, he could spend one night in the guest quarters, but he could definitely not stay for long. It was the same way when a nun came to a temple inhabited by monks.

When laypeople sought to spend the night at a Buddhist temple, it was not called "hanging up the bag." The basis of Buddhism is compassion and sometimes, taking account of the situation, Buddhist temples would accept laypeople and allow them to stay there temporarily. In Tang and Song times, many poor and destitute students stayed in Buddhist temples while they pursued their studies. There were a considerable number of cases of this, like the famous Tang dynasty scholar Li Bi, the Duke of Nie.

During the Tang period, Wang Bowei stayed at a temple in Yangzhou while he was a student. The chief monk treated him contemptuously. One day, the chief monk deliberately struck the bell signaling the end of the meal, so Wang did not get to eat. Wang wrote a verse about this on the wall:

> The trip up to the hall is already over, and the monks are going
>   off in different directions
> I'm sorry the Reverend has already struck the bell ending the
>   meal.

Later on, Wang achieved fame and was posted to Yang-zhou as the official in charge of the area. When he passed through the temple again, he saw the verse he had written there previously: the monks of the temple had covered it with blue gauze in deference to Wang's present eminence. Wang then continued the verse saying:

> Twenty years ago, the dust blew in my face
> Only now do I get a blue gauze cover.

This event was altogether exceptional, and we cannot judge the whole situation on the basis of an unusual case and think that all Buddhist monks were snobbish.

At the very least, we can say that, after the Zen monastic system came into being, it indeed carried out on behalf of Chinese society the social-welfare work of caring for widows and orphans, supporting the young, and giving refuge to the elderly. This is an undeniable fact. When the Song emperor Renzong (r. 1023–1063) observed the life of the Zen communities, he was struck with admiration for its purity, and so he personally composed a poem in praise of the Buddhist sangha. Tradition has it that the Shunzhi Emperor (r. 1644–1661) of the Qing dynasty wanted to become a monk when he saw the standards of the Zen communities. He composed a poem in praise of the Zen monks which contained these lines:

> The Zen communities throughout the empire are like a
>   mountain of rice
> A bowl extending everywhere, letting good people eat
> I was originally a patchrobed one from the west

How did I fall into the imperial family?
Just because my initial thought went astray
I exchanged my monk's yellow for imperial purple.

Some say this was written by the Kangxi Emperor (r. 1662–1722). It is very hard to determine the real truth about this. But from this verse, it is obvious what an atmosphere prevailed in the Zen communities.

THE ZEN HALLS: CULTIVATION OF PRACTICE

When Baizhang established the *Pure Rules*, his most important contribution was to set up correct guidelines for the Zen school. Due to the widespread influence of this system of monastic regulations, most Chinese Buddhist temples in later generations, no matter to what sect of Buddhism they belonged, were labeled Zen temples. Zen monks led a simple plain life, traveling on foot, carrying their meditation cushions with them, wearing straw sandals and rainhats, so they could go to any of the famous Buddhist centers throughout the country. Everyone respected their austere practice, and so Zen temples and retreats were continually being built for them by lay devotees in the mountain valleys and glens.

But the principle purpose of the true Zen communities was not just the building of Zen temples and retreats. It was to have Zen halls proper for sitting in meditation, in order to provide Buddhist monks all over China with places where they could live in peace and devote themselves to cultivating practice.

The Scope of the Zen Hall

During the Tang, Song, Yuan, Ming, and Qing periods, there were Zen halls in the Zen communities that could accommodate from several hundred up to more than a thousand monks with places to sit and lie down. Every monk had a place to spread his mat, where he could sit peacefully in meditation, and where he could also lie down and rest. The places to spread the mats were arranged next to each other, so the ancients called this the *chang-lian-chuang,* "the long continuous seat." Each monk's name was written on his place, stuck to his mat. Usually the names of all the monks who were long-term residents of the temple were recorded in a register. The colloquial name for this register was the *cao-dan,* the "straw mat," and the technical term was the *jie-la-bu,* "the register of those who have taken the precepts and stay through the year." It was the equivalent of a modern-day population register.

The Zen hall was bright and plain and had harmonious proportions, in accord with the simple way of living that went on there, and adapted to

Zen skill in means. Buildings in the old days were built without much attention to ventilation, and were a bit deficient in air circulation.

The four sides of the Zen hall were all used for places to spread out mats. In the middle was a big empty area where the whole congregation assembled and which was used for slow walking. This slow walking is what the Buddhist scriptures say is the appropriate exercise for those who are practicing meditative concentration. The sutras call this *jing-xing,* "walking along," but in the Zen communities, the term was changed to *xing-xiang* or *pao-xiang,* which both mean "walking with incense." Thus the space in the middle of the Zen hall had to be large enough for the several hundred or more monks who lived in the hall to walk around. When the monks walked around, they walked in a circle. However, when it was necessary, the congregation would be divided up into two or three rings for this walking. Those who were old and weak were not able to walk in the outer ring: only the young and strong monks walked in the outer circle.

The Teacher in the Zen Hall

Since the Zen hall was the heart of the Zen temple, in modern parlance, it was like the educational center. Thus, it would seem that it should have been the place that was richest in colorful Buddhist imagery. But in fact, this was not the case. On the contrary, the Zen hall truly displayed the genuine spirit of the Buddha Dharma. It was completely free of all mystery and superstitious belief and starkly expressed the message of the Buddha Mind-Seal transmitted by the great teacher Bodhidharma. Originally in the Zen halls the practice of making offerings to images of Buddha was absent because, according to the teaching of the Zen school, "mind itself is buddha," "there is no difference between mind, buddha, and sentient beings," and "it is not mind, not buddha, and not things."

So what then was the Zen hall in the last analysis? We can say that it was where people were taught to understand and awaken to the essence and function of the true identity of their own bodies and minds, the so-called original face: the Tao is right before our eyes and is to be sought in daily activities, not externally.

In later generations, it gradually became the custom in the Zen hall to make offerings to images of the venerable Kashyapa or of the ancestral teacher Bodhidharma. A large seat was positioned in the place of honor in the Zen hall, facing the main door: this was the abbot's place.

Sometimes the abbot had to lead the congregation in their practice of sitting meditation, or else explain the Dharma in the morning or evening to give guidance to their cultivation of practice. Therefore, it was necessary to select as the abbot an enlightened teacher who had already awakened to the Path and attained the Dharma and who could really guide everyone in cultivating realization. Mind itself is buddha, and the teacher is the present buddha. Thus the abbot was the heart of the Zen community. Sometimes the abbot was called "the teacher in the hall."

If the abbot was unable to come to the Zen hall to give guidance, then the head monk of the meditation hall, of the rear hall, or of the west hall (i.e., the *tang-zhu*, the *hou-tang*, or the *xi-tang*) would assist the abbot and oversee the community's practice. These monks were seated at the head of the left row near the door. Besides these monks, sometimes the monk who held the sounding board (the *jian-xiang*) would take on the duty of overseeing the practice. He and the monk in charge of over-seeing discipline in the congregation (the *yue-zhong*) both had the respon-sibility of overseeing the congregation's cultivation of practice and medita-tion work.

In ancient times, the sounding board was a bamboo staff. One end was wrapped in cotton cloth. It was used to alert and spur on the meditat-ing monks. In the old Buddhist system, it was called the "meditation staff." In later generations, a wooden board was used as a sounding board made in the shape of a sword: it was called the "fragrant board," *xiang-ban*.

There were also several monks on duty in the Zen hall to bring tea and water to the monks. Sometimes this job was done by novice monks.

Life in the Zen Hall

As the name implies, the Zen hall provided the monks a place where they could devote themselves to the practice of meditation. The aim of Zen monks was to find the highest realm where enlightenment in the mind-ground really becomes manifest. To this end, they detached from sensory experience, abandoned their desires, and decisively cut off all entangle-ments. They also had to take great pains to be diligent and regulate their conduct until it was as pure as ice and snow. There were many monks who buried their heads in the Zen hall their whole lives and, even if they died without achieving enlightenment, they still sacrificed themselves to the Path without regrets.

All those who lived in the Zen hall had to maintain the discipline of the *Pure Rules* strictly in regard to food and drink and daily activities. They arose at three or four o'clock in the predawn hours and, after wash-ing and going to the toilet, went to their seats to meditate. Because there were no mechanical clocks in olden times, each meditation session lasted as long as it took for a long stick of incense to burn down, which was about an hour and a half. Then the monks would leave their seats and walk around inside the Zen hall in a long file. Though their bodies relaxed as they walked, their minds did not. They walked like this while another stick of incense burned down, then they returned to their seats. There were uniform rules for eating and drinking, sleeping, and visiting the privies. Thus the monks were always practicing Zen, no matter what they were doing. Each day was measured out with ten or more large sticks of incense.

In winter, when the agricultural work was finished, the weather was cold, and there was no other work to do, the monks would adopt the method of setting a time limit for realization. They would adopt a seven-day period of intensive practice: this was called "seven days of Zen," or "seven days of quiet sitting." During this seven-day period, the monks worked harder than usual on their meditation work. Usually during such periods, they sat in meditation every day for thirteen or fourteen periods measured by the burning down of a long stick of incense. Altogether, their combined rest time and sleep time during the day and night was no more than three or four hours.

The other schools of Buddhism, reflecting on the perfection of this method of hard practice, also began to hold various kinds of seven-day sessions: seven-day buddha-name recitation sessions are one example. With this spirit of seeking the Path diligently through arduous efforts, and persisting in this over the days and months, the Zen communities were sure to produce at least one or two people of unusual abilities.

When a Zen community undertook a period of seven days of intensive meditation, during which the abbot had to appoint someone to take the post of *jian-xiang* (the monk who held the sounding board and signaled the intervals in the session) in the Zen hall, he had to follow the same procedure as that for appointing monks to responsible posts in the community. After holding a meeting and discussing the appointment, the name of the candidate was posted and he was installed in his post with the same formalities as when one of the temple's administrative posts was filled. But installing him in his post was only a matter of escorting him to the *jian-xiang's* seat in the Zen hall, because this duty was centered on the Zen hall. Sometimes the abbot appointed seven or eight monks to take turns serving as the *jian-xiang*, so that it would not be too laborious for any one of them.

The Zen school emphasized the sudden method of seeing real nature, illuminating mind, and becoming enlightened then and there. It did not emphasize the method of cultivating the practices of *samadhi* and liberation. Nevertheless, from the time of Shakyamuni Buddha back in India long ago, up through the transmission of Zen to China, from ancient times until today, there has never been a Zen master who did not attain the fruit of enlightenment through diligent practice of *samadhi* and wholehearted devotion to meditation work.

At the start of Summer every year, the Zen monks settled down for three months, in accordance with the Vinaya prohibition on traveling during that period: this was called "commencing the summer retreat," *jie-xia*. The summer retreat was completed three months later on the fifteenth day of the seventh lunar month, approximately the middle of September. This was called *xia-man*, "the completion of the summer," or *jie-xia*, "release from the summer retreat." Thus in the old days, when one asked how long someone had been a monk, one asked him how many summers he had been a monk.

These guidelines established by the Zen communities for the Zen hall were exactly suited to the true correct road of the Buddha Dharma. The common saying went: "Sit in meditation for a long time, and you are sure to have Zen," and this was not unreasonable. During the Song dynasty, many of the great Confucians were influenced by the guidelines and teaching methods of the Zen halls. They switched their underpinnings and changed over to what became the Neo-Confucian styles of quiet sitting, lecturing, sincere conduct, and real practice.

The door of the Zen hall was hung with curtains and the fragrant scent of burning incense gently wafted out from inside. When the congregation went to their seats to sit in meditation, it was commonly called *shou-dan*, "receiving the mats." At such times, a signboard was hung by the door saying that quiet sitting was in progress inside. People passing by outside walked quietly and no one dared to talk in a loud voice for fear of disturbing the pure practice of the monks inside the Zen hall. When it was time to rest, the sign on the door was switched to one that said there was a break in the study. Then passersby could behave more as they pleased. The common term for this was *kai-jing*, "opening up the silence."

Teaching Methods Inside and Outside the Zen Hall

Since the Zen hall was the teaching center of the Zen temple, there had to be a constant course of study going on there. Certainly, the constant course of study of the Zen monks was real study and realization, genuine cultivation of their own fundamental matter, and not a daily routine of lectures and explanations. In the Zen school, they considered lectures on the sutras and shastras to be in the province of the doctrinal studies teachers. Their own emphasis was on cultivating practice.

In the evenings when the monks were released from their studies, the abbot would go to the Zen hall and talk about methods for meditating and studying Zen. Sometimes, some of the monks would have doubts and difficulties and ask the abbot for instruction. Then the abbot would explain the Dharma and offer guidance according to the occasion. This was called *xiao-can*, the "small gathering." In later generations, as Zen declined, sometimes the abbot would be lazy and ask the chief of the hall to ascend to the teacher's seat and expound the Dharma, and this too was called *jian-xiang*.

Formally, there was another building apart from the Zen hall where the Dharma was expounded, which was called the Dharma hall, and to which the abbot was invited according to a fixed ceremony to ascend the seat and preach the Dharma. At such times, the bell was generally rung and the drum was beaten in a ceremonial style to inform all the monks in the entire temple that they should come to listen to the Dharma. The solemnity of this ceremony and the reverent behavior of the congregation gave this a very formal and solemn religious atmosphere. But the way that the Zen abbots expounded the Dharma was not the same as that of the Dharma teachers who lectured on the scriptures, who were sure to use Buddhist principles expressed in the technical language of the scriptures. Nor did the Zen abbots only preach in a religious style. Their guiding educational principle was to adapt to the occasion and the place, and seize opportunities as they arose, setting up teachings according to the situation without any fixed doctrine or methods. Their disciples and the temple secretary faithfully recorded what they said as they explained the Dharma. These records became the later genre of books of recorded sayings, *yu-lu*.

If Dharma teachers lectured on the sutras and shastras, this had to take place in the lecture hall. Dharma teachers who specialized in explaining the sutras and shastras were called *cuo-zhu*, or "lecturers."

Certainly, the Zen hall was the center for the Zen temple's cultivation of practice and educational work. The abbot, who acted as the teacher and guide, had to monitor at all times the process and the progress of the congregation of monks who were sincerely cultivating practice. If there happened to be a certain event or a certain expression that could stimulate them to develop wisdom, the abbot had to seize the opportunity and give them the appropriate teaching.

Sometimes, the witty, seemingly light-hearted teaching methods used by brilliant Zen teachers achieved great results with certain people, enabling them to be transformed and realize enlightenment. Even if they could not achieve this goal, these teaching methods sometimes produced very humorous and charming episodes. Later generations recorded these events and called them "public cases," *gong-an*. The Neo-Confucians took up this style and changed the term to "study cases," *xue-an*. These unusual and wondrous sayings appeared later in the recorded sayings of the Zen masters and became known as *ji-feng*, "witty barbs," and *zhuan-yu*, "turning words."

From this, we can see how important were the teaching responsibilities of the teacher who served as the abbot of a Zen temple. The Buddhist scriptures say that the great teacher's duty lies precisely in taking on the responsibility of the correct Dharma of the Tathagata. Taking on this responsibility meant continuing the work of the enlightened teachers of the past and developing the enlightened teachers of the future, taking charge of the treasury of the correct Dharma eye, and perpetuating the work of the life of wisdom. In the Tang and Song periods, there were many cases of eminent monks who judged that their own merit, wisdom, and ability to teach did not qualify them to act as teachers, and so modestly confined themselves to tending to their own development and declined the position of abbot.

The Transformation of the Zen Hall

During the Yuan and Ming periods, the monastic system of the Zen temples gradually lost its shape. At the same time, various other sects began to create their own monastic systems, modeled on the guidelines of the Zen school. In the temples of the other sects, the Zen hall was transformed into a buddha-name recitation hall in Pure Land sects, or into a contemplation hall in Taoist temples, and so on. Genuine Zen halls and Zen teachers became few and far between. If people happened to see a real one, they would feel they were getting a remote view of some lofty style, and they could not repress their sighs.

Since the Republican period, the fashion for studying Buddhist learning has arisen in response to the times, and so many Zen temples have established institutes for Buddhist studies. The Zen school has been changing and has already turned into "Zen studies." Some Zen temples have tried to revive the declining system and reform its abuses, and others have invented new rules. All we can do is look up in expectation of worthy sages yet to come.

THE LEGACY OF THE ZEN COMMUNITY *PURE RULES*

The *Pure Rules* were established by Zen master Baizhang, to become the pure guidelines to which later Zen communities adhered. Though other Zen masters in later generations also established rules and guidelines at times, they all acknowledge the *Pure Rules* of Baizhang as their chief source. Moreover, the instructions to the people issued by the first emperor of the Ming dynasty, Zhu Yuanzhang, and by the Kangxi Emperor of the Qing dynasty both drew their stylistic inspiration from the *Chanmen Qinggui (Zen Community Pure Rules)* and the *Chanlin Baoxun Precious (Lessons for the Zen Communities)*.

The original articles of Baizhang's *Pure Rules* were lost long ago, and the *Pure Rules* that are extant today are later versions such as the *Baizhang Qinggui (Pure Rules of Baizhang)*, composed by imperial decree in the

Yuan dynasty, the *Baizhang Qinggui Zhengyi (Textual Exegesis of the Pure Rules of Baizhang)*, the *Chanyuan Qinggui (Pure Rules of the Zen Gardens)*, *Ruzhong Riyong (Daily Functions of the Monastic Community)*, *Ruzhong Xuzhi (Essential Knowledge for the Monastic Community)*, *Huanzhu Qinggui (Pure Rules of Huanzhu)*, *Conglin Jiaoding Qinggui Zongyao (Compendium of Essentials from Comparative Editions of the Pure Rules of the Zen Communities)*, *Chanlin Beiyong Qinggui (Practical Pure Rules for the Zen Forests)*, *Riyong Qinggui (Daily Use Pure Rules)*, and *Chanlin Liangxu Xuzhi (Essential Knowledge for the Two Echelons of Zen Monks)*. Besides these, in Japan there are such books as the *Daikan Seiki (Pure Rules of Daikan)*, *Eihei Seiki (Pure Rules of Eihei)*, and *Ozan Seiki (Pure Rules of Ozan)*. But today, over a thousand years later, these versions we have are not in the original form from the time of Baizhang. The contents of these texts mix in elements from the Zen monastic rules of recent times and have incorporated much of the atmosphere of the period. So we will select several relevant texts to consult.

Zen Master Baizhang's Biography

From the Song dynasty *Gaoseng Zhuan* or *Biographies of Eminent Monks:*

The Buddhist monk [Baizhang] Huaihai was a native of Fujian province. In his youth he left behind the decaying house [of worldly existence] and travelled to many Zen centers. He was very spontaneous by nature, and did not follow the urgings of others. He heard that Mazu had begun to teach in Nankang, and he made up his mind to become his disciple. He went to Mazu's place empty and returned full, and indeed became a Zen adept, a craftsman of the Zen school.

Subsequently Huaihai was invited by patrons who believed in Buddhism to take up residence at Xinwujie. There was a steep mountain there some thousand feet high, and it was called Baizhang Promontory (Baizhang means "a hundred rods," the equivalent of a thousand feet, since a rod was a measure of length equal to ten Chinese feet). Once Huaihai was living there, Zen travelers came there from near and far, and crowded the teaching hall.

Baizhang said: "We are practicing the Mahayana Dharma. How could it be appropriate to follow the disciplinary practices of the Hinayana scriptures?" Someone asked him: "There are Mahayana precepts of discipline in the *Yogacarabhumi Shastra and the Scripture on the Necklace of the Fundamental Deeds of Bodhisattvas.* Why don't we follow these?"

Baizhang said: "I have studied widely in the Hinayana and Mahayana scriptures, and combined elements from both of them to establish a set of rules and duties, and hark back to what is good in them. Thus I have decided not to follow the old system of discipline, but to set up a separate one for the Zen communities."

Ever since Bodhidharma transmitted the Dharma to China, and up through the Sixth Patriarch, those who attained the Dharma Eye were called "elders." This is the same as the practice in the western regions [Central Asia and India] of calling those who who have been monks for a long time and reached a high standing in the Path a name that connotes "elders." Still, many of the monks who live in Vinaya temples think that the other Buddhist temples are deviant.

Baizhang also directed that no matter what their standing, all monks should enter the monks' hall. In the hall was set up a long continuous meditation bench, and wooden frames for them to hang up their bags and their bowls and robes. When they lay down they had to use a slanted pillow at the head of the bed: this was called sleeping with a sword. Those who had done sitting meditation for a long time could only rest briefly. The monks were to practice meditation in a group from morning to night, and take meals when appropriate.

Baizhang taught the Zen monks discipline and frugality. He instituted the practice of the general call to labor, and taught that all monks high and low were to work on an equal footing. The elder of the community lived in a room ten feet square, like Vimalakirti's room. Zen temples were not to establish a shrine with an image of Buddha, but only a Dharma hall, to show that the Dharma went beyond verbal expressions and images. The other rules [Baizhang laid down] were twice as rigorous as those taught by the Vinaya teachers.

All the Zen communities throughout China submitted to Baizhang's *Pure Rules* like grass bending down before the wind. The special practices of the Zen school began with Baizhang.

Baizhang died in the ninth year of the Yuanhe era (A.D. 814), on the seventeenth day of the first month. He was 85 years old. He was born in the sixteenth year of the Kaiyuan era [728]. In the first year of the Changqing era of Emperor Muzong [821], by imperial edict he was given the title "Zen Master of Great Wisdom."

Zen Master Baizhang's Enlightenment

The Zen history called *The Record of Pointing to the Moon (Zhi Yue Lu)* says:

> Zen master Huaihai of Baizhang Mountain in Hongzhou was a native of Changle in Fuzhou, a son of the Wang family.
>
> When he was a boy he accompanied his mother to a temple where they bowed to an image of Buddha. He pointed to the image of Buddha and asked his mother: "Who is this?" His mother said, "Buddha." He said, "He is not different in form than a man. Later I too will be a buddha."
>
> When Baizhang was a young man he left behind the dusts of worldly life, and practiced the three studies of discipline, concentration, and wisdom. He studied with Mazu and served as his attendant. Whenever the donors made offerings of vegetarian food, as soon as Baizhang lifted the lid of the bowl, Mazu would pick up a fried cake and show it to the assembly and say, "What is this?" This happened again and again.
>
> One day as Baizhang was accompanying Mazu on a walk, they saw a flock of wild ducks flying by. Mazu said, "What are those?" Baizhang said, "Wild ducks." Mazu said, "Where have they gone?" Baizhang said, "They've flown by." Mazu then twisted Baizhang's nose and Baizhang groaned in pain. Mazu said, "Do you still say it's flown away?" At these words Baizhang had insight.
>
> Baizhang returned to the attendants' quarters, crying loudly. Another of the attendants asked him, "Are you thinking of your parents?" Baizhang said, "No." "Did someone scold you?" Baizhang said, "No." "Then why are you crying?" Baizhang said, "My nose was twisted by our teacher and it still hurts." The other attendant said, "Was there some misunderstanding?" Baizhang said, "Go ask our teacher yourself." The attendant went and asked Mazu, "Was there some misunderstanding with attendant Huaihai? He is back in the attendants' quarters crying. I hope you will explain this for me, Master." Mazu said, "He understands this. Go ask him." When the other attendant got back to their quarters he said to Baizhang, "Our master says you understand, and he told me to ask you." Baizhang then laughed out loud. The other attendant said, "A little while ago you were crying, so why are you laughing now?" Baizhang said, "A little while ago I was crying, and now I'm laughing." The other attendant was at a loss.

The next day, when Mazu went up to the teacher's seat [in the Dharma hall], as soon as the congregation had gathered, Baizhang came forward and rolled up his mat. Mazu then left the seat. Immediately thereafter Baizhang came to Mazu's private quarters. Mazu said, "Just now why did you roll up your mat before I had preached the Dharma?" Baizhang said, "Yesterday I got my nose twisted by you, master, and it hurt." Mazu said, "Where were you keeping your mind yesterday?" Baizhang said, "Today my nose no longer hurts." Mazu said, "You deeply understand yesterday's business." Baizhang bowed and withdrew.

Another time when Baizhang was standing in attendance on Mazu, Mazu's eyes fell on the whisk hanging from the corner of the meditation bench. Baizhang said, "Do you function merged with this or detached from this?" Mazu said, "In the future when you open your mouth, what will you use to teach people?" Baizhang took the whisk and held it upright. Mazu said, "Will you function detached from this or merged with this?" Baizhang hung the whisk back up where it had been before. Mazu gave an awesome shout, which left Baizhang deaf for three days.

Not long after, when Baizhang was staying on Daxiong Mountain, his dwelling place was on a steep cliff, so it was called Baizhang. Students flocked to him from all over. One day Baizhang said to the assembly, "The Buddha Dharma is not a small thing. In the past I was shouted at by Mazu, and I was deaf for three days."

Preface to the *Pure Rules of Baizhang* by the Song Dynasty Literatus Yang Yi

The Zen school began [with Bodhidharma] on Shaoshi Mountain, and was transmitted through [the Sixth Patriarch Huineng] at Caoqi. Zen master Baizhang was concerned because most Zen monks lived at Vinaya temples, and even though they established separate halls for themselves, they did not adhere to the guidelines in expounding the Dharma and directing practice. So Baizhang said, "Hopefully the Path of the buddhas and patriarchs will continue to spread its teaching into the future and not be destroyed. How could it be appropriate for the Zen school to follow the Hinayana teachings?" Some said, "There are Mahayana precepts of discipline in the

Yogacarabhumi Shastra and the *Scripture on the Necklace of the Fundamental Deeds of Bodhisattvas.* Why not follow these?" Baizhang said, "Our school is not confined to Mahayana or Hinayana, nor is it different from them. We must take the best elements from both, and establish a system of guidelines, and follow what is appropriate in them." So he decided to establish a separate system for the Zen communities.

[Baizhang's *Pure Rules* contained the following provisions.] All those whose virtue is to be honored all call elders. This is like the practice in the western regions of calling those who have been monks for a long time and have reached lofty levels in the Path such names as *acharya.* The one who acts as the chief teacher should dwell in a room ten feet square, the same as Vimalakirti's room. This is not a private sleeping room.

At Zen temples no other shrines [besides the Dharma hall] should be established. The Dharma hall is built first, to show that the personal instruction passed from buddha to buddha and patriarch to patriarch is to be honored throughout the ages.

The congregation of monks, no matter whether many or few, are all to enter the monks' hall, with no distinctions of high or low, and be arranged according to how long they have been monks. In the hall was set up a long continuous meditation bench, and wooden frames for the monks to hang up their bags and their bowls and robes. When the monks lay down, they had to use a slanted pillow at the head of the bed. They slept auspiciously on their right sides. Those who had done sitting meditation for a long time could only rest briefly. The monks had to keep decorum whether sitting, standing, walking, or lying down. Other than when entering the abbot's room for instruction, monks who were working diligently at their studies, regardless of rank, were not kept to a constant standard.

The whole congregation gathered together for group study from morning to evening. The abbot would go up to the Dharma hall, ascend to the teacher's seat, and take charge of the congregation, who stood there in order by his side listening. There would be questions and answers between the host [abbot] and the guests [the disciples], in which he expounded the essential principles of Zen, and taught the monks how to live according to the Dharma.

Two vegetarian meals were served equally to the whole congregation as appropriate. The congregation observed restraint and frugality [in regard to food], to show that the Wheel of the Dharma and the wheel of food were both turning.

Zen temples carried out the practice of the general call to labor, in which all monks high and low had to take part equally in manual labor.

Ten duty offices were established, each with one monk in charge directing several monks in the performance of the appointed tasks.

If miscreants took refuge in Zen temples under false pretenses, and mixed in with the pure congregation [of monks devoted to practice], and caused trouble, then it was up to the duty distributor *wei-na* to investigate and expose them and expel them from the temple, so that the pure congregation could be at peace.

If any of the monks committed infractions [against the *Pure Rules*], the whole congregation was assembled for a public discussion of the case. Then the offenders were beaten with the staff and driven out of the temple in disgrace. There were four regulations under this heading. First, not to defile the pure congregation, but to live with respect and faith. Second, not to betray the monk's form, but to follow the Buddha's regulations. Third, not to cause trouble with the government authorities, but to avoid lawsuits and trials. Fourth, not to spread rumors outside the temple, but to preserve the good order of the Zen school.

Whole congregations live together, and no one distinguishes between the sagely and the ordinary. Even when the Tathagata was in the world, there were sectarian differences, so how could they be entirely absent nowadays, in the period of the Semblance Dharma and the period of the Dharma Ending Age? But if we see one monk at fault, and then make a fuss ridiculing all monks, without realizing it we are denigrating the sangha and damaging the Dharma, and the harm is very great. If the present day Zen school is to be preserved from harm, it should adhere to the guidelines of Baizhang's *Pure Rules*, and decide matters accordingly to establish the Dharma and prevent treachery. We may not be worthy people, but better there should be standards and no transgressions, than transgressions and no teaching.

Indeed Baizhang, the "Zen master of Great Wisdom," made great contributions to protecting the Dharma. The distinctive system of the Zen monastic communities started with this. The essence of the *Pure Rules* is taught to all later students, so they will not forget the basis of Zen. These rules and standards have been collected in full detail. I have carried out the intent of [Hui]rui: he has edited the *Transmission of the Lamp*, and so I have composed this preface.

[Signed by] the Hanlin scholar Yang Yi.

Twenty Essential Rules for the Zen Community by Zen Master Baizhang

The Zen community flourishes by having no mundane concerns. Cultivation of practice becomes solid and secure through mindfulness of Buddha.

Upholding discipline is of first importance in making energetic progress. Fasting is the cure for sickness.

Affliction becomes enlightenment through patient endurance of insult. Liberation comes through not separating affirmation and denial.

Genuine sincerity is the real condition of community living. Doing one's utmost brings success in carrying out duties.

Talk should be kept to a minimum in order to become direct. When old and young are compassionate to each other and live in harmony, then there is advance in virtue.

The entry into learning is through diligent study. Having no faults comes from clearly understanding cause and effect.

Old age and death warn of impermanence and alert us. Buddhist activities become real through an impeccable pure spirit.

Dealing with visitors becomes an offering through true sincerity. The Zen temple is adorned by its old veterans.

All affairs should be planned for in advance so they do not become laborious. The proper etiquette for community living is humility and respect.

The power of concentration enables one to meet danger without becoming confused. Compassion is the basis for helping all beings.

The Treatise of the Samadhi of the Precious King

By mindfulness of Buddha we do not seek to be free from sickness. If the body were without sickness, then cravings and desires would easily arise.

In dealing with the world we do not seek to have no difficulties. If the world were without difficulties, then arrogance and sloth would surely arise.

In investigating mind we do not seek to be absent of obstructions. If the mind were without obstructions, then we would overstep the proper stages in our studies.

In our conduct we do not seek to have no delusions. If our conduct were without delusion, then our vows would not be firm. In making plans for things, we do not seek easy success. If we have easy success in affairs, then the will stays slack and proud.

When we form relationships with people, we do not seek to benefit ourselves. If we form relationships for self-aggrandizement, this damages morality.

We do not seek to have other people accommodate us. If other people accommodate us, our hearts are sure to grow complacent.

When we practice generosity, we do not expect a reward. If we expect to be rewarded for meritorious deeds, then we have ulterior motives.

When we see something beneficial, we do not seek to profit from it. If we seek to profit from what is beneficial, the mind of ignorance is active.

When we are oppressed, we do not seek speedy vindication. If we seek speedy vindication, then animosity and resentment increase.

Thus, when the sages established their teachings, they considered sickness and suffering as medicines, troubles and difficulties as freedom and ease, obstacles and barriers as liberation, and the multitude of delusions as the companions to Reality. They considered being bogged down in difficulties as success, broken relationships as sustenance, disagreeable people as gardens and forests, and the merit of generosity as worn-out shoes. They considered keeping away from profit as riches, and suffering oppression as a method of practice.

Thus dwelling amidst obstacles nevertheless brings a way through them, and seeking a way through on the contrary brings obstructions. Thus the Tathagata attained the path of enlightenment amidst obstacles and obstructions. The likes of [the murderer] Angulimalya and [the renegade] Devadatta came to do him harm, but our Buddha gave them predictions of salvation, and transformed them so they became enlightened. Is it not the case that [for those who truly follow Buddha's example], when others go against us, it is really favorable to us, and that when others try to damage us, it really helps us succeed? But at the present time, if conventional worldly people studying the Path do not first dwell amidst obstacles, then when

obstacles do arrive, they will not be able to push them aside.
Thus the great jewel of the Dharma King will be lost. Is this not
lamentable?

THE ZEN COMMUNITY AND PATRIARCHAL
CLAN SOCIETY

"When a method or teaching has been around for a long time, abuses accumulate around it." This is a famous traditional saying in China. As it was
passed down over long ages, the Zen monastic system, which was originally honored as a specially pure and noble thing, nevertheless could not
escape from this rule.

Because the Zen monastic system was a system that considered the
whole world as a single family, there was absolutely no room within it for
selfish interests. But the result of the traditional value system, with its duties to one's sovereign, to one's teacher, and to one's kin, was often that
the feeling among kinsmen outweighed the sense of duty toward sovereign and teacher, and thus self-centered egotistical views arose. Buddha
prohibited clinging to the self and taught people that they must genuinely
practice until they reached the realm of selflessness. The Zen monastic system forbade acting out of self-interest and considered itself to be the common possession of all sentient beings in the ten directions. Thus the Zen
temples were commonly called *shi-fang cong-lin,* "the Zen communities of
the ten directions." Because of this, monks in the Zen communities were
not allowed to accept disciples as they pleased. Even if they made special
efforts to accept disciples, this kind of relationship between teacher and
disciple could only be reckoned as a kind of individual act, not as a relationship involving the whole temple.

If the abbot of a *cong-lin* Zen temple accepted a disciple, the disciple
could not automatically succeed to the abbot's position. The next abbot
still had to be chosen from among the eminent monks of all the Zen communities. From a moral or legal point of view, there was nothing at all
wrong with such a procedure. But people are still people, and from the
standpoint of human feelings and behavior, gradually this procedure could
not always work.

Thus, standing outside the Zen monastic community known as the
cong-lin, a system of hereditary temples gradually came into being, along
with private hermitages, teaching halls, and small temples. In the so-called
hereditary temples, teachers were succeeded by their disciples as abbots in
charge of the temple, much like the practice of hereditary succession in
the ordinary clan system, though not through blood ties. Since the disciple could succeed to his teacher's position, at the same time he also assumed control of the temple's property. Moreover, the property of a tem-

ple was considered to belong to that temple alone, and not be held and enjoyed in common by all the Zen communities of the ten directions. In other respects, such as the formal appointment of monks to administrative posts and the practice of giving visiting monks food and a place to stay, the hereditary temples in form were the same as the *cong-lin* Zen temples. But in fact, resources of the hereditary temples were subject to the limitation of private property rights and could not be entirely shared with all the monks under heaven. In the hereditary temples, if an abbot had several disciples, they were ranked in the order in which they had joined the temple. As the disciples in their turn accepted their own disciples, the temple property was further subdivided, as it would be among the various uncles and brothers in the ordinary clan system. In this way, as time went on, abuses multiplied and unworthy disciples launched struggles for power and control of property. Things went so far that the behavior of these so-called monks was the same as that of ordinary worldly people.

In the final analysis, is human civilization progressing? Or is it regressing? This is a major question in philosophy, which is very difficult to decide.

From the social standpoint, any religion can only be considered as a particular social formation. Social formations are man-made. Can you deny that humans are not just ordinary living beings? This being so, there is nothing strange about the transformation in social forms. In the establishment of hereditary temples, private retreats, and small temples, we can see that the deep roots of China's traditional culture, with its patriarchal clan ideas and organizational forms, were still planted deeply in every kind of social formation in China.

Hereditary temples were the product of roughly the same time period as the *cong-lin* Zen monastic system created by Baizhang. Because the Zen school emphasized succession to a teacher, the establishment of various subschools was a logical result. Especially by the time of the late Tang and Five Dynasties periods, the Five Houses of Zen had become separately established and the idea of being the disciple of the teaching of a particular Zen House had already become firmly planted in people's mind. Thus each of the Five Houses—Linji, Caodong, Guiyang, Yunmen, and Fayan—had its own charts of its lines of succession, which were passed down through the generations. Even today, such charts are still in use. Sometimes the Zen schools finished a line of succession and began to count again from the beginning, and thus continued indefinitely. This was not the same as the clan system of the patriarchal clan society, which always emphasized generational continuity.

During the Ming and Qing periods, most of the Zen temples in China were descended from the Linji school. The other schools of Zen had already declined to the point that they were hanging by a thread.

As the hereditary temples arose in the course of the evolution of Chinese Buddhism, they became like small family lines of monks. Apart from the fact that there were no marital bonds and that they gave their allegiance to Buddhism, in all other practices the monks in these temples were not very different from people in secular life. They were nothing more than religious groups for unmarried people. At a level below this, the rise of the family temple system in Japan, whereby the son of the abbot inherits the control of the temple, verges on a complete change in the character of Buddhism in eastern Asia. As for the pernicious influence of this on the Zen monastic system, all I can do is quote from Confucius (*Analects* 3.10): "At the great sacrifice, after the libation is done, I no longer wish to look on."

THE ZEN MONASTIC SYSTEM AND CHINESE CULTURE

Obviously, the Zen monastic system was a product of Chinese culture. When Buddhism was transmitted to China, it was synthesized with Chinese culture and this produced a reformed current within Buddhism, the Zen school. This has already been discussed above and does not have to be explained again. Strictly speaking, as Buddhism passed through its interchange with Chinese culture, there were two major developments that were enough to influence the future fate of the Buddha Dharma and add to the glory of its life of wisdom.

First, there was a reordering of Buddhist theory. The Tiantai school and the Huayan school presented an orderly critique of Buddhist doctrines. The Tiantai school encompassed the whole system of diverse Buddhist teachings in terms of the five periods of Buddha's teaching career and the eight levels of the teaching. The Xianshou school of Huayan philosophy did this in terms of five teachings and ten schools of thought. This was the famous analysis and differentiation of the teachings.

The second major development, in the area of forms of practice, was the establishment of the Zen monastic system. This synthesized Buddhism with the spirit of traditional Chinese culture, including the Confucian system with its emphasis on proper norms of behavior and adapting to the Taoist philosophy of taking joy in natural spontaneity. More than a thousand years ago, the Zen communities had already put into practice the norms of true Chinese-style democracy and liberty. The Zen system was obviously not the same as the religious despotism of the autocratic system. Indeed, it established dignified standards guided by the Buddhist Path for freedom of learning and democratic life.

Beyond China, in the countries that received the southern tradition of primitive Buddhism, like Thailand, Cambodia, Laos, Sri Lanka, and Burma, where this has been transmitted up to the present day, although there have been many changes from the ancient forms, Buddhism still more or less keeps some of its original style. But the survival of Buddhism in these countries is still dependent on the government and the remnants of popular faith. Knowledgeable people will see how unfavorably this compares to the solid basis for the genuine cultivation of the Dharma offered by the Zen monastic system without my having to say any more.

In the opposite case, the Buddhism of the northern tradition in Tibet has taken on a mystical coloration that sets off its religious aspect, and for more than a thousand years has won a privileged position in a theocratic political system. Although this is somewhat similar to the power of the Catholic Church and the pope in the West, Tibetan Buddhism differs from it in lacking an international organization on a world scale. In politics, it is not based on a comprehensive and long-established system of thought, and in terms of religion, it is still locked up within a culturally backward region.

With a deep understanding of the totality of Shakyamuni Buddha's teaching, we can see that neither the Buddhism of the southern tradition nor the northern tradition is true to his original intention. Only the Zen monastic system is really capable of not going against Shakyamuni's basic intent. Thus we can see that neither the southern tradition nor the northern tradition has achieved the great success of Buddhism in China. What is the reason for this? Even though the light of the Buddha shines everywhere, a people without its own all-encompassing age-old cultural tradition will not have the strength to make Buddhism prosper and grow great. Thus it is said that, when the great teacher Bodhidharma was in India, he saw from afar that, in China, conditions were right for Mahayana. Not shrinking from the hardships of the journey, he crossed the seas and came to the East, where he put down his robe and bowl and transmitted the mind-seal of the Buddha Dharma to China.

In a nation with an age-old culture like China, the legacy of history displayed against the backdrop of famous mountains and rivers is already enough to show the glory of the whole civilization. The monastic system established by the Zen communities has added quite a bit to the poetic and artistic feeling of China's wonderful scenery.

Expressing the style of Chinese culture, the Tang dynasty poet Du Mu wrote:

> Four hundred and eighty Buddhist temples dot the south
> So many towers and platforms in the mist and rain.

Here he was only describing the achievements of Buddhism in Jiangnan in the Northern and Southern dynasties period. In the Tang dynasty and thereafter, with the rise of the Zen monastic system, it could be said that there were Buddhist temples and Buddhist communities along every river and lake and on every mountain in the whole country. Later there was the lyric: "Buddhist monks have occupied most of the famous mountains in the country."

The bold spirit of the people of Tang times and the generous spirit of the people of Song times were combined and synthesized in the building style of Buddhist temples. In every part of China we can see beautiful and magnificent stupas and temples. When we read through the provincial and local gazetteers, we will find famous ancient sites and Buddhist and Taoist temples and shrines taking up half the book.

As we consider from afar the earlier sages and think back on the legacy that has come to us over two or three thousand years, it certainly makes us resent those half-educated people who falsely look down on Chinese culture. We must realize how long the experience of a deep-rooted civilization has been, and how many wise people have spent their heart's blood to create it. To make the changes needed to adapt to the trend of the times and insure China's survival takes learning and technical knowledge, and careful strategic consideration before we undertake to act. This mission cannot be accomplished by a course of action that is shallow and false and rash.

THE ZEN MONASTIC SYSTEM AND THE SECRET SOCIETIES

The Zen monastic communities were Buddhist social organizations of monks living collectively and concentrating on religious practice. In the last analysis, they were religious organizations, administered by means of a code of disciplinary precepts. If not for these, then probably it would have been even more difficult for the Zen monastic communities than for ordinary society to deal with the disputes that arise in the course of human affairs. This is the sense of the traditional saying: "Better to bring along a thousand soldiers than a hundred monks," because monks are more quarrelsome even than soldiers. As for the abbots and the other monks entrusted with administrative posts in the Zen communities, for now let's not discuss their virtue and wisdom. But as for their personal experience in the world, most of them had had some worldly involvements. Thus the ancients said of Zen communities that "Dragons and snakes were mixed together [in them] and ordinary people and sages lived together [there]." In fact, monks with concealed worldly concerns and monks truly committed to the Dharma for its own sake were very hard to tell apart.

Over the course of Chinese history, there were many cases where brave men frustrated in their worldly ambitions, loyalists of fallen dynasties, and people who had suffered things in life too painful to speak of, took refuge in Zen communities out of despair. They sought to finish the remainder of their lives seeking enlightenment in a serene environment. Indeed there were many people like this.

When the Zen school was flourishing in the Tang and Song periods, the congregations of Zen temples often numbered over a thousand. Thus, apart from the monks who were rigorously upholding the disciplinary code of the Zen *Pure Rules*, there were sure to be some monks who secretly devoted themselves to the martial arts and military exercises. When Li Shimin established the Tang dynasty, when Zhao Guangyin established the Song dynasty, and Zhu Yuanzhang established the Ming dynasty, Buddhist monks skilled in the martial arts from such places as Shaolin Temple assisted the dynastic founders in conquering and pacifying the country. They did not accept official position as a reward for their services, but just withdrew back into the Buddhist communities. This, too, is a historical fact.

Tian Wen's *Record of a Journey to Shaolin Temple* says:

> The Tang period monk Tanzong lived at Shaolin Temple in Henan province. He was an expert in the martial arts. In 621, when Tang Taizong [i.e. Li Shimin] was not yet emperor, but still the Prince of Qin, he was given the mission of leading a punitive expedition against Wang Shichong (a Sui general who had usurped the throne after the assassination of Emperor Sui Yangdi). Some thirteen Shaolin monks, including Tanzong, joined the forces of Taizong. Because of their awesome ferocity and skills in combat, they defeated the enemy and achieved victory. Taizong appointed Tanzong as a general, but the other monks were not willing to serve as officials, so Tiazong awarded them each a purple robe as a mark of honor. An inscription in stone recording this event is set into a wall at Shaolin Temple.

The essay on the soldier-monks of Huguang province found in volume nine of the second part of the *Qiao Shu* says:

> In 1553 pirates were ravaging the seacoast in the Yangzi delta area. The militia tried to ward them off, but were defeated in thirty-seven engagements. Cai Kelian, who was the official in charge of the area, recruited soldier-monks to annihilate the pirates. From then on, our forces won many victories over the pirates. The victories began when [the monk] Tianyuan and his cohorts joined the fighting . . . When the pirates attacked the city of Hangzhou, the local officials assembled a force of forty

soldier-monks to resist them. Their commanders were Tianzhen and Tianchi. Tianchi was a Shaolin monk. When the soldier-monks joined battle with the pirates, they routed them.

The pirates fled and took refuge at Taicang in Shanghai [which was then still a small town]. Mister Cai had his head-quarters in Suzhou. He sent money to Hangzhou to recruit sol-dier-monks, but discipline was strict [among the monks] in the Hangzhou area, and none of them agreed to join [the military force]. Luyuan, a monk, with no other way to thank Mr. Cai, sent someone to recruit Yuekong and eighteen other monks who had not previously been among the forty monks fighting against the pirates. The local officials then gave permission for this. Luyuan said to Yuekong: "Since you are presently in charge of a temple, you should tell [Mr. Cai] that your soldier-monks have been recruited and are irresistible. If he offers you money, it would be better to decline. If he does not accept your refusal, you should recommend the Shaolin monk Tianyuan to be the commander [of the soldier-monks]. He is presently lec-turing on the *Surangama Sutra* at Tianchi Mountain, and he has the ability to command troops." When Yuekong met with Mr. Cai, he tried to decline the commission, but this was not accepted. So he recommended Tianyuan [to lead the soldier-monks]. Tianyuan accepted the appointment and left Tianchi Mountain. This was the tenth day of the fifth month. Mr. Cai took up residence at Ruiguang Temple, and stayed there with Yuekong. Yuekong led a band of eighteen soldier-monks from the Hangzhou area, and Tianyuan led a band of forty-eight sol-dier-monks from the Suzhou area. They joined forces and at-tacked the pirates. There were also ten soldiers from Xuanshe Mountain who joined Yuekong's force. On the tenth day of the sixth month they sent out six groups of fighters against more than a hundred of the pirates. They attacked the pirates fero-ciously, and the pirates were terrified and fled. After this they fought the pirates many times and won every battle. They at-tacked all the coves where the pirates fled and destroyed all their encampments, until none remained. Forty of the pirates were slain or wounded by the soldier-monks.

Zhu Yuanzhang, the founder of the Ming dynasty, in his youth had been a monk in Huangjue Temple, and he naturally knew the regulations of the Zen monastic communities. Thus, in the bureaucratic system he set up in the early part of his reign, some of the official titles retained the feeling of the names of the administrative posts of the Zen monastic system. The

Ming bureaucratic system was derived with some changes by following the old system of the preceding Yuan dynasty, with some reference to the Tang and Song systems.

The Yuan system of official posts had been influenced by Lamaism and by the Buddhist-Confucian statesman Liu Bingzhong and, in many respects, was imbued with the flavor of the monastic community and its forms. Even for a man of great talent like Yelu Chucai, the Jin dynasty nobleman and Buddhist adept who influenced the nature of the regime set up by Mongols after their conquest of North China, it was hard to get away from this pattern.

During the period of the Southern Song, Jin, and Yuan dynasties (12th through mid-14th centuries), the Taoist master Qiu Chuji and his disciples established the Complete Reality school of Taoism, following the example of the Zen monastic system, in order to preserve the national culture of the Chinese in the face of barbarian conquest by the Jurchen and the Mongols.

When the Manchus entered China and founded the Qing dynasty in the 17th century, many of the leading figures of the fallen Ming dynasty, along with many of the Chinese intelligentsia, maintained their allegiance to the fallen dynasty and, out of a sense of duty, refused to submit to the Qing. Some of them wanted to overthrow the Qing and restore the Ming. Seeing how easily many of the Chinese elite had switched their allegiance to the new regime, these Ming loyalists began secretly to form networks of the brave fighters in the Yangzi Valley region. Thus the secret society organizations gradually formed among the common people. Tradition has it that leading intellectuals like Gu Yanwu, Li Erqu, Huang Zongxi, and Fu Qingzhu were the hard core who directed this movement behind the scenes. Naturally, those who joined these secret groups included many surviving officials of the Ming dynasty who had changed their names, gone into hiding, and lived under the guise of Buddhist or Taoist monks.

Thus, these kinds of secret society organizations had as their backbone the traditional culture's values of loyalty, filial piety, human fellow-feeling, and duty, and were dedicated to overthrowing the Qing and restoring the Ming. But apart from this, in terms of their rules and forms, they were all patterned on the forms of the Zen monastic regulations.

Examples of such secret societies are the Gelao ("Brothers and Elders") Society of the early Qing (also called the Hong Bang), and its later offshoots, the Qing Bang ("Green Gang"), the Hong Bang ("Red Gang"), and so on. Externally, they were social organizations, but their inner objective was to plan the restoration of Chinese sovereignty on behalf of the people and the nation. Other examples are the Li Men in North China, which merged elements from Confucianism, Buddhism, and Taoism. Later it was called the Li Jiao ("the teaching of the inner design"). Its organization was also modeled on the Zen monastic regulations.

At a lower level were the various religious sects of the Ming and Qing periods, such as the Dadao Hui ("the Big Knife Society") and the Hongjiang Hui ("the Red Spear Society"), and the various similar sects based on Taoist techniques that resembled Taoism but were not. All of these were more or less organized according to the rules of the Zen monastic system.

From these examples we can see that the Zen monastic system indeed had a major historical influence on all levels of Chinese society.

CLOSING COMMENTS

Confucianism was always the main current in traditional Chinese culture. Confucianism put forward the social aim of great harmony under heaven, and its central teachings took proper social and cultural norms as the guide for political order. Good order achieved through the proper social and cultural norms would be able to realize the objective of everyone under heaven acting for the common good enunciated in the *Book of Rites*.

But the kind of social organization where everyone acts for the common good only appeared after several thousand years of transmission and practice during the Tang dynasty, in the form of the monastic system of the Zen school of Buddhism. To be sure, in form this was a community of Buddhist monks, but in spirit it was a model for the synthesis of the true meaning of the Confucian ideal of proper social norms with Buddhist precepts of discipline.

Confucius said: "When the proper norms have been lost [at the court of the ruler], seek them in the countryside." As for social norms that were genuinely good and fair, I'm afraid these could only be found in the Zen communities. But even so, these could not serve as a model for bringing political order to the whole country, because the task of properly managing the affairs of the whole country is many hundreds of times as difficult and complicated as the task of regulating the Zen community. Human beings are creatures of both emotion and reason, and if we lean too heavily toward either side and cannot properly balance the two, the result will be an inability to make human life peaceful and secure.

There were four reasons that the Zen monastic system was able to extend so widely and become popular. First, the Buddhist monks had left the secular world and had already resolved to abandon the emotional ties and troubles of worldly affairs and human desires. Even though life in a Zen temple was communal, it was also an absolutely free search for one's own ideal realm. Second, given the monks' religious faith and the concepts that came from a clear understanding of cause and effect, it was already unnecessary to add a controlling system of rules and regulations. Third, each monk had already resolved within himself to purify his own mind and made this his rule, so this was the highest principle by which the monks governed themselves. Fourth, the economic system of the Zen communities, which supported the monks and provided their livelihood, already met the needs of their material welfare, so all they had to attend to was their own physical and mental cultivation. They could abandon all other concerns.

For these reasons, the Zen monks could achieve the highest goal of the Confucians, which was to uphold the proper social norms, as well as the demands of the Mohists, which was to dedicate themselves fully to the welfare of all under heaven.

What of ordinary human society? There the power of desires for sex and food and drink and material things continually expands and develops further. As human affairs proceed and worldly concerns operate, conflicts arise between people. There are many doctrines that are certainly correct in terms of theory and as educational devices, but when they encounter the demands of human emotions and human desires, they are entirely unworkable.

The Zen monastic system was perfect, but outside of teaching and offering guidance, it employed no punishments or sanctions. Without the exemplary moral conduct of the Zen monks to uphold it, it would have been absolutely impossible for it to set an example for more than a thousand years. In the Southern Song period, Zen master Dahui Zonggao of Jingshan Temple in Hangzhou and Zen master Zhu-an Dagui of Longxiang Temple in Wenzhou feared that, in the future, the Zen monastic community would go into decline, so they collaborated to put together an account of the excellent sayings and doings of the leaders of the Zen communities down through the generations. To set a standard for later generations, they wrote the book called *Chanlin Baoxun [Precious Lessons from the Zen Communities].* The models of lofty style, sterling discipline, honesty, and rigorous practice contained in this book have been good enough to match the study books of the Song Neo-Confucians down through the ages. If we put aside the monastic exterior of the Zen teachers whose deeds are recorded in *Chanlin Baoxun,* and look upon them as models of cultivating the human personality and perfecting action in the world, this book can be put to unlimited uses and can stimulate our infinite natural potential.

When Zen master Baizhang established the Zen monastic system, his original fundamental intent was to enable Buddhist monks to be able to carry out genuine cultivation of practice, unhindered by life, without worries or cares to drag them down, and give them the peace of mind to seek the Path of enlightenment. He was not thinking of establishing any kind of social organization, nor did he have any ambition to form a religious organization. He did have the state of mind described in the Confucian maxim: "A profound person cherishes the people by virtuous conduct." But he certainly had no intention of aggrandizing himself.

Indeed, Baizhang had no worldly ambitions at all, and that's why all that he did was very spontaneous and natural and in perfect accord with the Confucian and Buddhist principles of compassion, human fellow-feeling, and righteousness. If Baizhang had had any worldly desires, then it would have been as the Buddhist scriptures say: "When the causal ground is not genuine, the results obtained are twisted." If that had been the case, how could he have become a protean teacher for the ages?

When Baizhang was in the world, the reason people denounced him as a monk who was breaking the precepts was because they were clinging rigidly to the code of discipline of primitive Indian Buddhism, and they thought that Buddhist monks should not engage in agriculture to earn their living. Looking back from our standpoint a thousand years later, we can see that, if Baizhang had not courageously reformed the monastic system and had allowed the Zen monks to persist in the original Indian pattern of begging for food, Buddhism in China would not have been able to preserve its standards and remain widespread up through the present day.

The Zen school emphasizes that people must have a genuine perception of reality. The Buddhist scriptures call Buddha "the Great Hero." Times change and the world changes too. Over time, the world has moved from an agrarian society and way of life to the social order of the present day, which has been transformed by industry, commerce, and science. As we think back to the earlier sages, we really lament that we don't know to whom among them we can turn for guidance in this unprecedented situation.

Index

Zen Master Nan Huai-Chin a native of China is considered one of the world's foremost experts on Chinese history and culture who combines the highest level of theoretical knowledge with practical experience. Master Nan is unusual in that he is an expert on the cultivation schools of Confucianism, as well as being a tripartite Master of Zen, Taoism and Esoteric Buddhism. He resides in Hong Kong where he devotes his energies to China's economic development and to reintroducing Chinese culture, previously destroyed by the Cultural Revolution, into Mainland China.